MW00459536

THE MIDDLE MARKET

The MIDDLE MARKET

An Integrated Approach to Increasing Share and Profitability in Banking's Most Dynamic Market

Charles B. Wendel

A BankLine Publication

 PROBUS
P U B L I S H I N G

Chicago, Illinois
Cambridge, England

BANK**LINE**™
A BankLine Publication

ISBN 1-55738-718-4

Printed in the United States of America

BB

1 2 3 4 5 6 7 8 9 0

BH

Dedication

Elaine Svensson has contributed more to this book than anyone else. She has clarified muddled passages, improved convoluted syntax, and caused me to rethink many of my assumptions. More importantly, the same week I completed this book she became my wife.

Appropriately, I dedicate it to her.

Contents

Exhibits

xi

Acknowledgments

While this book may have one author's name on its cover, it is the result of the involvement, insights, and generosity of many. Therefore, I want to thank formally those who contributed to the making of this book.

Three companies allowed me to profile their approach to the financial services middle market in some depth. At Chemical Bank, Frank Lourenso and John Spressert responded to my queries and offered valuable insights about the marketplace. Andy Parton, who is featured in my chapter on Chemical, merits particular thanks for the time he spent with me and his willingness to share his past experiences.

A number of key GFC Financial Corporation employees—among them Bob Korte, Robert Radway, and Greg Smalis—contributed to my ability to understand that company's operations. Most particularly, Sam Eichenfield, chairman and chief executive officer of GFC, has been of invaluable assistance.

Norwest is a bank that epitomizes some key strengths for continued success: the ability to challenge traditional views about a business, the need to be flexible, and the willingness to reinvent the company as required. Ed Morsman has articulated these issues in his own book. He was kind enough to spend time with me to discuss his views. Scott Kisting, president of Norwest's Minneapolis bank, has long been a leader in encouraging increased banker productivity and improving customer focus. I thank him for his early involvement in a project that lead to this book.

In addition to these individuals, Ed Lyman and Jeff Butterfield of Harris Bank were willing to share an account of their bank's transformation process and their pursuit of a more efficient approach to technology.

David Fox, Pete Garrison, and Joel Molinoff of Greenwich Associates provided access to their extensive and powerful database and allowed me to use some of their data to support and deepen my perspective on the importance of account retention and cross-sell.

Robert Morris Associates, represented by Ned Miller, Clarence Reed, Nancy Welsh, and, especially, Charlie Huntington, gave me a forum for conducting ongoing research into the banking industry and an opportunity to test hypotheses with its leaders. Charlie played an important role in facilitating discussions among senior bankers on many of the topics reviewed in this book.

Many people from my own firm, Mercer Management Consulting, Inc., have played either a direct or indirect role in this book. Tom Waylett has played a major part in encouraging thought leadership in the firm, as has Paul Fulchino and Jim Down. James Quella of the Financial Services practice area has backed that culture up by committing himself and his team to establish the firm's capabilities in areas of particular importance to the industry's growth and ongoing profitability. My hope is that this book is viewed as a contribution to that effort.

Mark Argosh, Andy Cohen, Paul Cusenza, Ernie Berger, George Overholser, and Neal Pomroy helped to develop many of the concepts presented in this book. Sandy Berry has had significant impact on this book's perspective on business banking. Fields Wicker added the European slant on some key topics. Recently, Matt Blumberg, Carole Chinn, Lauren Green, Darren King, Caroline MacNaughton, Vivi Grossman, Peter Lehmann, Tammy Schulstad, Paul ter Weeme, Steve Warner, and Chris Wolf worked on major client projects that strengthened the conclusions presented here. Additionally, Jessica Kostner assisted in tracking down some often hard to find industry statistics.

Rob Duboff, Pat Pollino, and Judy Woodfin head our marketing effort and make certain that, based on reality, our capabilities are increasingly known by corporate executives. They have supported and encouraged my effort.

Our graphics group at Mercer produced and sometimes designed the exhibits presented in the book. I thank them for their patience as I thank Libby Ferrarini for proofing much of the text. Most importantly, I thank Soraida Vila who retyped and reformatted the text time and time again.

In addition, Jeffrey Kutler of *American Banker* has provided me with an important forum for discussing the ideas developed in this book. George Bollenbacher was an early encourager of this project. Thanks also to Joel Ackerman of Warburg Pincus and John Heeger of Prudential Securities.

Also, great thanks go to Don Carson of Wachovia, Tucker Hood, and Bruce Grossman for reading the manuscript in draft form and making comments. I consider that and all the above to be true acts of friendship.

Finally, the people at Probus Publishing encouraged this project and kept it on track. I appreciate the effort of Mark Butler, Kevin Thornton, Anne Hughes Keane, Andrea Rosenberg, Pam van Giessen and others on the Probus team.

Introduction

During the 1980s, middle market banking experienced a number of dramatic changes. Most of those changes involved either the customers, competitors, or product offerings. Virtually all changes had significant impact on corporate relationship managers, the bankers who play a supporting role in the financial infrastructure of corporate America.

Unfortunately, commercial banks face a tougher and tougher sell just to keep their current customers. An immediate, pro-active campaign to restructure the way business is done should be top priority for bank managers at all levels. But the middle market franchise is one area at particular risk. This book focuses on providing those bankers and their managers with a framework for assessing the way they do business in the middle market and presenting options for improving profitability.

This book also is intended to lead to change—change in the way bank management and the individual banker approach the middle market; change in how the bank assesses its customers and targets; change in how the bank defends itself against tougher competitors. The ultimate goal, of course, is to grow profitability and, where appropriate, increase market share.

Smarter and Tougher Customers

Change begins in the marketplace, in the customer's boardroom. For middle market companies change has been pervasive from the smallest $10 million operation to the largest $200 million company. Smarter and tougher than even five years ago, these companies have been making banks work extremely hard for their returns.

In recent years, an increasing number of these middle market companies have, in fact, found that they no longer need to rely on bank financing. By working with their investment bankers or with specialized groups at a handful of commercial banks, mid-sized corporations discovered it was possible to obtain lower-cost funding by using commercial paper, and some began entering the equity markets. Borrowing from an individual bank or a syndicate became an uneconomic option or a "fall-back" position. This process of disintermediation is now a fact of doing business. The disintermediation option will become available to more and more corporate borrowers, from small businesses to mid-sized and large corporate.

Corporations, of course, have not stopped doing business with banks; they have, however, begun to demand more. The quality of corporate staff members that handle financing and other banking needs has improved dramatically as MBAs have entered the corporate sector and as analytic software has become widely available and user friendly. In fact, analytic capabilities, particularly for larger companies, has begun to exceed the skill base of many banks. If the gap widens, bankers risk falling behind the customers with whom they are supposed to develop "consultative" relationships.

Stated bluntly, in many cases, the balance of power has shifted away from the banker to the customer. In many corporate market segments, this change is permanent.

The Competition

During the past decade, several waves of competition have hit commercial banks. Within the banking community itself, foreign banks found the level playing field of a growing U.S. economy a highly attractive market. The following brief story should illustrate the intensity of this competition.

When I was a banker at a foreign bank in the early 1980s, I made a marketing call in rural South Carolina. The marketing target I visited was a manufacturer located more than an hour away from any airport; in fact, the only nearby airport was serviced by what is commonly called "puddle jumpers."

Of course, I thought that my persistence in getting to this prospect would set me apart from other bankers. I had gone off the traditional big-city calling route and had even scheduled a visit during the middle of the summer, a period of high humidity and, I thought, fewer visiting bankers. Rather than being a pioneer, however, I was one in a long line of marketers. The company's treasurer told me that a Swiss banker was expected the next day and that a Japanese banker had called the day before. As the treasurer said, "We're a regular United Nations here."

The focus of the foreign bank community on the U.S. market and its concerted calling effort has lead to impressive market share growth, if not always strong returns. Throughout the '80s it also undercut the ability of many domestic banks to price their loans at an acceptable rate of return.

Non-banks have also emerged as a major threat to the U.S. commercial banking franchise. On both the consumer and corporate sides of the business, non-banks have conducted highly focused marketing campaigns for the specific financial products they sell to targeted market segments. For example, although non-banks may compete in only one or two retail product areas, the impact is substantial. Successful approaches include Travelers Express in money orders, AT&T in credit cards, and Fidelity in mutual funds.

Similar examples also abound on the commercial side of the business. Among the many players are GE Capital in leveraged buyouts and leasing, GFC Financial Corporation in commercial finance and asset-based lending, Thomas Cook in commercial foreign exchange, and Morgan Stanley in global custody. These companies have demonstrated an ability to pick market segments, make quick decisions, be flexible and market-sensitive in their approach, limit internal bureaucracy, and pay, without hesitation, for top-quality performers.

Non-banks also have shown their ability to "cherry-pick," selecting the most attractive opportunities. Further, because many are so selective in their focus, they, in effect, choose their competition. This approach is very different from commercial bank strategies that all too often seem to offer all products to all market segments.

Going forward, most industry observers rightfully view non-banks as the major competitive threat to banking's middle market franchise. Consequently, one of the major challenges banks face is how to operate more like their non-bank competitors. This book will discuss how banks can adapt themselves to combat this very tough group of competitors.

The Products

Not only did customer knowledge and capabilities increase during the 1980s, the product options available to them also expanded. More non-banks and banks from regions far from the customers' headquarters began to market both non-credit and credit products aggressively. This competitive atmosphere prompted some customers—primarily, but not exclusively, those in the upper end of the market—to name the terms and conditions acceptable to them, and to refuse to negotiate with the banks.

The gap between the needs of the customer and what the banker wants to sell is large and threatens to grow larger unless commercial banks take action. The typical corporate banker continues to emphasize credit. Tip back the hat of most relationship managers and you find the face of a lender who has been trained to make loans, whose strength is knowing how to do so, and who gets personal fulfillment from completing a loan transaction. Historically, bank compensation packages also have been based largely on success in lending, reinforcing this strategic focus.

Due to the lack of internal coordination, many banks also have failed to present one corporate "face" to the customer. Customers become confused by the number of calling officers, and banks fail to deepen relationships as far as possible by cross-selling multiple products.

The sources of this situation include the lack of coordination between the diverse product areas. For example, the trust, corporate finance, and treasury departments have different internal cultures, and the barriers of bank accounting and performance measurement systems do not encourage team marketing.

The Corporate Banker

Beyond the customers, competition, and products, the roles and responsibilities of calling officers, product specialists, credit personnel, and support staff call for fundamental changes.

In the early part of the decade, the banker controlled the relationship with a company. He determined (and it was still largely a *he*) what products were offered to which customers and when. Further, with only rudimentary profitability systems available, the banker also played the key role in determining whether the revenues generated from a customer relationship resulted in an acceptable profit return to the bank. During the 1980s, however, the corporate banker's job, as defined by the marketplace, changed fundamentally and permanently. Some banks, however, failed to realize it.

The factors reshaping the corporate banker's responsibilities are a central focus of this book. Importantly, that banker's success is now much more dependent on selling multiple credit and non-credit products. But, change involving products—their number and complexity—is just one factor. Today, the core relationship banker has to be a quarterback and facilitator, often yielding a leadership position with the customer to a bank colleague from a specialized product area while still maintaining overall responsibility for the account. This new definition of the traditional corporate banker's role necessitates a reconsideration of hiring, training, and compensation requirements.

Transforming the Corporate Bank

My experience as a consultant to the banking community has made it clear again and again that transforming the corporate bank is an imperative, not a choice, for continued profitability. Banks have no alternative but to change and keep pace with a faster-moving, always changing economy.

Those changes will be difficult for many institutions to accomplish. However, those banks that continue to operate as they have in the past will find reduced revenues and profits and limited options for growth. Some will find it necessary to merge with other banks or to cut back operations dramatically. Conversely, those banks that transition successfully to a focused, multi-product approach will be positioned for sustainable growth in tomorrow's economy, no matter what its shape. Banks can position themselves to generate increased fee income while decreasing their staffing levels and compensation costs.

Let me offer a final note. This book is written from my perspective as a former corporate banker as well as a management consultant. I have made cold calls, written credit memos, and closed loan transactions.

Much of this book's commentary on banking may be interpreted as critical and, in some cases, even uncomplimentary. As a former banker, that is certainly not my intent. In my view, the banking industry remains a business that is full of profitable opportunities over the longer term. That said, however, fewer banks will be around to capture those profits.

Transforming the middle market banking business is not an option; it is a mandate from shareholders and customers. My hope is that this book will provide insight into the changes required and a partial blueprint on how to implement them. The positive impact a farsighted senior management team can make on the corporate bank's bottom line more than justifies the effort required to effect change.

The Middle Market at a Glance

The imperative for a new approach to the middle market results from the opportunity to improve relationship manager productivity and the need for sustained growth.

Current Situation

Accounts managed per relationship manager (RM)	12-20 borrowers 12-30 in total
Percent of RM time spent on marketing	20-35
Percent of RM time spent on maintenance and customer service	30-40
Percentage of accounts that generate return on equities (ROEs) less than 10%	60
Average number of banks used by the $20-50 million company	1.7
Cost of generating and marketing credits for banks with commercial outstandings of $2-5 billion	$1,902-$5,774 per $1 million of loans outstanding

Improvement Opportunities from a Renewed Approach to the Middle Market

Cost savings post-renewal	20%+
Potential shift in RM marketing time	from 20-35% to 50%+
Potential improvement in cross-selling	50%+ higher revenues

Steps for Reengineering the RM

Step 1: Ensure success by including key internal groups.

Step 2: Analyze current activities and workflows.

Step 3: Obtain internal agreement on change.

Step 4: Create specific implementation plans.

Step 5: Reap the benefits.

Key Reasons Why Banks Need to Transform Themselves to Become More Like Non-Banks

- Increased productivity results from better motivated employees due to empowerment and incentive pay.

- Competition is based on value-added features and not pricing.

- Improved focus leads to improved profit.

How to Become a Non-Bank

- Reduce bureaucracy.

- Evaluate strategic focus—avoid trying to be "all things to all companies."

- Rethink compensation.

Time Required to Transform the Corporate Bank into a "Selling Machine"   *4-6 months*

1

Imperative for Change

"It's as if we are in the steel industry. Do we want to be Nucor or Bethlehem?"

—a chief credit officer at a $30 billion bank holding company

Many bank managers resist any detailed analysis of their institutions' corporate banks. At the core of this reluctance is the fact that a great number of bank managers still cannot quantify their returns from specific customers or products.

Resistance to this basic economic analysis—a mainstay of retail banking—remains widespread, particularly among bank groups targeting the middle and large corporate markets. Excuses abound. One hears, "Corporate banking is an art; it's not like retail banking." Or, "We can't change the way we do business until we have new information technology systems." And, of course, there's always the blind-hope excuse, "Our business is improving. Look at how our net interest margin has increased; it's the best in years."

A grain of truth can be found in each of these statements. Unfortunately, there is also a great deal of danger in accepting them without question. Corporate banking, while not an art, often does involve a high degree of customization due to the varied financial needs and expectations of companies. Nonetheless, account profitability and cross-product accounting systems, a streamlined organ-

1

izational approach and clear definitions of roles and responsibilities across the corporate bank can have a dramatic impact on profit.

Likewise, top-quality database systems are without a doubt the critical component in a bank's ability to change profitability assessment, upgrade customer service, and improve productivity. But, waiting for new systems to come online 12 to 18 months down the road simply avoids rethinking what can be done with existing technology.

Poor Market Indicators

Admittedly, corporate banking returns did improve during the early 1990s. Much of that high profitability, however, was driven by the huge gap between the cost of funds to banks and the prime rate. That gap began to narrow in late 1993 and, although fortuitous, it is not in any way a solid foundation for future business planning.

Therefore, the realization that banks are not insulated from the realities of the marketplace has prompted senior corporate-account managers at many banks to take action. They have launched an examination of how their corporate groups operate and are seriously considering fundamental changes in their approach to the business.

An announcement by CS First Boston and Merrill Lynch that they intend to originate large commercial loans should only heighten commercial bank anxiety. Merrill reportedly already has $600 million in loans outstanding to small business.

More demanding and sophisticated customers and more aggressive bank and non-bank competitors are only two reasons why senior managers of corporate banking groups now may be willing to reexamine their operations.

Loan Decline

Perhaps one specific statistic has had the strongest impact upon corporate bankers: the declining volume in commercial and industrial loans.

As Exhibit 1.1 illustrates, bank loan outstandings have decreased each year since 1990. Prior to that, consistent loan growth was an occurrence that bankers had long taken for granted.

The decline is particularly disturbing in light of the contrasting growth in total private debt found in the credit market, as reported by the Federal Reserve Board. In 1993, bank debt was approximately 30 percent of total private debt, down from 35 percent in 1990 and about 40 percent in 1980.

Market Share Decline

Not only has the lending originated by domestic corporate banks declined, but competitors also have registered strong growth in corporate market share. For example, the commercial paper market has exploded. Outstandings in 1993 were approximately $5.75 trillion, representing a 3 percent compound annual growth rate

Exhibit 1.1   Commercial and Industrial Loan Volume, 1989-1993

Commercial and industrial loans are flat.

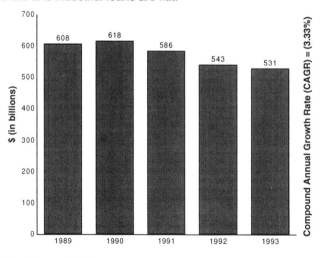

Source: Federal Reserve Bulletin.

3

(CAGR) from 1990. In other words, the continued growth in commercial paper is at the expense of the banking industry.

However, a different group of lenders has thrived in the same environment that has hurt traditional corporate banks. Commercial finance companies, many of them owned by banks but managed as separate companies, have increased their outstandings and profitability in the same slow growth economy that has dealt a blow to the banks. Why?

Commercial finance companies concentrate on secured financings and focus on a market segment that is almost solely dependent upon them to meet their borrowing needs. In fact, this target market is actively downplayed or walked away from by many traditional banks, which do not consider these companies to be the right type of borrowers for them. Additionally, the commercial finance approach to conducting business encourages a strong, continuous sales effort. Conversely, many banks deliberately focus on market segments that either no longer need to borrow or try very hard to go the disintermediation route by working with their investment banks. (Commercial finance companies have not always been acknowledged as serious threats to traditional corporate banks, but the lessons they offer are highly relevant to banks and will be discussed in detail in Chapter 13.)

While there has been some growth in commercial loan volume in 1994, most economists agree that corporate loan growth will show little significant increase in the foreseeable future. Virtually no one predicts the likelihood of a near-term return to a super-heated economy that could drive borrowing needs up and, with that surge, create significant loan growth opportunities for banks.

Faced with limited loan growth, banks, like their own corporate clients, have two levers to manipulate. They can increase productivity and cut expenses—in effect, doing more with less. Or, as an alternative, they can increase the number of dollars of revenue generated by each customer.

The best strategy is to cross-sell products in cooperation with other parts of the bank—that is, to sell more credit and non-credit products to current customers and targets.

More than likely, both strategies will be needed. Failing to act in these two areas will lead to reduced profits and, ultimately, to the bank becoming less and less relevant to its customers and targets.

Lack of Productivity Improvement

Improvement in productivity, one of the most basic performance measurements, has been minimal at most corporate banks since my days as a banker. In the late 1970s and early 1980s, my account responsibilities at a money center bank included approximately 25 borrowers and 10 to 15 non-borrowers. In addition, I was given a list of 25 or more prospects, only 5 to 10 of which could be considered "hot" targets.

Back then, we faced a number of impediments that today's bankers would look upon with horror. There were no laptop computers available; financial statement spreading was done largely by hand and on paper; telecommunications capabilities were often by telex with rudimentary or limited fax availability, and there were no cellular phones.

Today's banker can take advantage of many labor saving and analytically rigorous tools that can free up time for managing increased account loads or marketing more intensely. Computer-generated spreadsheets and the ability to delegate to trainees now make credit analysis less onerous. Fax machines, overnight mail, and cellular phones can increase a banker's responsiveness and ability to keep in touch with customers. Furthermore, many banks now have designated product specialists on staff who are available for co-calling.

One might think that such technology and resource capabilities now available to relationship managers (RMs) would have automatically led to a number of improvements. Higher productivity, increased account loads, and a higher number of marketing calls are logical expectations.

Unfortunately, that conclusion could not be further from what an analysis of banking industry best practices and my work with bank clients indicate. While individual bank exceptions exist, no research that I have seen suggests that on an industry-wide basis, individual banker productivity for the corporate market has shown noteworthy improvement.

Banker anecdote upon anecdote supports this dismal view of productivity. Individual and group productivity is poorer today than it has ever been. Why? Regulatory requirements, tougher credit hurdles, and increased internal paperwork are some of the reasons offered. Perhaps, however, the real answer is that few banks place any emphasis on selling. Some banks, in fact, appear to consider a dedicated sales focus unprofessional rather than at the heart of the corporate banker's job.

Three points underscore how far bankers are from where they should be given advances in technology and, even more critically, the threat from competitors. First, many bankers are handling account loads similar to those of 10 years ago. Relatively few are handling substantially more clients. Second, in spite of the marketing focus that many banks claim to have, account calling is at a dismally low level—in many instances lower than five years ago. Third, relationship managers simply do not give enough priority to marketing.

Static Account Management

The low level of account loads points to the underlying infrastructure problems faced today by many banks, even when they try to grow market share and improve profitability.

Exhibit 1.2 presents the number of accounts handled by relationship managers at six major regional banks operating in a variety of geographies across the U.S. The average account load ranges from 12 to 30 customers. Even taking into consideration variations in customer service and credit requirements, this small sample shows a wide variance in what is expected of a banker. Across the board, a relatively low level of productivity exists.

Within an individual bank as well, disparity exists among account management numbers. Whenever a bank looks behind an aggregate number to evaluate individual unit or relationship manager performance, the result is quite similar to the data presented in Exhibit 1.3.

Exhibit 1.2   Relationship Manager Account Loads

In general, account loads vary widely.

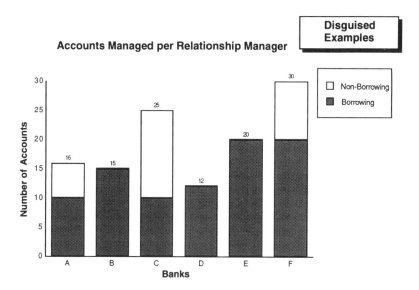

Bank A—disguised for reasons of confidentiality—is one of the 20 largest U.S. banks and operates in a major urban area. It ranks third or fourth in overall market share but leads in certain regions within its market.

The account officers of Bank A manage from 3 to 17 active accounts. Their prospecting responsibilities also differ widely, ranging from 6 to 15 targets. Of course, relationship bankers' account loads will legitimately differ; some of the disparity can be explained away by market differences or customer service intensity. Significantly, however, at this bank and at multiple others, individual account and prospecting responsibilities are not determined by unit management. A review of current and target accounts is not part of the yearly planning cycle.

Some banks have focused on rebalancing account responsibilities by taking into account the size and demand of accounts, the complexity of relationships and other factors. That exercise, valuable because it encourages consistency and tries to bring all bank officers

Exhibit 1.3   Intra-Bank Account Management Comparison

Account management responsibilities differ significantly within the same bank.

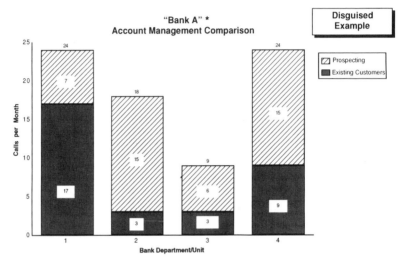

"Bank A" *
Account Management Comparison

Disguised Example

☑ Prospecting
■ Existing Customers

Calls per Month

Bank Department/Unit

* Not normalized for complexity

up to a similar level of performance, did not occur at Bank A. Without planning or analysis, that bank experienced wide swings in performance. At the source of this disparity is the fact that disciplined account management had not been established as a value within the bank's culture. (Account rebalancing strategies will be discussed in Chapter 10.)

This lack of consistency results in part from senior management's literal failure to manage. Lack of a uniform definition and understanding of the roles and responsibilities of relationship officers means that the bankers are not all moving in the same direction at the same time. Plus, this *laissez faire* approach leaves too much discretion to inexperienced officers. Examples of this lack of consistency and its detrimental impact on the corporate bank will appear throughout this book.

Low Account Prospecting

In view of the relatively light level of account loads found in middle market corporate banking groups, it is perhaps no surprise that account calling levels, that is, in-person visits or well-planned phone contacts with customers and targets, also are low. To illustrate the impact of this pattern, let us begin by looking at an industry best-practice.

One bank that appears to be more market-focused than any of its peers requires a 40-call-per-month goal in addition to managing a full load of accounts. In this bank, the quota can be met by a minimum number of approximately 20 in-person visits combined with telephone contacts. Telephone calls are credited as one-half of a personal visit. Therefore, up to 60 customers could be targeted within a month. Doing the simple math calculation, this plan generates approximately 600 contacts in a year, adjusting for vacation days, holidays, and other time off.

This best-practice example appears dramatically better than actual performances at most corporate banks, even those that report strong returns. Based upon a multi-bank survey and on-site work with bank clients, the typical corporate bank reports calling levels that range widely from six calls to a high of 40 calls per month. Approximately, 60 to 75 percent of those calls at the banks surveyed were made to current customers, ostensibly to ensure account retention and promote cross-selling opportunities. Similar to account loads, wide differences also exist. Exhibit 1.4 illustrates the vast contrast in calling intensity that can occur within the same bank.

One key reason for the disparity is the management vacuum, again similar to the lack of consistency in account load management. The decisions on which accounts to call and at what level of frequency are often left to the account officer's discretion. Not surprisingly, the judgment level of the account officer making the decisions also varies.

Marketing, A Low Priority

The demonstrated low level of account calling questions the importance of marketing to relationship managers.

Exhibit 1.4   Monthly Calling Levels

Monthly calling levels also vary widely.

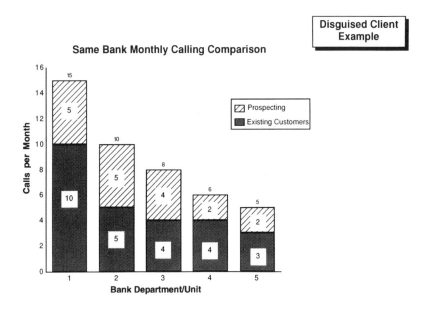

In the course of working with clients, industry consultants often take a quick snapshot of how bankers allocate their time for different tasks, including marketing. At my consulting firm, we frequently ask managers and individual account officers to separate their work time into four "buckets." Bucket 1 is new business development—that is, marketing the bank's services to prospects. Bucket 2 consists of time spent marketing to current customers. The third bucket is time spent on credit-related activities, including the loan underwriting process. The final bucket contains the time spent on account maintenance. This catch-all constitutes time spent on everything from customer complaints and inquiries to more routine customer service activities performed by the bankers.

We conducted this time management survey with more than 1,000 bankers at approximately 25 regional, super-regional, and money center banks during 1992 and 1993. These conclusions were reinforced recently by our 1994 survey for Robert Morris Associates, which summarized the activities of more than 5,000 RMs from 26 regional and super-regional banks.

The results of these surveys expose the root of corporate bankers' problems. Exhibit 1.5 gives a fair representation of the results we typically see.

Marketing usually makes up much less than half the account officer's day. In most cases, current account maintenance eats up a minimum of 40 percent of the banker's time. Understandably, credit analysis is also a major time commitment, upwards of 30 percent. The remainder, approximately 30 percent, is time left for marketing.

Management Vacuum

In analyzing relationship manager activities, the same lack of consistent planning within banks that was discussed earlier is further evident. In fact, this arrangement suits many bankers. Some bankers want to be account maintainers. Others prefer credit work, and a third group emphasizes the marketing and sales aspects of the job. As Exhibits 1.3, 1.4, and 1.5 indicate, all too often bankers define their jobs for themselves, determining how to spend their time and whether or not to make customer calls. Bank business strategy, unfortunately, only partially drives their decisions. This empowerment emerges, as we suspected, from a management vacuum.

While military analogies may be viewed as out-of-date in this post-confrontational era, the battlefield is still an appropriate metaphor for bankers. No army could possibly survive if its individual troops rather than its commanders were allowed to determine when they wanted to march, where they felt comfortable camping and if they wanted to attack. Commercial finance companies, non-banks such as GE Capital, and top-tier commercial banks such as Norwest, do march together, with the vast majority of their employees sharing clear objectives. Those employees who do not buy into

11

Exhibit 1.5   RM Activities

RMs are spending insufficient time on marketing activities.

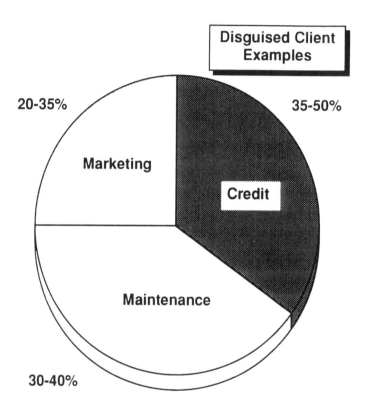

the direction envisioned by senior management simply do not fit in throughout the long-term.

Non-banks place significant emphasis on individual creativity and empowerment. They promote creativity and independence within the larger context of defined corporate goals, performance requirements and strategic direction. Some bankers say they regard such guidelines and specific goals as limits to the individual's responsibility, treating them as if they were not professionals.

Imbedded Job Assignments

One of my consulting firm's most disturbing findings relates to the experience level of the bankers who are assigned corporate calling. It is closely linked to the corporate banking culture.

As corporate banking careers progress, most experienced bankers become administrators, chained to their desks. That means that the marketers are relatively young and inexperienced. Ironically, the bankers who possess the most knowledge—valued by customers and prospects—are the ones that call the least.

Through both client studies and industry research, we also have seen multiple instances where experienced bankers, who are primarily assigned marketing responsibilities, allocate their time in the same way as their junior colleagues. They spend approximately the same time on administration and internal matters as their juniors do. Consequently, they spend just as little time marketing. The imbedded bank culture—departmentalized, political, and turf-protecting—plays a large part in this unfortunate pattern, repeating itself generation after generation.

Improving productivity is imperative now because there is a slow growth macro-economic environment, a more focused and aggressive group of bank and non-bank competitors, and the very human motivation to improve and enliven the banker's job. Recently, more relationship bankers have begun to realize that they are being underutilized by many of their banks. They are viewed as and paid as "paper pushers" and caretakers rather than dynamic marketers. Many of them, not only the younger bankers, welcome the reengineering of their jobs to free up time for revenue producing activities that are also intellectually challenging. In addition, we can almost guarantee that they will be particularly interested in increased time for revenue production if compensation is also reengineered to increase or establish an incentive-based, pay-for-performance system.

Cross-Selling Underemphasized

Given the low level of calling, it cannot be a surprise that today's level of cross-selling is far from what it must be and can become. One anecdote illustrates a key issue impeding effective, internal cross-selling.

A senior officer at a super-regional bank frankly discussed his dilemma. One member of his team recently made a significant sale of a Trust product. "That was terrific for him," the senior officer said. "The Trust group immediately gave this employee a bonus check for the sale. It was also terrific for the bank, which generated additional revenue. But for me, it meant nothing. In fact, it could even be a negative. Today, my compensation is based upon this unit's ability to increase loan volume. The retail side gets most of the benefit from increased deposits; non-credit product areas benefit from non-credit sales, as does the individual banker. But, my team has to generate a higher loan number. Until our division's accounting system takes other business into consideration, I am going to emphasize loans above all else."

As illustrated above, human nature and self-interest play a part in the low commitment to cross-sell. In the late 1970s and early 1980s, the banks' internal battlegrounds saw cash managers and the relationship manager fighting over what to do about the deposit side of the business. Traditional bankers feared cannibalism, that is, that they would lose whatever value they received for free balances to another part of the bank. The cash management sales force based its internal "pitch" on the premise that if its bank did not offer this set of products, some other bank would. The creditability of the relationship banker would, thereby, be damaged, and the relationship would be a potential loss for the bank.

Today, cash management is the most widely sold non-credit product marketed by corporate bankers. Competitive necessity and years of internal training have made most bankers enthusiastic salespersons for this product family.

With that skirmish over, the battleground within many banks has now shifted to other areas. For example, relationship managers are still acting as gatekeepers to control the corporate finance area's introduction of private placements and structured transactions rather than more traditional loans. In some instances, this gatekeeping extends to the trust area or the treasury desk.

The relationship banker's days as a gatekeeper, "allowing" some product salespersons to see "their" client while delaying or denying others, are limited. In fact, the related economics are too powerful to ignore. Exhibit 1.6, which compares the percentages of non-credit revenue and loan outstandings at a selected group of super-regionals, illustrates that point. (One note: this calculation was chosen to allow for comparability among banks.)

The top performer generates $7 of non-credit revenue for each $100 of loan outstandings. The bottom performer generates less than two dollars. That 500 basis point gap between the top and bottom performers translates roughly into an average 250 basis points in net pre-tax margin and demonstrates that the bottom-line impact of better cross-selling of non-credit products is dramatic.

Exhibit 1.6   The Value of Non-Credit Cross-Sell

Benchmarking shows that banks will benefit significantly from improving non-credit-related revenue levels.

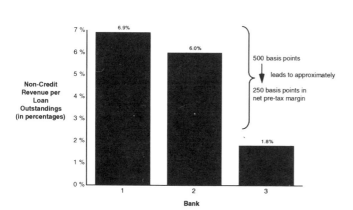

15

So why isn't cross-selling seen as an industry-wide imperative? While many bankers and their managers "talk the talk" most are still not "walking the walk." The traditional bias toward lending, based on comfort and experience, is one reason. The lack of accounting systems that can capture non-credit sales and link them to relationship profitability is another. Insufficient knowledge of those non-credit products, among both relationship managers and their senior managers, is a third.

Summary Thoughts

Until the roles and responsibilities of relationship managers are clarified and the infrastructure to support them is better aligned both to their needs and the marketplace's requirements, banks will fail to achieve the level of results required for success in tomorrow's marketplace.

The imperative for change follows from shifts in customer requirements and financing choices, competitor dynamics and business economics. Relationship managers, their activities, and the infrastructure around them should be the focus of the change process.

2

The Role of the Relationship Banker

"There is no consistency in what the RM does across our bank."
—*a senior bank executive of a northeastern regional bank*

At many banks the role being played by today's relationship manager (RM) reflects the accumulated history of banking since the Depression. Despite the advent of enhanced technology, responsibilities have not changed substantially during the past 20 or more years. From marketing to prospects and cross-selling products to current customers, to analyzing credit and conducting account maintenance, one person is still called upon to perform a series of tasks that involve different and sometimes conflicting core competencies.

While the job largely has remained the same, the job title has changed. The loan or account officer is now called a relationship manager, a word connoting a deep understanding of customer needs, a businessperson who offers consultative skills to the corporate executive. Unfortunately, the reality of the banker's job often diverges significantly from the dialogue promised by the new title.

Multi-Product Sales Expectations

The brokerage world provides a meaningful analogy for what has and has not happened to the role of the bank relationship manager.

For years, stockbrokers have been called account executives (AEs) within many investment firms. Much of the public, however, and, in fact, many brokers themselves continue to view AEs primarily as sellers of stock.

During the 1980s the senior management of leading brokerage firms, such as Merrill Lynch, repositioned their AEs to capture market share in emerging non-stock product areas, among them annuity/retirement accounts and money market funds. The job title was then changed from account executive to financial consultant, reflecting the intention to pursue consultative selling.

While the title change was part of the transformation process, it also was supported by a refocused training program, a new compensation structure and a management directive that gave the salesperson the mandate to sell a broader range of products to customers. The senior management of firms such as Merrill, which achieved this transition successfully, were strong leaders in this change process.

While to this day a number of brokers remain primarily stock sellers, the most successful have responded to customer needs by adding non-traditional products to their portfolios. They use these products—such as mortgages, credit cards, debit cards, and retirement accounts, which have historically been viewed as "bank" products—to retain key customers, take share-of-wallet away from competitors and increase their companies' importance to the customers. In banker's terms, these brokers have become "first-tier" service providers.

Conversely, those brokers who have not fit into the new multi-product framework have often lost a significant share of their customers' overall business to mutual fund companies and insurers. Further, as their firms continue to adapt to and anticipate customer needs, they, as individuals, are becoming the "square peg in the round hole."

In contrast to brokerages, at banks we often see a different situation both in terms of internal support available and the commitment of senior management to change. The banker's title has changed, and the end goals of the job have begun to shift. Yet, the relationship manager and the bank are still tied to the old ways of acting.

Similar to the brokerage financial consultant, the relationship manager is now supposed to introduce and sell many products beyond loans and cash management. Treasury-related interest rate management and trust and corporate finance products are only a few of the additional and diverse products that have been added to the RM's portfolio.

Now, management not only expects the banker to uncover, understand and meet increasingly complex customer problems but also address time-consuming regulatory requirements, such as those related to the Community Reinvestment Act. Of course, maintaining pristine files to avoid unfavorable Office of the Comptroller of the Currency (OCC), Federal Reserve, Federal Deposit Insurance Corporation (FDIC), state, and other examinations is a given.

At the same time, pay-for-performance still accounts for only a small percentage of the banker's total compensation package. While banks may be promoting a more aggressive approach to the market, in most cases their salary structures have remained largely the same.

This history, fossilized into organization bureaucracy, undercuts the ability of the banker to become a multi-product salesperson. That is true across the board, from the small business group up to the large corporate area.

Dysfunctional Corporate Bank Structure

A corporate banker's typical day, knowing full well that no days are in fact "typical," consists of a hodgepodge of mundane and sophisticated tasks, from "pencil pushing" to answering inquiries requiring detailed financial analysis.

Within the course of a day, a relationship manager may analyze a credit, coach junior officers, telephone customers on an in-process loan, and participate in multiple internal meetings. Oh yes, he also may have to fit in a client or target meeting to sell new or additional business.

Given the above smorgasbord of activities and the fact that approximately 50 to 75 percent of the work time of key sales producers is spent on work they do not personally need to do, it can hardly be surprising that productivity has not increased. The tools and approach provided to corporate bankers are simply dysfunctional—to use a currently popular term. Bankers are expected to meet and anticipate tomorrow's customer needs within the organizations of the past.

Bank management needs to realize a disconnection exists between the results expected of bankers and the current structure of the organizations within which they operate. When that level of understanding is reached, they can proceed to examine each component part of how their bank approaches its business and determine the level and type of internal support required to achieve higher performance.

The banker's job needs to be redesigned to focus more tightly on the highest value-added tasks by deemphasizing some tasks and delegating those which support staff can perform. Ideally, certain tasks should be eliminated entirely.

As stressed throughout this book, one primary question that senior management must ask when evaluating its corporate banking operation is: are the specific activities that credit-trained bankers are performing appropriate uses of their skills? Obviously, management can determine a priority job description and then eliminate certain tasks from the banker's task list. Could another specialist perform those tasks, freeing up the banker to concentrate on the major "deliverables" of the job? Again and again, the answer is that the net effect of transitioning selected tasks, such as preliminary prospecting, away from RMs does not diminish their role or take "power" or "responsibility" away from them. Rather, it allows RMs to concentrate their efforts on activities that can increase the payoff to the bank.

One senior banker from a highly respected regional bank summarized the need to reexamine not only the RM position but also all others related to it. His cynical comment was, "The reason we need to change our approach is that it takes a Superman to do all the things that are required of today's banker. We just don't see that many Supermen anymore."

Clearly, a new approach to the RM's job is needed. Today's corporate bankers must fulfill a number of roles that require a broad set of core competencies, including marketer, salesperson, credit analyst, negotiator, account maintainer, credit quality protector, trainer, mentor, and workout specialist. It is no wonder Superpersons are hard to find.

RM Business System

The typical activities in which the RM is involved can be described as a "business system" or "value-added chain." Exhibit 2-1 presents an overview of these activities and summarizes the functions that a bank must perform effectively to be a winner in corporate business.

The eight RM activities in Exhibit 2.1 can be grouped into four key areas:

1) Marketing—primarily prospecting

2) Cross-selling—selling additional loan and fee-based products

3) Credit underwriting—risk management

4) Account maintenance—customer service

Exhibit 2.1   Corporate Bank Business System

Corporate banking activities can be grouped into four distinct bid-related areas.

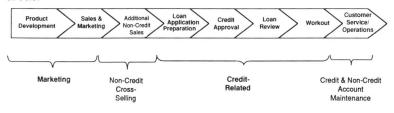

21

In examining these key areas, we will cover the key components of the activity, the current RM role and responsibilities within that activity, issues facing senior management and the value of industry best practices.

Marketing

Marketing encompasses both product development activities and sales management. Product development, in turn, involves the process of creating or improving already-existing bank products and services in response to customer needs and competitive pressures.

Sales management focuses on sales to new customers and includes target marketing, agreement on acceptable risk criteria, pre-screening, and development of aggressive calling programs and sales promotions. A strong sales management process with clear leadership needs to be instituted in those banks where it does not currently exist.

Cross-Selling

Product cross-sell is an area of concentration today for both aggressive and defensive reasons. From a marketing perspective, selling to companies that are already in-house is considerably easier and less expensive than establishing a relationship with a new target. One estimate is that it costs about five times as much to establish a new customer as it does to retain a current one. From a defensive posture, selling more to current customers is also a key strategy for customer retention.

Although exploiting (in the best sense of the word) the existing customer franchise appears essential, a majority of sales calls currently focus on new customers. This counter-intuitive sales tactic results, in part, from bank management considering only new sales to new customers when calculating incentive compensation. The result is that banks "disincent" what should be the easier and more profitable sale. In one manager's view, "Selling more to current customers is just part of the RM's everyday job."

Credit Underwriting

Credit activities center on booking the initial loan and encompass preparing a loan file, conducting analysis, applying a risk rating, making a recommendation, completing documentation, and closing the loan, among other steps.

The initial credit approval function, when combined with loan monitoring, often consumes up to half of a relationship manager's time. This concentration is a residue of banks "tightening the screws" as credit quality deteriorated in the late 1980s.

Despite the importance of fee-based income, these credit-related activities remain the foundation of most bank relationships. Even today, loans serve as the "lead" product, that is, the first sale to a new customer. Small business customers, while in many cases not active borrowers, expect their banks to make credit available to them. Large corporate clients, even if they are not direct borrowers from banks, are usually subject to credit assessment for products such as foreign exchange and money market trading, derivatives or trade finance. In addition, many middle market companies, of course, rely on banks as their major source of funds.

Although transforming the role of the relationship manger centers on the need for increased marketing, all that sales effort will be wasted if credit quality deteriorates at the same time. Credit quality functions involve monitoring, loan review, and workout to ensure that individual loans are repaid and that the overall risk profile of the portfolio remains acceptable to management, shareholders, and regulators.

Credit monitoring may include compliance tracking, collateral checking, and periodic credit review. Loan review concentrates on assessing the composition of the portfolio, setting reserve requirements, and "sampling" individual loans in detail. Workouts usually involve a classified loan. Typically, the bank's goal demands exiting the customer from the bank as soon as possible but occasionally involves "rehabilitating" the account and, then, returning it to the line.

Account Maintenance

This area includes multiple customer service activities, many of which are operationally intensive. The scope of tasks that the RM performs is often quite broad and can include taking deposits, making investments, answering routine customer inquiries, and completing management reporting requirements.

At some banks, these functions eat up close to half of the relationship manager's day, and reorganizing this one area can free up a significant amount of time for marketing. As will be detailed in Chapter 7, bank management should establish a clerical infrastructure to accomplish many of these "monitoring" tasks at a much reduced cost. The bottom line impact of this change, when combined with an effective sales management process, is increased customer calling and, ultimately, increased profits.

The levers that a bank can pull to increase the focus on marketing and sales are limited. As discussed in Chapter 1, bankers spend most of their time on credit-related or account maintenance activities. Therefore, if a bank wishes to emphasize a customer-driven, market-focused approach, senior management needs to evaluate these two areas in particular and, as appropriate, change the type and amount of effort that their bank officers apply to them. The chapters that follow offer practical approaches for this restructuring based upon industry best practices and years of experience with corporate banking clients.

A Note on Benchmarking and Best Practices

Much has been written, both positively and negatively, on the value of companies benchmarking themselves against their competitors. One key value of benchmarking is that, when conducted in an effective and rigorous manner, it allows a bank to assess performance against its peers on both a quantitative and qualitative basis, as seen in Exhibit 2.2.

Rigorous benchmarking results in a profile of industry best practices. We define best practices as an approach that has generated strong and demonstrable results from which other banks can

Exhibit 2.2　Implementing a Best Practices Approach

Evaluating best practices allows organizations to adopt tactics and approaches that have been proven to be effective.

CONCEPTS BEHIND DEMONSTRATED BEST PRACTICES

Demonstrated:
- Proven to work in the real world; not just a theory
- "De-bugged," so emulators don't have to repeat mistakes

Best:
- Fits with a strategic vision of the industry and the bank
- May be one of several "best" alternatives
- Approach leads to outperforming

Objective Criteria:	e.g., Productivity, Growth, Marketing Activity, Loss Recovery, Loyalty
Subjective Criteria:	e.g., Innovation, Credit Culture, Simplicity, Ease of Implementation

Practices:
- Can be codified and transferred from one organization to another

learn and, ideally, apply to themselves. Best practices are always actual, not theoretical, and are based on detailed analysis of and interviews with leading bank and non-bank players.

Relevant quantitative measurements for the corporate bank, for example, can include the number of accounts managed, the number of marketing calls per month, the number of non-credit products cross-sold or the cost of the loan approval process. Qualitative benchmarks can include how a peer bank conducts its credit underwriting process or the role of the loan review area.

Relevant benchmarks also may exist outside of banking. One of the most notable and often repeated benchmarking examples for consumer banking is to review how Disney manages customer lines and relate that system to speeding up branch teller lines.

On the corporate side banks indeed need to look beyond their direct peer competitors to find innovative practices for areas such as job redesign and incentive compensation. For example, a number of commercial finance companies have a distinctly non-bank approach to the way they organize marketing, credit, and account monitoring. How they incent their front-line employees also shows an appreciation of sales, planning, and relationship building. For example, press reports indicate that the new IBM sales force compensation plan is based 40 percent on customer satisfaction and 60 percent on product sales.

Oftentimes, even more valuable results come from analyzing a bank's own internal best practices, an approach that is frequently overlooked. Within an institution, at least one group usually outperforms all others. While factors such as location or industry concentration may play a role, in most instances a number of factors that can be influenced or controlled by management are responsible for this success. This includes a unit's culture or a reward system that encourages increased selling. These factors often can be applied to other areas within a bank. Practices that work internally also have the benefit of being less easily dismissed as irrelevant or theoretical.

Of course, benchmarking is not the "Holy Grail" or "silver bullet" for all companies. In fact, considering benchmarking as a simple solution to all problems distorts its value. Understanding how well your company is performing versus others and evaluating new tactics that might improve performance is a meaningful tool leading to action.

Benchmarking often results in a Chinese menu-like approach. It requires judging the value of different approaches from internal and external industry and non-industry sources, rather than direct imitation of another institution, no matter how impressive that company might be. Blindly adopting another bank's approach can, in fact, be disastrous, unless it fits into a specific strategy and culture. Too many banks try to transform themselves into a Morgan Guaranty or a Wachovia by imitation and find little success.

Benchmarking also can be limiting if a peer company's results are viewed as a ceiling or upper limit of performance. Ideally, benchmarking provides a knowledge base that can be used to leverage improvement in a bank's performance. When done effectively, it should lead to a performance level that leapfrogs peers rather than merely mimics them.

Summary Thoughts

Rethinking the RM's role is the foundation of achieving long-term success in the middle market. Freeing up the bankers and transforming them into "marketing machines" while maintaining excellent credit quality and customer services means enhanced profitability and stronger customer relationships.

3

Economic Analysis: The Foundation of Growth

"You should not linger in desolate ground."
—Sun Tzu, The Art of War

Perhaps the most compelling arguments supporting a decision to increase the productivity of RMs—the group that, in effect, serves as a bank's product distribution and delivery system—can be found in an economic analysis of customer profitability. Unfortunately, many banks still equate revenues with profit and stop their economic assessment of the customer relationship at that level. In some cases, I suspect that senior managers avoid calculating profitability so that they will not be forced to take the hard steps that the acknowledgment of poor profits demands, such as, cost reduction, repricing, and downsizing.

However, an economic analysis will prove that banks need to redirect RM marketing time in pursuit of high profit opportunities and drop those relationships with either low current profit or minimal potential. Not only will this data validate restructuring, it also will provide a clear-cut outline for change.

A detailed understanding of wholesale bank performance—by geography, product, market, and individual relationship—should

29

provide both the foundation and the ongoing guidance for refocusing a bank's marketing efforts. Segmented analysis of the current wholesale business will uncover the potential bottom-line payoff, a key factor in persuading bank managers to redirect their RMs into areas of higher revenues and net income, both on an absolute and per-employee basis.

Senior managers of some banks will remain skeptical, of course, about the validity of basing business decisions on any one number, such as return on equity (ROE) or return on assets (ROA). They are right to be skeptical. Their concern results from a reasonable fear that although the ROE or ROA calculation might accurately represent current performance, the actions these numbers dictate may improve the group's profitability only in the short term and sacrifice the bank's longer-term performance.

My approach does not, in fact, suggest that management blindly base its decisions upon one number. Rather, I view economic data as only one factor for input into the decision-making database used to determine allocation of resources, from capital and personnel to technology development.

The issues raised by such economic analysis range from the broad to the detailed. They will include but are not limited to several areas of critical importance to management:

- Whether and how the bank should reevaluate its pricing policies;

- How to balance the time and dollars spent servicing a customer versus the return that customer generates for the bank;

- Which segments and products should be selected for concentrated marketing efforts.

Simply stated, this process can lead to "invest, maintain, or exit" decisions about specific geographies, products, and customers. It will provide bank management with an understanding of profitability according to market segment. It also can raise key tactical and strategic issues for the institution to consider and, ultimately, can result in significant action for a bank to take.

To ensure that the bank takes full advantage of this analysis, management must obviously be comfortable with the methodology employed. Unfortunately, some consultants recommend profitability analysis systems whose complexity seems to exceed practical value. These approaches fail to gain the "buy-in" of unit managers and often quickly fall into disuse. In other instances, profitability projects can take up to 12 to 18 months before deliverables are achieved.

This "complexification" of economic analysis is unnecessary. In most cases, a "good enuf" analysis—that is, an analysis that is viewed by most managers as providing significant value—will generate clear implications for business units while being accomplished in a relatively short time frame and at a limited cost.

A Profit-Assessment Example

To develop an appreciation of how bank managers can benefit from a detailed examination of the economic performance of a business, it helps to look outside the banking industry for an example.

Several years ago, my consulting firm was asked to assist in improving the profitability of a company that provided technology-related products and services to the banking industry. Our experiences at this company capture the challenges facing bankers who wish to perform a similar exercise. As part of our analysis, we assessed the effectiveness and profitability of the in-field group that services ongoing customer needs, largely based upon a fixed-price contract. A primary objective was to determine whether customers were paying their "fair share" commensurate with the level of services received.

Fortunately, we knew the revenues that each customer generated for the technology company, and we had access to an internal company database that captured the time each employee spent with a customer. These direct labor costs and the allocated overhead represented the vast majority of the cost structure for this particular business. Using that information, we constructed a "rough cut" profit number for each account, equal to customer revenues minus direct labor costs and allocated overhead expenses.

We then proceeded to "cut" the data multiple ways, including by size, by individual services performed (to see if some services were money-losers company-wide), and by geography. Our analysis showed that the company was, in fact, overservicing many accounts at the expense of customers with a greater long-term potential.

Small accounts that paid relatively little for services consumed the most time. They often demanded much hand-holding and personalized attention. Some of these accounts, which offered minimal long-term potential to our client, frequently threatened to shift to third-party service providers. In response, they received a preferential rate, even though the technology company's bottom line actually would have improved if the complaining customers had moved their business. In other words, we found that the fees charged to this small account segment did not adequately compensate for the customer support level required. Losing some customers would have been preferable to retaining them.

The principle guiding the technology service company's approach to business appeared to be to fix the squeaky wheel that made the most noise. The accounts that demanded service received it, no matter what the account's actual requirements or fees charged. Conversely, high-potential accounts that did not demand attention or hesitated to call the company remained underserved. In some instances, these quiet customers shifted their businesses to more attentive competitors.

This relatively straightforward analysis, which required about six to eight weeks to complete, led senior management to undertake a repricing program for "underwater" accounts, outsource servicing in some geographies where no critical customer mass existed, reduce the number of in-field personnel, and refocus its sales efforts on more profitable user segments.

Given the availability of the revenue and cost data for this company and the relative simplicity of the business's cost structure, account-specific profitability, widely viewed as "correct" by key internal groups, developed fairly quickly. We all knew that from an accountant's perspective the numbers were either "wrong" or at best "incomplete." Estimates of time spent per account were often fudged by employees; allocations were by their very nature inaccurate; and some costs were omitted. Nonetheless, we were in the correct sphere of operations, and we were on track. In a matter of weeks, we crystallized key issues for management and provided a highly implementable road map for increased profitability.

Bank Profit Modeling

Shifting to the world of banking, profitability modeling is a diagnostic tool that enables a bank to quantify not only current performance but also the impact of changing cost of product delivery, pricing structures, or risk and return on capital requirements. The outputs of profitability modeling may include but are not limited to:

- Determination of cost-to-serve and key cost drivers on a product and customer segment basis;

- Agreement on key business segments for future marketing focus;

- Focus on areas that require additional analysis and perhaps difficult decisions due to poorly performing products and below-hurdle rate returns for specific business units or lines of business; and

- Recommendations concerning pricing initiatives and cost-reduction opportunities required to achieve the desired internal hurdle rate.

As you can imagine, reaching even an approximate level of accuracy when analyzing a bank's profitability requires surmounting multiple hurdles, some of which are highlighted below.

- *Consistent management information systems (MIS) may not be readily available, and departmental policies and procedures may vary.*
    Banks often are unable to access all the data required to profile an individual customer relationship. For example, corporate bankers usually go to one information source for loan and cash management information on a customer. Other prod-

uct areas such as trust and corporate finance, however, need to be queried department by department. Capturing retail and private banking information involves crossing yet another organizational boundary. A substantial degree of calling around and hand calculating may be required to develop a profile of a customer's full relationship with the bank.

- *Shared expenses permeate bank cost structures.*

 Typically, an estimated 30 to 40 percent of the total expenses of most bank departments are shared with other areas within the bank. For example, costs related to wholesale banking could involve operations and MIS, the retail branch system, and the investment areas, to name a few. This situation can frustrate managers attempting to gather accurate cost data and cause them to throw up their hands in frustration.

- *A standard for risk adjustment is required. Banks also need to factor in more than one performance measure.*

 Given their historic dependence on lending and other capital committing businesses, banks—unlike the technology service business profiled above—can evaluate their returns only in light of the risks required to generate profits.

 While the determination of ROE targets and equity allocation methodologies are critical, it is beyond the scope of this discussion to present a detailed system for risk-based performance measurement. Of course, chief financial officers, accountants, and almost every consulting firm will have approaches that they recommend. That said, ROE and not ROA should be the prime focus of a measurement system. The need for capital allocation modeling and a high return on risk-adjusted capital will only increase in importance in the future.

 Ralph C. Kimball, a professor from Babson College has, however, synthesized many of the key issues that senior managers need to consider when building an ROE model. Kimball effectively discusses how to determine and use ROE to evaluate line-of-business performance. He focuses on three related approaches to measurement: economic measures, primarily

ROE and ROA; periodic profit measures, such as quarterly earnings; and operating statistics, which could include productivity measurements.

- *Some of the required information may not exist.*

Remarkably, banks may keep no records of the time RMs and administrators spend originating transactions and servicing accounts. Intuition and gut feelings may be the only data initially available. A data collection process can, however, be introduced and much of the necessary information obtained within one to two months.

Segmenting and Costing Customer Data

Customer information can be segmented based on characteristics such as annual revenue, relationship breadth (that is, type and number of product use), and business type. These numbers should add up to total product and business unit profit numbers.

To complete such an analysis, however, it is necessary to allocate all operating expenses fully, whether they are of a direct or indirect nature. A risk-adjusted reserve must be applied to each borrowing customer and capital allocated to various product lines based on the level of potential loss. Depending on the business, those losses might result from a combination of interest rate risk in the case of derivatives; market risk, such as for energy or offshore loans; or credit risk, as based on customer cash flow and collateral position.

Ultimately, each corporate relationship should be evaluated on the basis of the ROE it generates for the bank. The "profitability matrix" presented in Exhibit 3.1 begins with a profit calculation for each customer by product. Its goal should be segmented profit analysis by customer type, geography, and product.

Data sources that contribute to this economic analysis may include existing customer and product reports, cost center reports, and interviews with local and corporate financial management personnel. Such a cost-assignment process will demand the involvement of internal staff members throughout the bank. Direct costs are usually straightforward and easily determined and ob-

Exhibit 3.1   Elements of Profit Modeling

Profit modeling allows for meaningful benchmarking across the bank and quantifies the impact of repricing and/or additional cross-selling.

Illustrative

Geography 2			
Geography 1			
Customer Segments	Commercial Loans	Corporate Services – Cash Mgmt – Trade Svcs – Investment Banking	Other Linked Products/ Accounts – Private banking – Retail – Trust
Customer size	Product Profitability $ and ROE		
Relationship Breadth/ Product Usage			
Customer Type			

Customer/product profitability will be evaluated for each geography

Local market conditions will be reflected

tained. Agreeing on indirect costs, however, is more of an art and is often subject to negotiation. But it can be done and provides meaningful insight for managers.

The outcome of this exercise is summarized in the two tables shown in Exhibit 3.2. In the table on the left, key support functions are listed in the columns. This exhibit indicates the need for two sets of data: one capturing head count for each functional group serving a business department and the other capturing related costs.

For example, with the help of internal staff and line personnel, the number of marketing personnel or the full-time equivalents (FTEs) working for the middle market, large corporate, and business banking areas can be determined. The approximate dollar amounts spent by marketing to support the middle market will result from determining salary, bonus, and benefit figures as well as any overhead costs.

Exhibit 3.2 Approaches to Cost Allocation

All support expenses are assigned to departments and also to product groups.

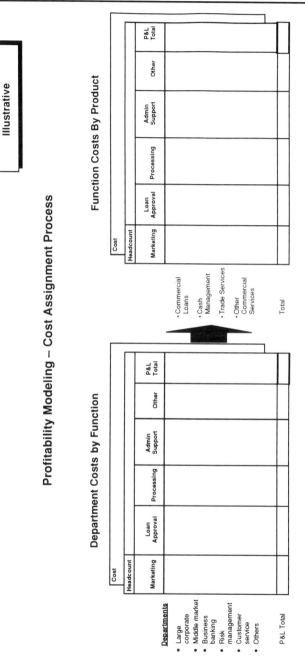

Illustrative

Profitability Modeling – Cost Assignment Process

Department Costs by Function

		Cost					
	Headcount						
Departments		Marketing	Loan Approval	Processing	Admin Support	Other	P&L Total
• Large corporate							
• Middle market							
• Business banking							
• Risk management							
• Customer service							
• Others							
P&L Total							

Function Costs By Product

		Cost					
	Headcount						
		Marketing	Loan Approval	Processing	Admin Support	Other	P&L Total
• Commercial Loans							
• Cash Management							
• Trade Services							
• Other Commercial Services							
Total							

To follow up on the marketing example, four FTEs who are part of the marketing support group are in fact working for the middle market unit. Personnel related costs total $75,000 each, resulting in a total cost to the middle market group of $300,000. Similarly, the chart on the right side of Exhibit 3.2 totals the costs generated by major functional support areas for key products.

Other methodologies also can be developed with bank management and applied to provisions for risk-adjusted capital allocations by individual customer and by specific products/services.

Bringing Profitability into Focus

Perhaps the hardest lesson to learn from economic analysis is that businesses that add dollars to the bottom line can still be value destroyers for shareholders. These businesses, in effect, misuse capital that should be put to work supporting higher profit businesses or, alternatively, returned to shareholders in the form of dividends.

Exhibit 3.3 gives an example of how economic analysis can shed new light on profitability. The exhibit breaks out the details behind the economics of lending for the middle market effort of one bank we analyzed.

The y-axis represents income in basis points (BPs) or expenses divided by funds employed. Beginning with the left-hand side of the chart, operating expenses total approximately 145 basis points. The estimated loan loss provision for this unit at the time of our work was 150 basis points, a number that will rise and fall with economic cycles.

The 400 BPs represent the income level required to generate the hurdle rate of return, given the expense base of this bank. The next two columns show income from loans and fee-based products. In this case, as in most others, loan income dwarfs non-lending, fee-related income.

The far right of the chart shows what could be called the "return gap." Assuming a pre-tax ROE hurdle of 17.5 percent, an 80 BP gap exists between actual income generated by the business and desired

Exhibit 3.3 The Economics of Lending

In many cases businesses that make a positive return fail to meet hurdle rates.

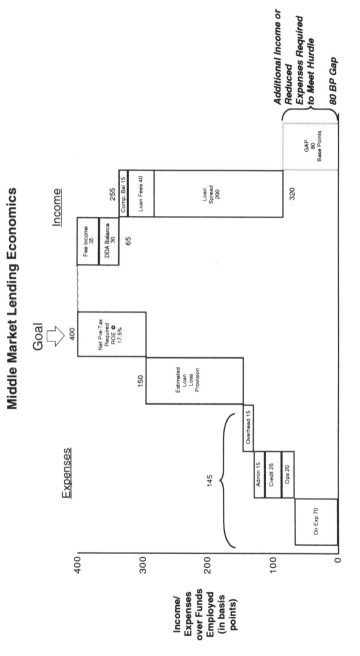

Middle Market Lending Economics

performance. Obviously, the gap between desired and actual performance will depend on the quality of the costing methodology, the extent of shared costs within the bank, and the accuracy of the loan provision applied.

Given the broad-based assumptions required, this calculation will never be 100-percent accurate. However, it does clearly make two points:

1) This bank's middle market business is a money maker in absolute terms and generates a positive ROE.

2) Given its failure to meet the bank's 17.5 percent ROE hurdle rate, arguably, this business creates little, if any, value for the bank's shareholders.

Determining Action Steps

The next step in economic analysis is to go beyond the macro-numbers to look at individual customers and determine specific action steps. In the disguised but realistic example presented in Exhibit 3.4, only 25 percent of this bank's customers exceeded the desired hurdle rate.

In excess of 30 percent of these customers failed to generate any profit at all. Most other customers provided mediocre returns for this bank. The gap between customer groups appears even more pronounced when the top 25 customers of this bank's unit are compared with its bottom 25. The message sent to management by such an analysis is usually not debated. Quick and strong action is required to stop the flow of an institution's life blood onto the bottom line. Certain customers are value killers.

Once this analytic methodology has been established, banks can analyze their profit numbers by product, business unit, geography, or whatever other segment makes practical sense. Similar analysis can be developed for other wholesale or related businesses.

In the case of the middle market performance gap of approximately 100 basis points shown in Exhibit 3.3, management addressed its gap with a three-step plan.

Exhibit 3.4   Customer Segmentation by Hurdle Rates

Economic analysis of middle market portfolios shows that a substantial number of accounts lose money for the bank in absolute terms. Others are ROE "value destroyers."

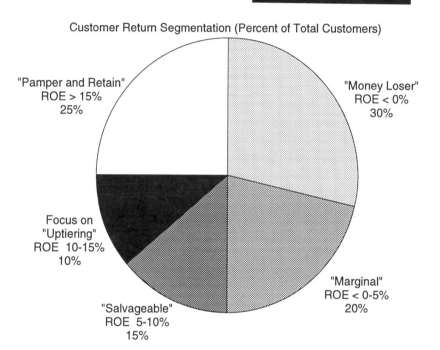

Disguised Bank Example

Customer Return Segmentation (Percent of Total Customers)

"Pamper and Retain"
ROE > 15%
25%

"Money Loser"
ROE < 0%
30%

Focus on
"Uptiering"
ROE 10-15%
10%

"Marginal"
ROE < 0-5%
20%

"Salvageable"
ROE 5-10%
15%

- Operating expenses were reduced by about 20 basis points by the centralization of a number of administrative activities.

- Credit quality improved, not only because of increased supervision and greater consistency in the underwriting process, but also because of the improvement in the overall economy. (Luck is always welcome.) The impact was significant, close to 50 basis points.

- A more rigorous approach to pricing, increasing the involvement of senior management in the pricing process, combined with an increased emphasis on cross-selling generated another 50-plus basis points for the bank.

In the case of this bank and others like it, performing a detailed evaluation of current performance will allow management to focus on opportunities for improving the bottom line and will assist in creating the imperative for change which is so important in many banks.

Creating an Economic Focus

The levers of performance, whether they involve economics or RM productivity, are limited. Banks have relatively few options when attempting to improve their bottom lines. Refocusing the marketing effort on high potential markets and products, improving pricing, and reducing costs are the major choices available to bring about improvement. Conducting a detailed economic analysis allows management to make each of the following disciplines part of a bank's culture.

- *Focus on the best potential current customers and targets.*

   Exhibit 3.5 summarizes the results of evaluating one company's portfolio when it segmented its ROEs by customer industry.

   This disguised bank example reveals that for this particular bank, two industries—communications and health care—generate significantly higher profits than two other areas—insurance and general corporate lending.

   The message of this analysis is not to abandon certain industries or to concentrate on only a few. That may, of course, be the ultimate conclusion, but only after management develops the information base to support such a decision. In the case of the laggard industries, the bank must determine why the poor returns occur. For example, is pricing for this business too low versus other industries? If pricing is, indeed, the key reason for inadequate returns, is low pricing endemic to that

Exhibit 3.5   ROE-Based Industry Analysis

Industry analysis highlights those areas that may merit increased marketing or, conversely, a fundamental reevaluation.

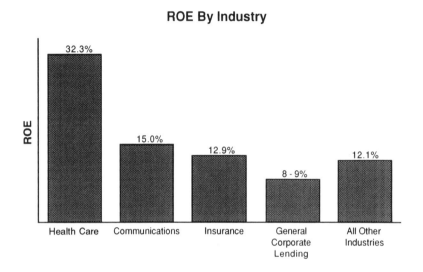

ROE By Industry

particular industry or has the unit's management not been aggressive enough in raising fees?

- *Instill a pricing discipline throughout the corporate bank.*

    Historically banks allow the RM to determine the appropriate pricing structure for loans and related products. ROE often is deliberately omitted from the credit proposal to avoid prejudice. In contrast, most non-banks have specific and well-communicated hurdle rates that must be achieved, or business is not added to the books.

    For example, GFC Financial Corporation (GFC), a non-bank secured lender—which will be profiled as a case study in

Chapter 14—limits the pricing flexibility of its salespersons based on risk/return parameters.

GFC sets a minimum goal of a 15 percent risk-adjusted ROE. Inputs into the pricing required to meet that hurdle include the type of industry (e.g., communications or transportation) and loan, the one-time selling expense required to generate the transaction, yearly maintenance expenses for that type of borrower, lender leverage, type of payment (balloon or amortized, fixed or floating), current and projected costs of funds, and, last but hardly least, the borrower's risk rating. Either the business development officer or an assistant can input this information.

One example of output based on this data appears in Exhibit 3.6; any individual calculation would show substantial differences. This unit of GFC specializes in longer-term loans; obviously, its cost structure and pricing hurdles leads to that type of transaction.

A one-year loan for $1 million requires close to a 30-percent interest rate to reach the company's 15-percent hurdle. That contrasts with rates below 10 percent for loans above $5 million or for maturities beyond four years.

GFC has demonstrated expertise with both the dollar amount and the time frame necessary to meet or exceed its hurdles. A GFC salesperson will focus on those loans that meet the rigorous criteria of the company and will use the pricing model—which is regularly updated—as a screen to determine whether a potential borrower merits additional attention and to determine the degree of negotiating room for an individual deal.

GFC's approach does not simply rely on the "answer" being displayed on a computer screen. Rather, the pricing model offers an important input into the marketing and credit decision process. Recommending a transaction that fails to meet return requirements needs to have a very strong, profit-driven rationale behind it.

Exhibit 3.6   Modeling the Loan Pricing Decision

Loan pricing models allow business generators to focus on companies that meet or exceed hurdle rates of return.

Disguised — Directionally Correct Data

**Loan Pricing Model
Minimum Required Fixed Rates**

Amount (in $ millions)	Year of Loan Maturity			
	1	3	4	5
1	28.8%	18.2	16.7	15.8
2	18.5	13.1	12.4	11.9
3	15.0	11.5	11.0	10.7
4	13.3	10.6	10.2	10.0
5	12.2	10.1	9.8	9.6
10	10.2	9.1	9.0	8.9

- *Evaluate cost reduction opportunities.*

   Benchmarking an area's cost performance against other relevant units and competitors will highlight opportunities for change. The high beams will be pointed toward outlying areas that need management attention.

- *Emphasize high return products.*

   Exhibit 3.7 presents a summary chart that encapsulates how certain businesses are performing today and how they are expected to perform in the future.

Opportunity Mapping

The analytic exercise outlined in this chapter can build internal consensus concerning those industries, geographies, or products

Exhibit 3.7   Opportunity Mapping

Internal agreement on opportunities results from an assessment of product strengths, bank capabilities, and industry potential.

Disguised Bank Example

Areas of Opportunity

Product Area	Consumer Needs	Likely Future Profitability	Degree of Roles for the Bank	Likelihood of Bank Success	Priority for Focus
Asset-Based Lending	High	Medium	Medium	Medium	Medium to High
Private Placements	Low	Medium	Low	Low	Low
Derivatives	Medium	High	High	Low	Low and Limited in Scope (e.g., Broker only
Retirement Plans	High	Medium	Medium	Medium	Medium to High

that the bank should emphasize or, conversely, where it should pull back. Thus, a number of my firm's clients have created detailed assessments of overall business potential by region and industry, leading to the creation of an opportunity map.

Such an approach takes stock of where the bank is today and, as appropriate, repositions it for the future, based upon where higher profits appear to exist. Of course, this approach also demands customization to a particular bank's strengths. This process begins but does not end with the foundation of internal numbers crunching. It also includes a detailed perspective on external market factors and a qualitative assessment of a company's capabilities.

Exhibit 3.8 presents an estimate for the total loan market for one regional bank's key geographic markets. Similar charts can and should be developed for deposit income and major fee-based products such as cash management, trust, and corporate. Once completed, this market sizing map allows banks to generate projected "theoretical" revenue and profit numbers by product, geography, and marketing activities such as cross-sell versus new customer sales, leading to an evaluation of the current versus potential share of wallet for each customer.

While certainly not 100-percent accurate, opportunity mapping allows banks to rely on more guesswork and intuition in judging where to allocate scarce resources. Sources for such an analysis can include Dun & Bradstreet and Equifax reports, Robert Morris Associates studies, bank call reports, and local research, as well as internally developed analyses.

This analysis can play a powerful role in redirecting management. For example, in terms of geography for this bank, city A generates 30 percent of the state's loan volume but only 10 percent of the volume for our client bank. Because the bank appears to be an underachiever in that market and assuming that loan volume translates into profits, management needs to determine whether to invest further to build share or, conversely, to sell its existing business to another bank and concentrate its use of capital to increase its position in another area, such as city B, where the bank is in a stronger competitive position. Again, such analysis initially leads to more questions than it does definitive answers. But the questions are focused and driven by a profit orientation.

This same chart also prompts questions about the bank's need to develop industry specializations further. While the bank already has a number of specialists, several industries that borrow actively, such as textiles and mining, have been overlooked by the bank. In this case, management should determine whether and how to invest personnel in marketing to these industries or, alternatively, reaffirm its desire to minimize exposure to those businesses.

Exhibit 3.8 Assessing Overall Market and Industry Potential

Developing a market-sizing map highlights opportunities for rethinking strategies based upon business potential.

Illustrative

Total Loan Market (in $ millions) Selected Industries

City	Service Industries	Textiles	Communications	Manufacturing	Mining	Percentage of Total Loans	Percent of Current Bank Portfolio
A	3,500	750	900	1,500	500	34	25
B	1,500	500	550	1,200	1,000	23	20
C	1,540	600	400	700	300	17	15
D	1,100	500	450	550	200	13	25
E	1,000	800	300	450	200	13	15
Total	$8,640	$3,150	$2,600	$4,300	$2,200	100%	100%
Percent of All Industries	41	15	12	21	11	100%	

Summary Thoughts

Detailed economic analysis of products and customers is an important input into developing a successful strategy for the middle market. Generating profit or return numbers, however, are not the end of the process. Management actions must be based on an understanding of the dynamics of the banking business and its specific organization. Further, management needs to develop an economic model which evaluates a transaction and a customer on a "life of the deal" (or Present Value) as well as a GAAP basis.

The analysis outlined in this chapter should be second nature to chief financial officers. In too many instances, however, financial analysis activities center on non-interpretive reporting and fails to generate the management information required to run the bank profitably. Those banks that do develop a hard-nosed quantitative approach to assessing their business strategy on a risk-adjusted basis will be at a distinct advantage when matching up against other non-banks. Make no mistake, the GE Capitals and American Expresses of the world have had these skills in place for many years.

4

Marketing: Finding New Customers

"Prospecting is what I do after I've finished everything else."
— *a relationship manager from a southern regional bank*

Recently, a senior banker described his institution's middle market banking philosophy in terms of a pendulum. The arc of the pendulum, never stopping in the middle, swings from credit to marketing, depending on the performance and needs of the bank.

"When the bank was in a credit mode," he said, "the new business effort was virtually ignored. Conversely, when marketing was in the spotlight, additional RMs were hired and higher call goals for new targets were set. The emphasis on marketing usually lasted for two to three years," he said cynically, "until the loans generated by the big marketing push began to sour. Of course, at that point the pendulum then swung back to credit. And, so on."

Contrast that cyclical approach with another bank where a senior banker told me, "We stay in the market at all times and are constantly looking for new targets. Even during periods of tougher credit requirements, we will market aggressively. We do that for several reasons. This lets us keep our finger on the market's pulse, plus we get to know what competitors are doing and how they are changing their focus. Consistent marketing has allowed us to up-grade the quality of our loan portfolio. Another advantage is that we aren't viewed as being in and out of our markets."

It is our contention that rather than illustrating conscious choices in marketing strategies, these two approaches to the market originate in the banks' approach to the process of prospecting.

How much time should be spent prospecting for new customers versus developing current relationships is a conundrum facing every corporate banker: 50:50? 60:40? 30:70?

We recognize that successful banks constantly re-emphasize the importance of their current customers and devote more time to that group. However, new prospects are an important testing ground for the reevaluation of products, offerings, and staff capabilities. Generating high quality, new customers is also an area that is vital to the continued growth of corporate banks.

By quality customers, we are not simply referring to investment-grade credits. Too many banks are focusing on that limited market. We define "quality" as those customers that can generate a level of profitability exceeding the bank's hurdle rate of return through their purchase of bank products. Furthermore, once identified, these targets should make the transition to full-fledged customers within a finite period of time ranging from less than six months to two years. How to determine the highest priority target and, then, convert that target to an established customer is this chapter's focus.

The foundations of effective cross-selling and account planning, which are essential to sustained profitability, begin with prospecting. That process begins with a review not only of "how" a bank currently undertakes its prospecting process but also "why" it focuses on particular prospects.

The Prospecting Process: An Overview

To gain increased efficiency and to achieve rigorous and bank-wide consistency in securing target prospects, banks need to increase reliance on centralized product specialists as well as recognize the role technology can play in screening, pre-qualification, and follow-up. The net result of rethinking the prospecting process and approaching it as a system improves the RM's chance for success when meeting a target. Further, the promise of success can, of course, increase the RM's enthusiasm for what is usually referred to as "cold calling," an activity that is often neglected or actively avoided by many bankers. What the banker quoted at the beginning of this chapter means, of course, is that he did virtually no cold calling.

Prospecting consists of four related steps (Exhibit 4.1). As with other aspects of corporate banking, these incremental activities need to be evaluated holistically and with a clear understanding of their interrelationship.

The first step for target prospecting requires *identifying a "live" prospect name,* that is, simply finding the name of a company that is either new to the bank or has not been evaluated by the banker for a minimum of six months to a year. Name generation leads to the second step, prequalifying the prospect for acceptability and the likelihood of success. After the target name is prequalified, the third step is to make the first call. That call determines the level and type of follow up appropriate and should lead to the final part of the process—an assessment of the time required to convert the prospect and conduct the pursuit or, alternatively, a reconsideration of its priority as a target.

Step 1: Identification

Bank management often loses a rich opportunity to strengthen the effectiveness of its overall marketing program by virtually ignoring this first step of prospecting: identifying viable targets. Typically, the prospect name-generation process is left up to individual bankers who often possess minimal experience in target identification and even less training. While bankers may obtain some names from a centralized marketing group, it is left up to the RMs to determine on whom to call and how to make an approach.

This undirected independence is not employee empowerment. Skimming a stack of D&B reports, making a list and, then, beginning the time-intensive process of cold calling those names amounts to

Exhibit 4.1   Prospecting Process

Success at prospecting requires effective leveraging of the RM.

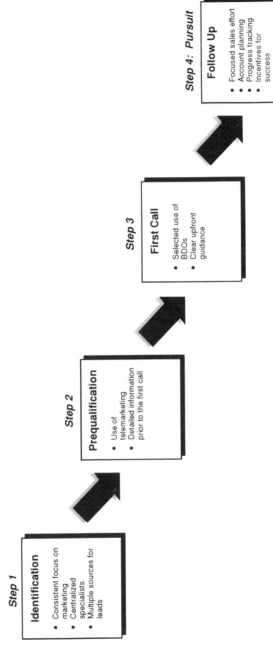

Step 1

Identification

- Consistent focus on marketing
- Centralized specialists
- Multiple sources for leads

Step 2

Prequalification

- Use of telemarketing
- Detailed information prior to the first call

Step 3

First Call

- Selected use of BDOs
- Clear upfront guidance

Step 4: *Pursuit*

Follow Up

- Focused sales effort
- Account planning
- Progress tracking
- Incentives for success

virtual anarchy. The results are invariably low in contrast to banks that use marketing specialists to develop sophisticated databases on prospects. Throughout this chapter, we will be promoting the value of centralizing selected aspects of prospecting, particularly target generation and screening.

As our earlier discussion of the RM's role makes clear, assigned tasks can range from the sophisticated to the mundane. Looking for prospects has to fall into the mundane category. Although its importance as a foundation for successful selling cannot be underestimated, for the most part, prospect identification easily can be shifted away from the RM.

Conducting basic research is an excellent example of a low-value-added task. Those banks with the most consistent marketing effort have dedicated groups working to generate "clean" prospects for the bankers. A centralized source of marketing information also can generate consistently higher quality data on an ongoing basis. Bankers, who are being pulled in many directions, can be deployed more effectively if they concentrate on preparing for pre-screened target calls, making those calls, and then following up, to secure a sale.

Sourcing with Databases

Many banks remain largely dependent on two sources for prospects: either a centralized database purchased from an outside vendor, such as Dun & Bradstreet, Equifax, or Lotus One Source or the inherited prospect files of bankers who have since moved on or out of the bank. Either of these sources of information usually fail to provide sufficient leverage to a banker making the initial cold call.

Virtually every sizable corporate bank does purchase an outside database. Its appropriate use is to provide a foundation for further knowledge gathering, not as the sole source of data about a target prior to making an in-person call. Few bankers who have relied on these databases and, as a result, experienced frustration would disagree that they can be incomplete or inaccurate concerning such fundamentals as company size, financials, and current management. For example, too often, credit-trained bankers spend up to 10 phone calls—one hour or more of a workday—dialing their way through a target company to update information on management and to determine the person or persons whom they should, in fact, have called first.

A marketing support group can perform that time-consuming task at least as well. Plus the generally lower per-employee cost will reduce the cost of prospecting. In any case, banks need to develop a procedure for systematically capturing refinements to the information databases.

One personal anecdote will point out that another regularly used source of names—old prospect files—also frequently leads to frustration and low productivity. When I completed my corporate bank training program in the late 1970s and joined a line unit, I "inherited" a set of prospects that had been called upon in the past. Among those somewhat crusty files, I saw one name that had been on the prospect list since the 1930s. I pulled a D&B report, overcame my trepidation, and telephoned that target. After bouncing around the company because previous bank contacts had moved on, I finally reached a decision maker. Out of pity or perversity, he agreed to a meeting. At that meeting, he made clear that yet another generation of bankers from my bank would fail to gain his company as a customer.

Although I received "credit" for the call, I realized that the meeting had delivered zero value to my bank, which—if it had instituted a better screening and priority setting system—would have demoted that prospect years ago. Generations of newly minted bankers had called on that target, all with the same lack of success. Was the company a "real" prospect? Unlikely. Should that name have been on anyone's list? Also, unlikely.

Alternative Approaches

Other, more creative sources for generating prospects exist—some more time consuming and effective than others. Scanning regional business periodicals can uncover new names in a geographic area and spotlight growing companies.

Similarly, some banks use what they term "drive-bys" or "windshield surveys" of local business parks to find unknown potential targets. We suspect that most of these mobile surveys take place on sunny Friday afternoons. In either case, both these approaches are likely to lead to targets more suitable to the small business area.

As will be discussed in a separate chapter, applying a middle market or large corporate organization or marketing approach to the small business effort is economically unfeasible. Even if the drive-bys do by chance uncover middle market names, racking up expense mileage is, without a doubt, an inefficient use of the RM's expensive professional time.

In a market where more and more customers regard traditional bank services as commodities, a bank's prospecting effort has to focus on tactics that can distinguish it from "the pack of gray suits." For example, RMs can play an important role in using current customer contacts to reach targets who otherwise might be inaccessible. Making the current customer a salesperson for the bank has relevance to all markets, small and large, but surprisingly, this opportunity remains largely ignored by most banks and is used inconsistently at best.

One bank of note regularly organizes informal dinners for clients where an internal bank economist or external guest speaker may be the main attraction. RMs invite selected customers also asking them to nominate a friend to attend, someone who is an executive with a company that may be an attractive target for the bank. Importantly, the bank pre-screens invitees to make certain that, at least on a preliminary basis, they appear creditworthy and also offer the bank multiple selling opportunities beyond lending. The current customer becomes part of the bank's sales team, albeit in an informal way. Because the bank has, in effect, received a stamp of approval from a peer who is also a bank customer, the target views the bank more favorably from day one.

The benefits of such creative marketing approaches are numerous. From the customer perspective, those who provide the "leads" are usually pleased at being singled out for a special event. Further, they respond positively to the confidence that the RM exhibits by asking for their help in suggesting a target. While the prospects may not know the bank or the RM, they do trust their business associate and will consider attending. The RM makes points with his current customer and has an excellent chance for quality follow-up meetings with the target.

Any negative fallout from such a prospecting tactic would result from factors that good execution should be able to avoid—for example, inviting a marginally attractive prospect or one who has received a prior credit turn-down from the bank. Of course, the worst-case situation and one reason why some banks will not try this method of prospect generation would be a situation where the current customer feels that his friend had been treated unfairly by the bank. That eventuality can be avoided with careful upfront planning, again suggesting the value of RMs working with an experienced, dedicated team within the bank to focus on the "nitty gritty" aspects of marketing.

Even before looking outside to customers' references or to data-bases, banks need to make certain that they are fully leveraged off internal contacts. For example, do the small business and middle market groups interact regularly with private banking to obtain internal referrals? The Trust group, which often operates with great independence within banks, should not be forgotten as an excellent source of referrals. Breaking down these internal communications boundaries to find additional leads should be a very high priority for bank management. As will be discussed in the next chapter in the context of cross-selling, any internal constraints related to business unit accounting or compensation credit need to be resolved quickly without rancor to ensure cooperation.

Prospect identification requires a great deal of creativity as well as a reliance on old fashioned "blocking and tackling." As the case example of Chemical Bank in the next chapter illustrates, one top performer can transform a task that many banks fail to perceive as important into a real competitive advantage. Going forward, developing a rigorous prospect-generation system where the RM's activities are limited to key high value areas, will only increase in importance and ultimate payback.

Step 2: Prequalification

As with prospect identification, the banker is usually personally responsible for qualifying a prospect and refining the prospect list, receiving little outside assistance either from a team leader or areas outside his unit. Unfortunately, history shows that banks have not been successful at building cross-matrix teams.

Based upon the database and information on file, the banker may eliminate a few names that appear to be unattractive from his list—for example, those with a history of negative net income—and then proceed to contact one of the companies to set up an appointment. While the banker may have a rough idea about the customer's interest in the bank's capabilities and products, the first call is really a scouting mission with low odds of near-term success.

Support areas in most banks—such as centralized marketing units, if they exist—usually play a passive role in the screening process, acting on specific officer requests, rather than functioning as a pro-active member of a relationship team. Marketing groups usually are located both organizationally and physically distant from the line bankers and are often viewed as part of the amorphous "staff" whose salaries the line bankers work to generate.

In contrast to this tedious and somewhat random process of screening targets, a more effective prequalification process can yield quick results. Innovative banks have already largely removed the corporate banker from the cold-call process, employing instead a centralized group of experienced telemarketers to conduct an initial assessment of the attractiveness of a target and the high priority product areas. The on-site first call, then, can take on the content of a "second" or "third" call, greatly improving the chances for a high impact meeting.

Broadly, this approach to prospect identification and prequalification works as follows:

A marketing group, reporting to the head of the corporate bank or another senior line executive, develops a detailed prospect list. (Scale and expertise should determine who runs this group and where it reports.) The starting point for this list is a database, such as D&B or Equifax, supplemented by lists from local Chambers of Commerce or business newspapers. The marketing group then focuses on gaining additional information on the prospect names to prequalify them as potential customers. Their methodology is not industrial espionage or even detailed spread sheet analysis; they simply telephone the targets and ask a set of pre-determined questions.

Telemarketing, whether operated by an internal group or purchased from an outside vendor (outsourced) can increase productivity in sales calling dramatically. This is one of several approaches for warming up the cold call. Telemarketing can be applied across all the commercial banking segments from small business to middle market and large corporate. While telemarketing can be extremely helpful for the middle and large corporate markets, the economics of small business banking—as will be reviewed in Chapter 15—make telemarketing and other techniques to avoid cold calling essential to success.

When banks use marketing specialists, the professional telemarketers usually are able to reach a decision maker or at least someone who knows the company's current use of bank products. Within a five to 10-minute conversation, professionals can elicit key information, including: current bank or banks, recent profit or losses, borrowing status, use of other non-credit products, product needs, and the relationship with current banks. Importantly, the telemarketers usually work with a banker's schedule in front of them so that they can immediately arrange a first appointment for the banker to call in person. This eliminates both the impact of the banker's potential—although understandable—hesitancy to make a cold call and his inexperience in doing so unsuccessfully.

The degree of leverage that this process provides to the calling effort cannot be underestimated. The approach removes the nervousness of the initial cold call from the banker's shoulders, allows the bank to differentiate itself positively with the target when the first in-person call occurs, and sends a clear message to the banker from senior management about the significance of the customer calling effort. The development of this prospect generation and qualification "engine" is a key building block for creating a sales culture within a bank.

Step 3: The Initial Call

Banks need to view the initial prospect call as the beginning of a multi-month or multi-year investment process. All too often, bankers make one or two calls, fail to generate business and then go on to another prospect. Few banks have the procedures in place to support a rigorous, longer-term process. This discipline is particularly important in light of the generally lower experience level of bankers responsible for earning their stripes by generating new business.

Our analysis for clients and industry associations of multiple banks indicates that less-experienced bankers—those with less than five years of experience—do most of the prospect calling as part of their on-the-job training. By the time they are promoted to vice-president they are experienced bankers who ideally should be able to develop a more consultative relationship with corporate business managers and be better able to speak for the bank. All too often, however, they have been rotated to staff, credit, or account management positions that severely limit or even eliminate their selling time. Even senior bankers who regularly call on established customers are rare commodities.

Further, while the prequalification process weeds out some unqualified prospects—based upon public data and any information the telemarketers are able to obtain—that process only functions as a preliminary screen. Additional calls are needed to qualify and prioritize prospects. That being the case, the banker needs to be armed with an internal checklist of information to obtain from the company as well as a tool kit of sales and negotiation tactics.

Here is where the guidance of an experienced banker can be invaluable. In Chapter 6, one of the topics is managing the sales process. We will discuss the importance of a team leader's role as sales manager as well as cultural change agent, one who supports and "lights a fire" under the calling team. As key players on the front lines, these team leaders play a critical role in nurturing a sales mentality throughout the corporate bank. Their effectiveness needs to be evaluated, and their compensation package should reflect their contribution.

Business Development Officers

A small but increasing number of banks, both money center and regionals, use Business Development Officers (BDOs) to cover their middle market and upper-end small business accounts. For example, one major southeast super-regional, First Union, is now piloting the use of BDOs.

The role of BDOs is highly focused and straightforward. Typical RMs divide their time into three buckets, marketing, credit, and account maintenance—a job description rife with inherent conflicts. The BDOs, in contrast, have one primary task; they spend almost all their time marketing. They make the initial calls, cultivate the prospect, and involve a relationship manager only after a lead gets hot. Typically, BDOs have no credit authority, and they are not involved in the ongoing account monitoring or cross-selling. Although they usually focus on loan sales, they receive credit for fee-related business as well.

BDOs are professional salespersons or rainmakers. Some are line bankers transferred to this specialist role; others are former salespeople for manufacturing or service products. Since BDOs fill a non-traditional role, they are also often compensated non-traditionally. A program of 100-percent commission against a monthly draw is not atypical. A highly successful BDO can earn substantially more than an RM at the same bank. The BDO, in effect, builds the business stream supporting that compensation package.

Banks that use RMs for all marketing activities usually raise multiple objections to the introduction of the BDO role. One immediate objection raised by management is "Customers will not like it." In the words of one manager, "They want to deal with a decision-maker not an order-taker." Managers frequently mention the difficulty of transitioning accounts from one person to another. Additionally, traditional bankers express concern about cutting RMs out of the sales process and possibly decreasing their selling skills if their training time in front of potential customers is curtailed.

Bankers also view with distrust the possibility of internal conflicts between the sales and credit culture, and, as you might expect, objections are often raised about compensation, such as "You're creating a two-tier compensation system in the bank" or "They're salespeople who don't pay attention to the risks and credit quality."

Each of these objections can be dealt with. The target customer, of course, wants to understand the decision process a bank uses. If it is explained effectively and if the RM is transitioned into the relationship as it evolves, the customer will understand and accept the bank's approach. The customer simply wants to avoid any surprises and ensure both quality service and continuity. Few customers actually expect their bankers to be superpeople.

As for the internal politics, a team relationship needs to be cultivated between the BDOs and the RMs. In banks where this system has been introduced successfully, each group learns the challenges that the other group faces and exhibits respect for their colleagues. Interestingly, the BDO seldom yearns for the RM's job, or vice versa. As for the argument that the BDO structure will limit the RM's selling skills, this two-track system, in fact, increases the time available for the RM to market to current customers. The RM's responsibility for selling is not eliminated by the use of a BDO. The emphasis, however, may change. The RM's success criteria now can be geared to deepening relationships through the sale of additional credit and non-credit products.

Despite the objections raised, banks that use this approach speak highly of it and have encountered minimal customer confusion. Account transitions from BDO to RM occur with success because clear procedures and motivations exist for that transfer.

First, the RM meets with the target customer well before the bank approves a transaction, preparing the customer for any switch in account management. In fact at many banks, the RM takes over account responsibility as soon as a business opportunity arises. For example, at Wells Fargo, it is usually the RM who will shepherd a deal through the credit process, not the BDO. *Second*, both the BDO and the RM realize it is in their self-interest for the transition to work. *Third*, senior management makes sure that the BDO/RM structure works by getting involved quickly when problems occur.

As for BDOs' compensation, the 1990s will see increased variability in total compensation tied to performance. Bluntly, RMs cannot expect to receive automatic salary increases or a substantial incentive payout if their focus is primarily on internal monitoring activities. They will be paid at a "maintenance" level for the maintenance activities they perform. If they generate more bottom line income for the bank, both BDOs and RMs deserve to be rewarded.

BDOs may not be appropriate for all banks, and this change requires a major culture change for many banks. However, in instances where RMs, for whatever reason, have been slow to mount a consistent sales development program, the introduction of a BDO function, whether permanent or temporary, serves to "gin up" the sales effort. As one manager said, "Bankers gravitate toward paperwork." One workable response, in addition to eliminating or rerouting administrative paper away from the banker, is to establish a "paperwork-less" BDO group.

Bank Ambassadors

In lieu of a formal BDO structure, some banks employ bankers with long tenure and excellent community contacts to serve as ambassadors for the bank. The role of these bankers is to remain plugged into their local community and develop close ties with industry associations as well as intermediary groups, such as accountants and lawyers. While these ambassadors rarely have meaningful, if any, credit authority, they can be highly effective representatives and lead generators for the bank.

When I began my banking career in New York's garment district, we had one such experienced banker on our staff. He played an important role in assisting younger bankers, had an excellent ability to check out potential borrowers through his network, and basically knew just about everyone important to know in the garment, textile, and apparel businesses.

This approach worked because this gentleman understood and maintained the bank's screening criteria. This role has been tried often and then abandoned because the ambassador became a magnet for low-quality deals that clogged up the marketing and underwriting pipelines and created ill will through numerous turndowns.

The Need for Upfront Guidance

No matter who does the calling, front-line marketers need to be kept informed concerning the bank's changing appetite for borrowers and their profiles.

Norwest, a leading bank, focuses its calling program by employing an "upfront guidance system" across its holding company structure. This approach, which impacts both target calling and current customers, coordinates the bank's marketing effort with its overall goals for portfolio exposure to a particular company, industry, or type of risk. Norwest's system allows the bank to model specific prospects and determine the degree and type of exposure with which it would be comfortable prior to a formal request for credit. As one Norwest officer explained when describing the approach, "We try to marry loan policy and marketing." Again, the emphasis is on a holistic approach to both credit and marketing across the bank, dispelling any atmosphere of conflict.

One example of how a bank might use an upfront guidance system illustrates its value. On a 12 to 18 month basis, this example bank would review its exposure to key business segments. The line and credit officers would then make a joint determination concerning the level of ongoing exposure with which they were comfortable.

For instance, company-wide our example bank may have a $100 million risk exposure to the fast-food restaurant industry. Given a mediocre economy, the already high market share of fast-food restaurants, and stable-to-weakening financials, the bank may decide to reduce its industry exposure to the $75 million range. At the same time, another industry group may be assessed as ripe for expansion, based on the bank's knowledge about its market's likely performance. In that case, the bank could decide to grow its industry exposure from the current $100 million level to $150 million, encouraging an industry-focused marketing effort. This information would then become part of the screening and account planning process, driving the marketing strategy.

This scenario is fictional, but a similar process is followed at several banks. Clearly, this evaluation and planning system first requires that the holding company or bank be able to capture exposure information, cutting across business unit and geographic lines. The value of such an upfront guidance process is at least threefold:

- *First,* as part of the information collection process, the possibility of any unfortunate surprises is reduced. For example, "We had no idea that we had such a large exposure to that company bankwide," will not be an acceptable excuse.

- *Second,* upfront guidance provides a clear message to the calling officer on where the bank stands with certain industries, eliminating guesswork and wasted energy. Every banker can tell stories of writing up a credit only to learn that, while the credit appeared solid, its industry had fallen into disfavor.

- *Third,* having a systematic process for reviewing industries creates a consistent focus throughout the bank. Different product units or subsidiaries will assess the same industry segment with the same degrees of risk appetite.

Obviously, such a system is not a simple template; it must allow for special circumstances and an appeal process. Nonetheless, both the quality of the portfolio and the calling effort are brought into focus throughout the prospecting process.

Step 4: The Pursuit

Finally, after the prospect identification, prequalification, and the initial call are completed, a live prospect emerges. But as all bankers know, prospects can take a minimum of six months to one year or more to convert to meaningful clients.

There are three key elements to this follow-up process:

1) Focus the sales effort.

2) Reenergize the banker.

3) Track and reward progress.

Focus the Sales Effort

If banks establish a rigorous prospect-generation and prequalification process, the target names, when converted, should offer a substantial return to the bank.

Therefore, concentrating on fewer live prospects rather than filling a quota with a high number of poor quality calls should become a priority. Approximately 10 to 15 prospects appear to be an appropriate number for a banker to handle along with a full account load. In contrast, some bankers today have an overwhelming 50 to 100 prospects for which they are responsible.

A successful calling program involves more than a quarterly visit or semiannual lunch. Banks with a marketing orientation focus a much more intensive calling effort on their selected targets. Typically, managers encourage monthly contact, either a mailer on a topic of interest or a phone call, if not an information gathering meeting with a decision maker. Such an intensive program will distinguish a bank from others that show passing interest only two or three times a year.

Banks that are among the most successful at marketing believe that one key to winning business is simply being there when targets become dissatisfied with their current bank or when new business requirements arise. Persistency and consistency, hardly new concepts in sales and marketing, have a proven positive impact on relationship building. Banks that narrow the number of targets they are consistently calling on to the highest priority names, therefore, increase the likelihood that they will start a profitable relationship.

Reenergize the Banker

Many corporate bank RMs continue to view themselves as professionals who are a breed apart from their sales-oriented consumer bank colleagues. More than a few highly successful banks and non-banks, however, have achieved great success by borrowing techniques from the consumer side.

Corporate banks need to loosen up on their self-images and reach out to middle market customers. Companies like Chemical, Norwest, and CIT regularly use sales promotion techniques, some internally focused and others directed at the customer. These pitches both differentiate the bank and the RM from the competition as well as unite an internal bank culture that supports the marketing effort. Any significant resistance to sales gimmicks melts when management learns how well targets and customers react to them.

Here is one example of how Chemical Bank exploited media speculation that there was a credit crunch in 1992. Not surprisingly, banks had been accused of being unwilling to lend, and numerous horror stories about the impact of bank reluctance made headlines across the country. While the media wrote articles on how the banks were negatively affecting the already struggling economy, Chemical's Middle Market Banking Group turned a potential crisis into a marketing coup. The bank mailed out thousands of Nestle Crunch bars to customers and high-priority prospects. Along with the candy came a letter signed by Frank Lourenso, the executive vice-president in charge of Chemical's Middle Market Group, stating that the only "crunch" a qualified borrower would find at Chemical was from the enclosed candy bar.

This inexpensive promotion delivered a clear message. Potential borrowers learned that at least one bank was interested in lending to them, and the message was delivered in a non-threatening, humorous way. Competitors were put on the defensive. By inference, if Chemical was not tightening lending and if a lending crunch existed, then, it had to be the other banks that were slow to lend. Those banks had to develop their own defensive response or be placed in a negative light. And, if they had any doubts, Chemical's own bankers had received a clear message from senior management that the bank intended to grow its business, including lending to new customers.

The promotion was even picked up in the local press, providing free and highly attractive publicity for the bank. Unprofessional? Hardly. In fact this tactic is a sign of a new breed of hard-charging, customer-focused professionals who work to anticipate the needs of customers and targets.

Another energizing technique used at Chemical and other banks builds internal enthusiasm for increasing monthly call totals. It is called a "blitz" and occurs on a day specifically dedicated to calling. A blitz day has a marketing theme, and all the bankers across the Middle Market Group call on five or more targets during the eight-hour time frame. Depending upon the customer focus of a particular blitz, the calling effort may even employ the highest-level managers within the bank.

Blitz campaigns can be used for multiple purposes. For example, the campaign may take advantage of another bank's misfortunes or may sell a specific product. A bank can organize a blitz day in reaction to the announcement of unfavorable news about a competitor, perhaps lower earnings or a publicized change of direction, such as pulling out of or de-emphasizing a particular industry.

If the blitzing bank has created a rigorous target database, it can generate a list of those companies that bank with specific competitors, organized by unit or banker. Management can then launch a calling effort on that "wounded" competitor's customers, taking advantage of concerns about that bank's ability or willingness to service needs. If this seems like war, it is.

Alternatively, banks have blitz days that spotlight one product, such as a cash management service or an investment offering. In preparation for that event, the bankers learn more about the product, its applications, and customer benefits. This knowledge will prove to be of value long after the blitz is completed and reinforces other training.

When the blitz day arrives, the bankers sell that one product while still, of course, addressing other needs if they arise. It is important to note that the appointment set-up process for a blitz day is best handled by a telemarketing group. Taking that time-consuming responsibility away from the RM further illustrates the value that this market support group can offer.

Blitz campaigns send a dramatic message to bank officers on the importance of marketing and can be a catalytic agent in changing corporate culture to emphasize teamwork. If a bank's chairman and president takes part in a blitz or in regular business calling in addition to the occasional golf tournament, the message is clear: this bank wants to sell and refuses to sit passively sitting on the sidelines waiting for the phone to ring.

Track and Reward Progress

Increased calling alone does not ensure marketing success. Management must continually track calling programs to analyze the success of each approach, the volume of products sold, and the level of banker effectiveness. Without an effective tracking mechanism, banks will never gain full value from their field experience. Again, such performance tracking is second nature on the consumer side of the bank. To reinforce the learning process, it is important to enlist bankers in the tracking process. A number of banks allow RMs to count a call as contributing to that banker's monthly goals only after they enter it into the MIS system.

Of course, even with required reporting, bankers can "game" any system. In one case, a well-respected regional bank hired a new head for its corporate bank. He quickly established calling goals based on those he had implemented at his previous bank.

But these targets were considered too aggressive by some RMs. To paraphrase one skeptical banker, "This is not a big city like the one he came from. It's just not possible to make the number of calls he wants each month."

The banker making that comment applied various creative approaches to circumvent the higher calling requirements. For example, she invited 10 prospects to a sporting event, using the bank's private box. Ten invitees equated to 10 target calls during that month for her, even though little business was discussed. This was a clever approach to reach call goals but clearly not what the senior banker intended. This circumvention shows the need for multi-dimensional performance goals, a topic to be discussed in Chapter 11.

To avoid the gaming or "cooking" of numbers and to provide a safety net for bankers who are not succeeding, the tracking system must capture not only actual calls made but also successes. If over the course of six months of calling a banker fails to generate any substantial business, management should intervene. Assuming that the call gaming described above failed to lead to new business, the poor performer will be caught by the periodic analysis of performance by a seasoned senior manager reviewing the results. On the more positive side, it can lead to remedial steps to assist those bankers who are showing sincere effort but achieving little return.

A performance analysis should answer the following questions: Who is the RM calling on? Is additional training required? Which bankers should co-call with the RM to provide the benefit of their experience?

A training and support program can then be customized to meet individual needs, in sharp contrast to the situation at a majority of banks where sales training is usually limited (such as a one-time sales course) or, more likely, non-existent. "OTJ" (on-the-job training) is the industry standard with junior bankers relying on more experienced bankers as role models. Unfortunately, that senior banker has learned to sell in the same way and may not be an effective teacher for others. If after 12 months of supervision, returns are still not coming in, the diagnosis is clear and unambiguous.

Tracking systems can also lead to creating "pipeline reports" that forecast likely deal revenues and loan outstandings from prospects. Deals expected to close within 90 days or less should appear on that report. If they fail to close within that time, they are then dropped off and reinstated only after senior management review. Accurate pipeline reports aid the budgeting process and, once established, have proven highly accurate, that is, correct 80 percent or more of the time at banks where they are in use. Similarly, analysis of these reports also highlights the causes, whether infrequent or chronic, of differences between forecast and actual results.

Just as lack of success can lead to private remedial action, success should result in public celebration. A marketing "win" by an RM does not always have to be rewarded with cash or an expensive gift. That said, some banks publicly present a check each month to the most successful new business marketer or allow an immediate "tip" to be paid by a cross-sell product area, for example, whenever a middle management group makes a sizable trust or cash management sale.

As an alternative to immediate cash compensation, Norwest makes an inexpensive but highly visible symbolic gesture. In Minneapolis when a Norwest banker takes a customer away from another bank, a senior manager comes to that banker's desk and delivers a "Sting Bee," a stuffed animal signifying that the banker has helped Norwest "sting" the competition. This small token is presented with fanfare and highlights the bank's appreciation for the RM's achievement. The bee is proudly displayed at the desk. Obviously, its monetary worth is low, but the recognition effectively boosts morale and provides a corporate pat on the back.

Summary Thoughts

The retention of profitable accounts will gain in importance during this period of slow economic growth. Nonetheless, prospecting for new accounts needs to receive continued focus. Abandoning the traditional approach to prospecting will increase the quality of the marketing effort and reenergize the RM who often dreads the cold call process.

5

Creating a Sales Focus
Case Study: Chemical Bank

"Because its purpose is to create a customer, the business enter-
prise has two—and only these two—basic functions: marketing
and innovation. [They] produce results; all the rest are costs."
—Peter Drucker

Many bankers may not immediately view Chemical Bank or its
New York City-based Middle Market Banking Group as comparable to their own situations. Chemical is one of the five largest banks
in the United States with $149.9 billion in assets at the end 1993. The
bank operates in one of the most extraordinary U.S. markets—metropolitan New York—and also maintains a worldwide presence.
Perhaps most notably, following the merger with Manufacturers
Hanover, Chemical's market share in the middle market approaches approximately 56 percent, meaning that Chemical does
business with 56 percent of metropolitan area companies of $10
million to $500 million in revenues. On average, these companies
use three banks for their needs.

While the comparison may be unexpected, the organization,
focus, and accomplishments of Chemical's Middle Market Banking
Group provide highly relevant lessons about marketing and offer

an approach to prospecting and cross-selling that can be implemented at all banks, large or small.

Overview

Chemical may be the best example of a U.S. bank that has adopted sales and marketing practices typically considered appropriate only for retail and rarely for corporate, applying them consistently to a middle market customer base. Additionally, the bank has developed an infrastructure to help the RM plunge into the marketplace and "warm up" the cold call. Further, within a relatively short period of time, the bank has established a marketing machine that not only continues to generate prospects but also provides high-quality information about those prospects.

Given the size and complexity of its overall organization, Chemical's ability to develop a successful marketing program from a strategy based in part on flexibility and individual empowerment is all the more remarkable. Chemical's success in overcoming hurdles and institutionalizing a sales culture should provide encouragement to other managers who are in the early stages of creating a sales management system.

The thrust behind Chemical's marketing and sales promotion emphasizes the bank's fundamental belief that a "relationship" with the company's decision-makers is necessary "to make the sale." That relationship rests on finding a "common ground" with the principals and leaders of a company. Reaching that common ground provides a means of differentiation for any bank.

In contrast, as continued product commoditizing occurs, many competitor banks appear, from corporations' viewpoints, to be selling extremely similar services to their customers. Developing points of differentiation, by using sales promotions combined with a strong and continuous selling effort, should, therefore, not be viewed as a gimmick but as a necessity. In fact, this combination approach may become a requirement for bank managers who wish to design successful middle market marketing programs.

Current Organization

Chemical's Middle Market Group covers all corporations including non-profits operating in the metropolitan New York area with sales from $1 million to $500 million. Chemical divides its marketplace into small business ($1 million to $10 million), the broad middle market ($10 million to $500 million), and industry-focused groups, such as the textile and apparel industry centered in New York's garment district. Close to 500 relationship managers work out of 30 regions that are grouped into 10 divisions. Bank management reports that the Group handles approximately 25,000 active relationships. The bank estimates that its RMs made approximately 150,000 calls in 1993 with individual RMs in some regions averaging close to 40 prospect and customer calls per month.

Frank Lourenso, executive vice-president, heads the Middle Market Banking Group (Exhibit 5.1). Among the areas reporting to Lourenso are line business units and the marketing division headed by Andy Parton, a vice-president and director of marketing, who is based at Chemical's Park Avenue headquarters.

Parton describes his division's role as "driving the sales process." Broadly, his marketing group has the following responsibilities:

- Developing and now managing a 400,000-name customer and prospect database.

- Operating a telemarketing group that pre-screens prospects and sets up appointments for RMs.

- Running multiple sales blitzes.

- Designing sales promotions and advertising that is targeted at the overall small business and middle markets.

- Working with individual line managers and RMs to create target-specific marketing pitches.

- Coordinating new product introductions.

- Overseeing and analyzing prospect and customer call tracking.

Exhibit 5.1   Chemical's Middle Market Banking Group

Chemical's middle market has a dedicated credit officer and a structured finance group.

Chemical's Middle Market Organization

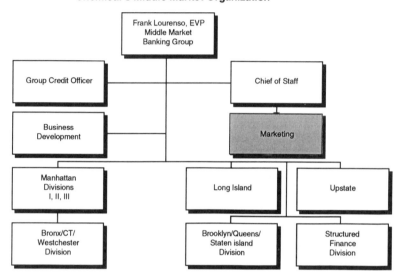

Parton has six employees that report directly to him: three marketing managers, a communications manager, a direct marketing manager, and a creative manager. General responsibilities for the marketing program are split among them. The *marketing managers* have geographic responsibility for providing all marketing support services to a number of the 10 regions for which they are individually responsible. They also have functional responsibility for one or more activities such as advertising, sports marketing, sales promotions, telemarketing, and merger integration.

The *communications manager* oversees all customer communications, including sales letters and brochures. The *direct marketing manager* oversees the operation of the telemarketing group and the customer/prospect database. And, the *creative manager* focuses on developing sales promotions, direct marketing projects, and the execution of other related sales initiatives.

The marketing group's mandate and the bank's overall middle market organization clearly show that Chemical has established a fairly seamless infrastructure that provides a significant level of internal support and external focus. Valuable insights can be gained, however, by examining how far Chemical's capabilities have progressed in less than 10 years. More than a decade ago in 1983, no corporate marketing group existed. The database consisted of files kept by individual RMs, and active marketing programs were avoided by most RMs who viewed themselves as fully occupied professionals reacting to customer requests.

Stages of Development

The three stages in the evolution of Chemical's marketing focus can provide senior bank management with a time frame and guidelines for introducing a sales management program into their banks. Changing a bank's sales culture starts with a renewed emphasis on selling and sales promotion and requires empowering a determined, creative individual "pioneer" as process manager. Next, it requires finding line managers, who may be skeptical, but are nonetheless willing to try non-traditional sales approaches to differentiate their calls. Finally, bank management must show a willingness to recast the RM's role and provide the tools to support a hard-driving sales culture.

Quick Wins, 1985–86

Until approximately 1985, no dedicated marketing resources were assigned to Chemical's middle market and small business groups. The bank's middle market marketing staff consisted of one person, Andy Parton, whose background was in consumer goods advertising and marketing for a retail brokerage firm. Until then, the bank's marketing needs had been served by the retail area, which did offer some capabilities and internal services to the corporate side of the bank. Given the internal hierarchy and allocation of resources, however, the corporate bankers could not gain the level of service they felt their market deserved.

One of Parton's first projects involved writing direct mail sales letters for managers in Chemical's Connecticut office and Westchester loan production offices. During that period, competitor banks operating in those geographic areas appeared to be reducing corporate lending activity as a result of performance problems. This created a growth opportunity for Chemical. But two problems remained: how to target prospects and how to get in the door?

At that point, no central database existed with prospect information; names were kept in hard copy files. The bankers' knowledge of their geographic market indicated that certain troubled banks concentrated their efforts in specific zip codes. Therefore, companies in those zip codes were judged receptive targets for a direct mail program that would emphasize Chemical's commitment to serve corporate needs. The plan was to articulate concerns that these local companies probably felt about their current bank and its willingness to lend. The letter served as an opening for the Chemical bankers to telephone and set up get-to-know-us meetings.

Writing sales letters can hardly be labeled a sophisticated marketing task. Nonetheless, it is time consuming and was a clear need on the part of the line managers. This project also provided an opening for Parton to develop a relationship with the bankers. It is also worth noting that the first offices to use this new resource were those units that were physically distant from headquarters and were beginning to operate in new markets. Opportunities to work with the more established bankers in mature markets of Manhattan took longer to develop.

Warming Up the Cold Call, 1986–87

Beyond the need for the basic sales tools such as letters, Parton discovered that RMs repeatedly expressed frustration with the process of cold calling. In their view, cold calling was a waste of time. It led to only a few meaningful appointments and demanded a level of banker proactivity that was clearly not the norm in the mid-1980s. But the markets were changing, and to achieve growth the bank began to experiment slowly with ways to warm up the cold call.

During 1986, Chemical produced its first testimonial advertisement featuring the head of David's Cookies, one of the first gourmet cookie franchisers. The second testimonial was from Prince Spaghetti. At year-end, the bank also decided to conduct its first sales promotion based upon a highly successful deal. Chemical had been the lead bank in New York-based Prince Spaghetti's acquisition of two related companies—Aunt Millie's, a sauce company, and Muller's, best known for its egg noodles. With three well-known consumer products in hand, the bank had the opportunity to invite customers to the table, so to speak.

One hundred prospects received gift boxes containing samples of products from the three companies. Prospects targeted were companies with sales in excess of $50 million and were spread out over 20 regions primarily in metropolitan New York. The targets for these mailings were attractive companies that had previously been unwilling to meet with a Chemical RM. With the samples came a letter that stated in effect, "Look what we did for Prince. Think what we can do for you." As a follow-up, the bankers called to set up appointments. The net result was that RMs arranged appointments with about 35 percent of those who received a promotion package. A response rate that high for a cold call pitch was considered unusual and a notable success by both RMs and line management.

With that pilot test under their collective belt, the marketing group teamed up with a line manager in one of the outer boroughs of New York who wanted to increase his selling effort. The result was Chemical's first, multi-part sales promotion in the spring of 1987. It began with the mailing of a tennis ball and a note reading, "The ball is in your court when you bank with Chemical." In the second mailing to the same target group was a golf ball and another accompanying letter stating, "As a bank, we're on the ball." Finally, a baseball was delivered with a letter stating "Here's the pitch" and requesting a meeting. All the balls were imprinted with the Chemical logo. Prospects "caught on," and a response rate of 50 percent was achieved when the bankers called to set up meetings.

As corny and unprofessional as these gimmicks may, at first, appear, they have proven to be successful ice-breakers and have provided points of differentiation time and time again. Based on these initial successes and the interest of more aggressive RMs, promotions are now institutionalized across the small business and middle market. Initial RM resistance has melted away in the face of success, and, in fact, bankers now regularly look for more promotions and events that they can use to differentiate themselves.

Events-based marketing, particularly tied to sports, has become increasingly important to Chemical. Although multiple examples exist, two provide significant insight into the power of this tactic.

Chemical is a major sponsor of the New York Mets. During the course of the baseball season, the Mets hold a number of sports clinics for children. At one, the bank invites the children of top customers and prospects, thereby making many mothers and fathers heroes in the eyes of their kids, who receive tips from their favorite ball players and go home with autographs. Obviously, the event generates good will, helping to create strong ties between the bank and its invitees.

In another case, an RM was calling on a new prospect who expressed satisfaction with his current bank, saying "You're all the same." The banker noticed the collection of New York Giants football memorabilia in the prospect's office, and she inquired about his interest. She decided to mention that Chemical sponsored lunches for customers and prospects with Giants team members also invited. The RM left the prospect's office at the end of her first call on the company with the financials, and she gives credit for her success to Chemical's events-based marketing program.

Certainly, customers will not sign on or remain at a bank simply because of lunches or other promotional events. Obviously, high quality service and excellent products are also required. Unique promotions, however, may provide banks with an edge, the one thing that singles them out from the pack and makes them less of a gray suit, and even friendly. Promotions by themselves, however, provide little benefit. They must be integrated into a larger program that emphasizes prospecting and cross-selling.

Emphasis on Selling, 1987 and Beyond

The third stage of Chemical Bank's marketing program institution-alized the processes into a sales culture and reconfigured the roles played by key members of the selling team.

Database Management

Prior to 1987, the only marketing "database" supporting the Chemical RM consisted of Dun & Bradstreet reports, which RMs had to request from the retail marketing area. This process was time-consuming and the information obtained on middle management companies was often inaccurate or incomplete. A rudimentary call-tracking system also existed; it required the RM to complete a four-part form that recorded the number of calls made during the month but did not update or refine the D&B information.

During 1987, the Middle Market Group took control of its call-tracking database, allowing the Group increased access to prospect names and giving the ability to add information of particular relevance to the corporate marketing effort. Physically, database operations were moved to the Long Island operations center where, to this day, the marketing database runs on a Wang computer system. At the same time, the marketing unit began to find new ways to answer RM complaints that, while they had increased the number of cold calls, the quality and yield of those calls remained low. Cold calling was still viewed as unproductive and with as much chance of success as finding the proverbial needle in a haystack.

Telemarketing

The solution the marketing group hit upon was pre-qualifying the cold call via telemarketing, and they found the resources right on their doorstep.

At that time, Chemical's retail group had an established in-bound telemarketing unit, answering inquiries from prospects who had seen advertisements that featured an 800 number. The in-bound calling pattern revealed that during certain periods of the day call frequency was extremely light. Seeing this gap as an opportunity, the Middle Market Group convinced retail to allow them to borrow two to three telemarketers who would focus on out-bound calling of prospects. This initial pre-screening pilot has become a key step in the sophisticated, multi-step marketing approach used today.

Chemical's middle market and small business telemarketing approach usually begins with a letter to the prospect, introducing the bank and promising that a representative will be calling. Prior to the RM making those calls, telemarketers are trained on how to obtain the desired information from the target prospect. The bank uses what it terms a "call flow" rather than a script to guide the calls. Goals of the conversation involve confirming information found in the D&B, including management, addresses, company focus, and obtaining additional background such as competitor banks, key products already used, and emerging needs. The telemarketer also tries to schedule an appointment for a banker to visit.

Appointments might be scheduled for an individual banker who has asked for assistance but is more likely part of a blitz day. Chemical has now created a "blitz machine," which supports 300 blitz campaigns a year. Of that number, only one blitz per year is bankwide; the remainder are spread among all 30 regions with many units conducting a monthly blitz. In fact, the blitz has become the engine fueling Chemical's current high monthly calling goals of 40 prospect and current customer calls per month.

Building on this part-time pilot effort, the middle market now has a telemarketing staff of 12 dedicated full-timers. Beyond screening prospects and setting up calls, they also are continually "cleaning up" the existing database, in effect creating an enhanced D&B database. The net result has been increased call efficiency and an improved knowledge of key geographic and business segments.

Chemical is currently centralizing all customer product data with the goal of improving customer segmentation and designing better cross-sell programs. The bank is already able to perform needs-based segmentation of current customers to highlight likely cross-sell opportunities. Surveys conducted by the Middle Market Group's market research department supply additional input into the existing segmentation strategies, tracking market share shifts as well as emerging customer needs.

New Business Development

The emphasis on selling also has been strengthened by the increased use of a new business development (NBD) specialist and by encouraging RMs to focus on relatively few names. Importantly, however, the RM remains the key link to the customer. The NBD officer drives the sales process in each region. He follows up on referrals from area accountants, lawyers, and others bringing the RM on calls as meaningful opportunities develop. Typically, the NBD has little or no credit authority, instead focusing on assessing and creating opportunities and then handing them off to the RM. The NBD often assumes the roles of a sales manager, co-calling with junior bankers and assigning new prospect names to bankers, as necessary.

Today, Chemical, among other banks, emphasizes quality in-depth calling and focus by encouraging a "5+5" program. Each banker selects five prospects and five current customers. In the case of prospects, the RMs focus on establishing a relationship with those companies during the next year and will develop plans to do so; with current customers, the emphasis is on cross-selling. This strategy leads into the need for an account planning process, as described in the next chapter.

Even with an aggressive marketing area, an NBD officer, and dedicated sales forces for each major product group, the RM continues to quarterback the customer relationship. Product areas are not allowed to solicit customers directly without the knowledge and go-ahead of the RMs. Further, cross-sell marketing initiatives cannot be introduced by product areas alone; they must be coordinated with the NBD or the marketing group.

Roadmap to Selling Success

Creating a sales-focused organization requires time and senior level commitment. Chemical's experience provides a number of lessons for other banks to consider.

1. *Initially, start small and set low expectations for the marketing initiative.* Andy Parton is not simply being humble when he says, "Anybody can do what we did here." The keys to success are start small; keep costs low; and set low expectations.

   Initially, Parton stuffed the boxes for early promotional mailings himself, and, at first, a "retail" call tracking system was used by the bank. A "skunk works" mentality helped build the team effort.

2. *At the beginning, leverage off other areas.* Similar to Chemical, many banks have retail-based telemarketing units that middle market bank managers can borrow to jump-start and pilot test a marketing program. It is likely that most in-bound retail groups have time gaps of low usage during the day, and out-bound retail telemarketers typically call at night when consumer prospects are home from work. The corporate group, with their need for out-bound calling during the daytime, can jump into the gap and use existing infrastructure to pilot a program.

3. *Find a "hungry" line banker to test pilot new approaches.* While Chemical's marketing group head was eager to work with the line, he needed to find bankers who wanted to improve their current performance and who were secure enough to look beyond the standard approach to new methods to grow market share. Older or even younger traditional bankers

were often too self-satisfied or set in their ways to consider somewhat unusual approaches when they involved telemarketing and promotions. Those bankers at Chemical who were willing to experiment were, at first, facing a challenge to grow a new customer base. As at Chemical, news of early wins should be publicized across the bank in news bulletins and other forums to encourage broader participation.

4. *Consistency in approach and in internal messages pays off.* Many banks have tried an occasional sales promotion or marketing blitz. Only a few banks, however, have developed a well-thought-out and consistent, long-term approach to promotions, telemarketing, and database management to transform their banks into selling organizations. Yet without consistency, cultural change is rarely achieved.

5. *Success reflects on the line, not on marketing.* The marketing group supports the line and serves as a tool for the line in generating the bank's income. Therefore, Chemical's marketing group deliberately emphasizes the RM's success rather than the marketing group's capabilities. Marketing should remain in the line's shadow to encourage RM cooperation and enthusiasm.

6. *Use existing technology.* Chemical, with its reliance on a Wang computer system, provides an excellent example of a bank that gets the job done without waiting for the ultimate hardware or software enhancements. Arguably, Chemical has developed and manages as good a customer and prospect database as exists for the middle market; it does so with relatively minimal requirements for additional hardware or software. The newest workshare software and computer networks may make this task even easier for start-up banks.

Summary Thoughts

Innovation in prospecting is not only a possibility; it should become a business imperative. As the Chemical case example shows, bringing a consumer marketing approach to the commercial market can improve efficiency while also making the marketing process more effective and, perhaps, even more enjoyable for the bankers.

When redesigned successfully, a corporate bank can become a marketing machine, continually generating, screening, evaluating, and prioritizing prospects—both for new business or cross-sell opportunities—while still maintaining a strong credit culture. What Chemical shows is that costly investments and new technology are not required. Creativity, a group of internal "champions," and senior management commitment are the genuine keys to success.

6

Cross-Selling: Building a Customer Franchise

"Selling appears to many bankers to be a departure from the profession they originally selected."

—Linda Richardson

Why is cross-selling—the selling of multiple non-credit products to corporate customers—critical to the long-term profitability and growth of banks? The reasons are both defensive—it is fundamental to bank survival—and offensive—cross-selling supports a profitable growth strategy. As a result, senior bank managers are giving increasingly higher priority to the cross-sell process.

The Reasons

Lending Undervalued

The above quote not withstanding, lending is widely viewed by many customers as a low value-added commodity product. As the Chapter 7 discussion on credit makes clear, however, lending remains a foundation product—one which is often essential to relationship development—across most customer segments. With many customer groups—particularly those traditionally most attractive for banks—bank credit as well as related services has declined in importance. This growing contingent of companies that no longer rely on commercial banks to fulfill funding needs includes not only the largest U.S. companies, but also many of the best credits in the small and middle markets. Often, these are the companies with sophisticated, multi-product needs.

One factor contributing to the commoditization of credit has been the ready availability of funds for good- or middle-quality credits. Many companies now can avoid the commercial banks entirely by issuing commercial paper or by securitizing receivables. In other instances, some domestic and foreign banks have demonstrated eagerness to lend near-term at below hurdle rates of return in the pursuit of a longer-term relationship with the company. Further, the corporate need to borrow has been reduced by better asset management, resulting in part from the restructuring exercises of the late 1980s and early 1990s as well as more sophisticated cash management procedures.

Shrinking Bank Groups

Many companies are reducing their total number of banks. Despite the growth in new product introductions, many banks are still viewed primarily as lenders by their customers. It should not be surprising, therefore, that companies are shrinking the total number of banks in their bank groups.

As shown in Exhibit 6.1, client data suggests that the average number of banks used by companies, whatever their size, is in decline. This 1989–1991 comparison indicated that companies are increasingly consolidating their business with fewer banks. Greenwich Associates data from 1993 shows that on average 1.6 banks now are used by companies from $10 million to $100 million in revenues and 2.6 banks for $100 million to $500 million companies.

Exhibit 6.1   Number of Banks Used by Companies

Companies are reducing their number of banks.

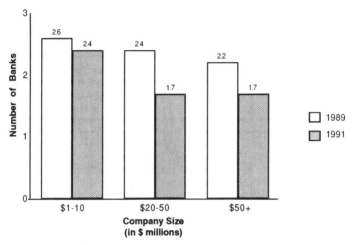

Source: Internal client data; Greenwich Associates.

First-Tier Status Equals Profitability

A lower-tier position is unacceptable to any bank concerned with its ROE because profitability is concentrated in top-tier banks. Even beyond customer requirements, internal bank economics point toward the necessity of building a multi-product relationship with a company. Banks achieving top-tier status outperform a company's other banks by a wide margin. In recent client work, my consulting firm has found that in cases where the bank is a first-tier player, per-account profitability is dramatically higher versus those instances in which the bank has only second-tier status.

This analysis is echoed by a Greenwich report (Exhibit 6.2) which shows that in 1993, close to 80 percent of the bank-related revenues of $10 million to $100 million companies were held by the lead bank.

89

Exhibit 6.2 The Value of Being the Lead Bank

In the middle market, being a company's primary bank is a key to profitability.

Revenues Held by Lead Banks

$10–100 million companies

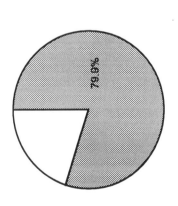

79.9%

$100–500 million companies

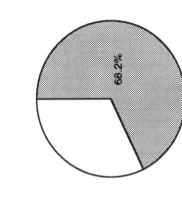

68.2%

$500 million companies

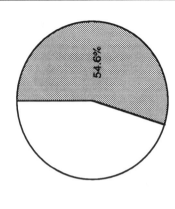

54.6%

Source: Greenwich Associates.

Revenues held by the lead bank declined to almost 55 percent for the largest U.S. corporations. Assuming a strong correlation exists between revenues and profits, the importance of high share of business is self-evident.

Disintermediation on the Increase

The profitability trends outlined above are not temporary. For example, Chapter 15 will discuss the expansion of securitization and disintermediation in the small business market. Much of the large corporate market and a substantial portion of higher quality mid-sized market names also have access to commercial paper. Current initiatives, such as the State Street/Lehman Brothers joint venture titled the Clipper Fund, will increase the ability of middle market companies to obtain funds from investors and, thereby, disintermediate the banks.

The Clipper Receivables Corporation was launched in 1992 as a $1 billion asset-based commercial paper program to fund selected lending by regional banks. The company is a joint venture between State Street Bank and five regional commercial banks: First Union of Charlotte, National City Bank of Cleveland, Norwest Bank of Minneapolis, Pittsburgh National, and U.S. Bancorp of Portland, Oregon.

Banks in the Clipper group make loans to companies with predictable cash flows, such as retailers and selected manufacturers. These loans are funded with A-1/P-1 commercial paper, which is collateralized by a pool of loans. Lehman Brothers places Clipper's commercial paper with institutional investors interested in money market-like investments.

This joint venture allows regional banks to enter a business that had previously been the domain of either investment or money center banks. Through Clipper, regionals can earn a fee for originating loans without the fixed costs of managing a commercial paper program. Borrowers can liquefy their working capital and raise funds at a cost that can be from 70 to 100 basis points below commercial bank lending rates. State Street as the group's leader, in effect, charges the banks for transaction processing. This business, similar to State Street's success in mutual fund processing, stresses fee generation over lending.

The bottom line impact of these disintermediation initiatives will be negative for bank market share unless management finds a way to participate as an originator and packager of loans, as discussed in Chapter 15. There is little doubt that the competitive landscape, particularly for lending, will continue to be cluttered with new competitors jockeying for business.

Hurdle Rates Unreliable

Historically, commercial lending alone has not generated an acceptable hurdle rate of return. Recently, banks have enjoyed record spreads between their funding costs and the prime rate. (For this purpose the Fed funds rate can be used as a rough approximation for funding costs.)

In 1991, that spread averaged approximately 480 basis points, while in 1993 it declined to 300 basis points. Looking back three to five years, however, a different situation existed. In 1990, spreads were in the 200 basis point range.

During that period the sale of additional fee-based products was the key to generate returns above 15 percent. While some additional spread cushion may exist today, lower spreads will certainly return. Events in 1993 began to suggest that spreads were already tightening and most bank managements saw the writing on the wall. In the past, market and regulatory pressures have not generally allowed lending rates to move up as fast as the banks' cost of funds increase. Management would be far wiser to exploit the gap for as long as it exists while simultaneously preparing for the time when the gap declines substantially from its present levels. Again, this emerging trend points to the need to cross-sell.

Account Retention Essential

Cross-selling is essential for account retention. Industry studies point to cross-sell as a key determinant of customers staying within an institution. Stated inelegantly, banks want to lock in both their retail and corporate customers to increase the pain involved when the customer contemplates switching to another bank.

One's own experience as a retail bank customer can offer some lessons to the corporate banker. Consumers are slow to switch banks just because of new products. Factors such as convenience and inertia usually put a halt to any momentum. Who wants to go through the inconveniences of moving a checking account with the associated need to change direct deposit and direct debit arrangements?

Other products, such as credit cards, are fungible commodities. Users face minimal hurdles in moving to another card provider and are easily convinced that they can gain substantial benefits from lower interest rates or fees. However, the inconvenience factor also can change. The ease of refinancing mortgages during the recent interest rate drop of 1991–93 pointed out to banks that products once viewed as stable (such as the 30-year fixed-rate mortgage) are also subject to volatility and competitive attack.

A similar situation exists on the corporate side. My firm's work with corporate banks suggests that cash management and trust products can serve as anchors for a relationship. Lending has become increasingly viewed as a transactional product, both by mid-sized and high-quality small business borrowers. Basically, money is readily available to those who need it the least.

Typically, more profits can be generated by selling additional products to current customers than by obtaining new accounts. The likelihood of achieving a sale is enhanced when selling to a current customer. Further, the margins from selling the same product to a current customer versus selling to a new customer are usually higher due to lower selling costs and the ability to avoid competing on price. For example, one client found that its profit in selling a cash management product to a current customer was more than two times the profit generated by making a new sale because selling expenses, the credit process, and internal set-up costs severely reduced profits.

The above example should not be taken to suggest that prospect marketing should be downplayed. Rather, RMs should make certain that they are getting as much "juice" as they can from current customers. RMs must balance their marketing time between customers and prospects depending on local market share and opportunities for growth.

Product and service needs differ by segment customer type. Exhibit 6.3 provides one perspective on possible needs by segment. Within each of the three market segments listed, sub-segments also exist. For example, within the lower middle market (Segment III) product requirements differ substantially depending upon whether the customer is a credit user.

Obstacles to Cross-Selling

As outlined above, the economic imperative supporting cross-sell could not be stronger. Unfortunately, while many customers prefer "fuller" relationships with their banks, it is often the banks themselves that create obstacles to deepening relationships. Some barriers are self-serving and arise from a desire to protect the RM's personal turf. Others are based on concern for maintaining an excellent customer relationship.

If a bank is to reach its cross-sell potential, each obstacle needs to be addressed. Internal obstacles include RM concerns about customer loss, product specialist resistance, undervalued product specialists, and compensation inequalities. Furthermore, management has often resisted the idea of reducing the number of RMs while increasing the number of product specialists.

Customer Loss Concerns

Ten years ago, many RMs believed that cash management sales would cannibalize balances and reduce the value of the accounts managed by the corporate banking division. The cash management group based its internal selling on the view that their products would help retain an account. If the bank did not offer them to customers, another bank could educate the customer and take the

Exhibit 6.3   Segmented Service/Product Requirements

Product and service requirements define key market segments.

Key Service/Product Requirements by Segment

Client-Based Example

Market Segments	Service/ Provider Requirements	Product Requirements						
		Basic Credit	Advanced Credit	DDA/Cash Mgmt.	Advanced Cash Mgmt.	Investment Banking	International	Other[1]
I. Upper Middle $50 million and up	• Highly skilled product specialists							
II. Core Middle $20 to $50 million	• Skilled credit officer • RM relationship • Private banking linkage					Emerging	Emerging	
III. Lower Middle below $20 million **Credit Intensive**	• Branch emphasis • Asset-based capabilities							
Service Oriented	• Transaction product support • Branch emphasis							

Legend:
- Critical
- Moderate priority
- Not central to relationship

[1] Includes Leasing, Trust, Investment Services

Source: Greenwich Associates; Mercer Management interviews.

relationship away. Today, cash management is, indeed, one of the most stable products of most banks' product sets.

Resistance has raised barriers to other areas, including corporate finance and products such as private placements and mergers and acquisitions (M&A). Private placements, of course, can reduce loan outstandings, just as cash management reduced investable balances; M&A requires a higher level of company contact (CEO or COO) than many day-to-day RMs have. The net effect is that some line bankers see their importance inside the bank declining as their status with customers is whittled away by the "new" fee-based areas.

Product Specialist Resistance

RMs often present deals to the product specialists that fail to meet key parameters, such as size or profit requirements. The deal may then be rejected, and the RM losses face with the customer as well as motivation to sell the product. This situation is worsened by the chronic understaffing of the non-lending areas of many banks and, perhaps as a result, a lack of continuity among specialists and a failure to build partnerships with the RMs. Without this relationship and with only working product knowledge, an RM may bring in the wrong specialist to see a customer. The net effect is that the bankers must then backtrack with their customers, potentially harming existing relationships.

Product Specialist vs. RM

Given most bank's histories, the RM controls the relationship and is the key source of corporate bank profits. In many banks the specialists are beholden to the RMs for gaining access to the customer. Ironically, however, the services offered by product specialists are often highly valued by the customer and a way for the bank to differentiate itself from others. Many banks, especially regionals, need to enhance the role of the specialist so that it is no longer considered "off-to-the-side" in career tracking or value.

In a few banks, the opposite situation occurs and non-traditional areas, such as corporate finance, are widely viewed as the prestige positions within the bank, a world apart from relationship management. This imbalance can also lead to a bank losing profit opportunities.

One example from a northeast regional illustrates the pitfalls when that occurs. That bank, seeking to carve out a position as a key regional player in corporate finance, hired a senior banker from a New York "bulge bracket" firm. That banker drove to the office in his Porsche and arrived on day one wearing a custom-made double-breasted suit and Wall-Street-style bright suspenders. He was the New England banker's worst nightmare of an overly aggressive New York investment banker. That was strike one.

Strike two resulted from the corporate finance officer's own attitude, which bordered on condescension, even though the RMs were his major referral source. In short, he looked down on the RMs and failed to develop a partnership approach in working with the RMs' customers. In this instance, the final strike happened when senior management got cold feet about entering the business, particularly given its slow start.

Compensation Inequalities

At some banks, the corporate finance personnel and other investment banking-type groups are compensated on a success fee basis, allowing them to generate all-in compensation levels far above those of the average RM. This inequality can create jealousy on the part of the RM and inhibit the RM's willingness to make referrals.

Overcoming Obstacles

Obstacles to cross-selling can be addressed by management by focusing on three key areas: internal communications, teaming, and performance measurement and compensation.

Communications

The product explosion that has occurred in financial services strains the capabilities of even the best RM. Senior management needs to ensure that their RMs possess both the training and the access to specialists required to prequalify cross-sell candidates—not unlike how companies are prescreened during the initial prospecting phase.

The RMs need to be clear on the criteria that make a company in their portfolio a likely private placement or derivatives candidate. In turn, the specialists need to give high priority to a quick turn-around for RM inquiries.

Teaming

Banks need to rethink how they can manage corporate banking relationships using the talents of every team member. The reliance on the RM as an all-around salesperson, credit underwriter, and account maintainer must give way to a more segmented team approach. RMs will still play the key role (quarterback is the sports cliché—usually applied) but others, including account administrators and product specialists, must be welcomed as full, contributing members of the team.

To encourage the teaming concept, specialists need to be aligned with individual RMs. Further, the RM and specialist jobs, along with credit, should be viewed as co-equals in status and career opportunity. Transfers from one group to another should be common and heralded across the bank.

Performance Measurement and Compensation

Chapter 11 focuses on why bank management must fundamentally rethink its approach to performance measurement and compensation. At a base level, these systems should encourage the RM to be indifferent regarding the products they sell, as long as those products meet the needs of their customers and attain an acceptable level of return for the bank. Whether the product is a loan or a private placement and even if the RM loses investable balances to a cash management account should be unimportant as long as those two, and related, criteria are met.

Sales incentives need to be introduced across most banks and tied to the sale of non-credit products. Formulas for incentives need to be straightforward and easy to understand. The more hoops bankers need to jump through to get a reward, the less their enthusiasm for the program will be, no matter what the carrot. Further, incentives should not create conflicts between RMs and specialists.

One option is to create a team selling incentive, split equally between the line officers and specialists. While much of the incentive compensation can be tied into the year-end review process, management should consider paying a portion of the incentive as soon as possible after a successful sale has been completed. That award should be made publicly—similar to Norwest's presentation of the "sting bee" discussed in Chapter 4—to underscore both the importance of the cross-sale to senior management and the immediate payoff to bankers who participate as team players.

Successful Cross-Selling

Specialized Product Development

As the corporate customer becomes more sophisticated and as many bank products become commoditized, developing products that address specific customer needs will become more important. The popular principles of "mass customization" and meeting the needs of the "segments of one" are as relevant to banking as to manufacturing.

Many banks, however, fail to leverage off the market knowledge that the line officer should possess. One specialist in product development at a regional bank explained that she does not involve her bankers in evaluating emerging customer needs or in designing products to meet them. She said, "The relationship manager is not involved in product development; he has no expertise." While this is a comment on the quality of the bankers, it says more about the inability of that product manager to develop a team approach.

Many other banks find value in including bankers as members of product development teams.

One of the best industry practices occurs at a southern regional bank that has formed product teams. These teams refer to themselves as a product's "board of directors." Their focus includes a regular assessment of market needs and emerging competitive issues as well as an evaluation of the operational and systems issues anticipated for new or changed products. The group also prepares a detailed *pro forma* profitability analysis for each product and key sub-service, allowing bankers to emphasize those products that serve the customer and generate a strong return for the bank.

One strength of this approach is that both internal bank and external customer perspectives are incorporated into product development. Importantly, the inclusiveness of this process eliminates many unhappy surprises in areas of concern such as back-office capabilities to support a product or RM willingness to market it.

Going forward, effective product development has become a factor differentiating excellent banks. Beyond development alone, however, it will become important for banks to access or acquire products and services that they do not currently offer and do not wish to develop internally, along the lines of the Clipper group. With increased sales to current customers playing an essential role in customer retention and relationship profitability, banks must offer a menu of high quality niche products along with the standards, even if they do not originate them in-house.

Some banks are failing to make certain that they can provide the necessary product set. During the past several years, one West Coast bank has eliminated a number of product areas that failed to generate a sufficient level of profits. As a result, until recently, that bank had no ability to offer private placements as a financing alternative or to act as an M&A advisor. When the need for such a capability occurred, the banker referred that customer to another bank, with no benefit to the originating bank. They ignored the opportunity to generate "no risk" referral income or to form an alliance with a specialist service provider.

Other banks have already discovered the advantage of outsourcing operations-intensive products such as securities safekeeping. At one high-profile money center bank, back-office account maintenance is contracted out while the bank retains the high-profile account management roles, such as American Depository Receipts (ADR) sponsorship of foreign companies listing on U.S. stock exchanges.

Clearly, most banks should not offer products, such as private placements or M&A, which require high investment and personnel expense, and expect to capture immediate market share. In many cases, outsourcing and alliances with outside banks or investment banks need to be considered. This type of outsourcing has a marketing focus rather than involving the back-office. Acting as a broker, in effect, for a transaction allows a bank to maintain a high profile with its customer and protect the relationship while obtaining a fee for servicing a need. In the future, as senior management evaluates the product development process, consideration must be given to redefining product development to include product "acquisition" from bank and non-bank alliances.

Account Planning

The account planning process plays an essential role in successful cross-selling.

While various approaches exist, the basics of this process require regular and, typically, annual reviews of at least the most significant accounts in each RM's portfolio. In a portfolio of 30 accounts, for example, detailed marketing reviews—separate from the credit process—should be conducted for at least five to six names. Account review meetings themselves can be scheduled monthly. Just as the RMs prepare detailed plans on their key accounts, the sales review process should have the same degree of rigor as the annual loan review.

Among the areas covered in this account "audit" are:

- Background on the customer and position of the industry.

- Total loan relationship, including exposure to all affiliates, joint ventures, key principals.

- Other product activities, including cash management, trust, and derivatives.

- Actual bank calling program during the past year, that is, frequency of calls and level of contact.

- Suggested calling program for the next 12 to 24 months, including product specialist and senior bank management involvement.

- Relationship profitability and trends, including a relationship ROE analysis.

- Recent trends in the company's business that could affect ongoing banking needs—for example, international expansion and increased client concentration.

- Specific new sales opportunities and sales goals.

From this list, it should be clear that the RM is not only providing a snapshot of the past but is also making a clear recommendation for the products to emphasize throughout the next year. The RM's understanding of the customer's business is critical in making clear requests as to the level and type of bank personnel involvement required during the marketing process to ensure success.

When completed, account plans are then reviewed on a rotational basis, monthly or every six weeks in a group meeting with relationship managers, team leaders, and key product salespeople. Credit officers should also be included to take advantage of their perspective and to avoid offering products with a credit risk component to companies that fail the credit screen. This team review is an extension of the concept termed "upfront guidance" discussed in Chapter 4 and Chapter 7.

The group meetings provide an opportunity to critique account plans constructively and to revise them to acceptable levels. In each case, specific salespersons are assigned to follow up within a limited time frame. By the end of the meeting, sales goals have been established for the accounts reviewed, with the new goals incorporated into revised product specialist and RM management objectives. The bankers and the product specialists both acknowledge that they have committed themselves to take action.

Customer Linkage

Reviewing account plans directly with customers can also have substantial value.

First, it can be an opportunity for senior management to meet with selected clients at least once a year. One of the enduring competitive advantages for a major northeast regional is senior bank managers' long-term relationship with key customers. The result is excellent customer retention and invitations to work on high fee-generating corporate finance deals, such as M&A.

While these strong relationships exist due to regular client meetings rather than once-a-year visits, the account planning meeting can be viewed as a mandatory senior-level call that is then supplemented by other calls, validating the customer's priority within the bank.

Besides providing an occasion to meet senior management, yearly account relationship meetings will also make clear the bank's current importance to them. Because of the decentralized decision-making process for managing bank relationships found in many corporations, bank customers are often surprised about how extensive a relationship they have with their lead banks. Simply summarizing the services that a bank performs may help differentiate the bank's value to the company's senior management and can also lead to expanding the relationship agenda for the next year.

Customer account planning meetings also serve as an opportunity to assess the relationship's profitability. In cases where profits are inadequate, banks will often show their profit numbers and the ROE calculations for the relationship to the customer. The banker then discusses how to increase the return, whether through additional product sales or increased pricing. Surprisingly, the response to this approach is often positive. Corporations understand profit dynamics and will usually give their bankers the opportunity to increase account penetration and returns.

Obviously, a confrontational approach should be avoided. That said, if the account has below hurdle rate profitability and in effect destroys shareholder value, the RM can use this meeting to discuss approaches for rectifying that untenable situation. If service has been good and the RM has built a rapport with management, corporates are often willing to bite the bullet rather than shop their business.

Client review also encourages the banker to move the relationship with the customer up to a more consultative sales approach, a step beyond to product pitching. Rather than throwing products on the wall and seeing what sticks, consultative selling focuses on assessing and anticipates the customer needs.

Account Planning Traps

The biggest negative of introducing the accounting planning process can be summed up in one word: bureaucracy. One banker captured the essence of this trap when he recounted his experience at a money-center bank that tried to institute a formal account planning process: "For several weeks, no one did any calling while we wrote up our plans." He went on to say that the plans took too long to complete because the systems infrastructure to generate background information did not exist. Ultimately, senior management showed no commitment to make a significant number of customer calls, killing the account planning process.

The circumstances that doomed this program to failure provide lessons for every bank considering the process. *First*, account planning became just another paper-pushing task. The banker's job was not changed in any way to *create* the time required to generate in-depth perspectives on the customers.

Second, the bank created a gridlock situation by making a fundamental mistake. Scheduling all the reviews for completion at the same time both tied up every banker and when the reports flooded in, their high number reduced the likelihood of effective review action being taken.

Third, and perhaps most damaging, was the lack of senior management commitment. While they had clearly latched onto a fad, the executives themselves were either unwilling or unable to focus more time on the customer.

The next two chapters, which discuss credit and account monitoring, offer insights into the prerequisites of successful account planning and cross-sell. Expecting RMs to add on account planning responsibilities without changing or reducing the volume of their other activities is at best naive.

Reassessing Staffing Requirements

The requirement for banks to cross-sell impacts hiring patterns, training requirements, and performance measurement systems. Criteria that were appropriate in the less-competitive environment of the 1970s are no longer appropriate.

Hiring

One senior bank manager recently recalled how his bank had traditionally screened MBA candidates for the RM position: "If someone had a sales background, he would immediately be viewed as less attractive to us; we did not feel comfortable. Instead, we focused on people we thought would be good credit analysts rather than good salespeople."

This bank believed that selling skills were relatively unimportant. Going forward, while credit and customer skills may still be important, the ability to market and sell will merit greater emphasis. While many bankers have denied the role over the years, the RM is, indeed, a salesperson. Bank management needs to act on their realization that the best banker for tomorrow may not be today's RM. Management must increase its commitment to hire individuals with an entrepreneurial spirit.

Training

Chapter 11 discusses the need for banks to change the training program for the corporate middle market group. The importance of training in creating a cultural change is widely underestimated.

One way to create a cross-sell culture involves increasing the number of rotations RM trainees serve in non-credit areas. A rotation into the cash management group is standard at many banks and needs to be complemented by rotations into corporate finance, trust, and other areas. Once the RM is on the line, cross-sell-related training is often sponsored by individual product areas trying to capture attention spans, differentiating themselves from other areas in the bank. Product area management should, however, establish informal methods as well as formal training programs to aid the RM in recognizing opportunities. Product specialists need to remember that, just as banks are fighting for a customer's "share of wallet," so too are product areas fighting for the RM's "share of mind" and attention.

At one bank, the corporate finance head meets with a group of five to six RMs on a weekly basis to review key products and discuss potential opportunities with specific customers. These meetings supplement the more formal annual planning process. The cash management area of this bank has introduced an even more informal method. This bank provides its RMs with a two-sided laminated sheet that coaches them on questions to ask customers, outlines customer needs and benefits, and suggests the appropriate product specialist for a follow-up call. Increased attention on the part of product groups as well as creativity in the methods they use will become more important in gaining marketing time.

Performance Measurement

A recommended corporate approach to performance measurement and compensation will be outlined in Chapter 11. The importance of new performance measurement systems and performance-based compensation is so significant that the topic could easily appear in each chapter of this book. One brief comment will suffice for now. Making the sale of a specific number of non-lending products, such as cash management, derivatives, and corporate finance part of performance goals will prompt RMs to examine their portfolios closely and should result in a number of joint calling opportunities with product areas. These goals not only need to be developed and actively reviewed with superiors but must also play a meaningful role in incentive compensation. All too often goals are set and then literally ignored when senior management makes its yearly RM bonus assessments. Hands-on review and compensation tied to results sends a clear message on the bank's commitment to sales.

Rebalancing

Chapter 10 focuses on how to reengineer the role of the RM. One result of analyzing the RM's role is a recognition that the ongoing need for RMs may diminish and the staffing requirement for product specialists may increase. As banks redefine the RM's role and clarify responsibilities, fewer RMs may be required to handle current accounts. Of course, some individuals can be shifted to a new business marketing role. However, the future bank environment will likely be one in which zero employee and salary growth needs to be matched with increased revenues per account. In that case, management may receive a higher yield on its employee dollar by increasing the number of sales specialists. Going forward, at many banks the balance of power will certainly shift slightly toward the product areas and away from the RMs.

Summary Thoughts

The appropriate cross-sell sales management system mirrors much of what has been discussed in the previous chapter. "Suspects" must be qualified as prospects for specific non-credit products. A combination of account planning conducted by the RM and product specialists, and database analysis, performed by a marketing support group, can spot candidates for the cross-sell of a particular product. Typically, the product specialists respond to RM leads rather than generate their own. In the case of cross-sell, preliminary contact is made by the RM who, after making certain that a cross-sell opportunity exists, arranges for a joint call with the product area. Proposals are sent out only after appropriate pricing has been determined; exceptions to pricing are evaluated by senior management of both areas. The results of the proposal are fed back into the individual customer and overall corporate database, enriching the quality of future analysis.

Introducing a sales management process without changing the RM's responsibilities and related support structure will marginally impact account profitability and RM productivity. As chapters 7 and 9 discuss, management must closely evaluate both the credit and customer service areas as part of its sales management process. The thrust of this analysis should center on uncovering opportunities to streamline or eliminate non-essential activities, particularly those that consume the RM's time.

Ultimately, management needs to break away from the mindset that allows past tradition to dictate future roles and responsibilities. Rethinking the nature of the credit and maintenance processes and the role of the RM in them can increase the amount of time available for marketing by 50 to 100 percent or more and favorably alter the economics of account management. Chapter 10 will show that, in fact, it is only by addressing these areas that a true holistic sales culture can be encouraged within a bank.

7

Leveraging Off the Credit Process

"There are two things that people should avoid seeing up close: the making of sausage and the way politicians make laws."
—*Otto von Bismarck*

Given the opportunity, Bismarck might have been tempted to add a third item: watching how bankers approve and review loans and related risk exposures.

The previous chapters have focused on the need for banks to emphasize selling and to transform their relationship managers from relatively passive order takers to proactive, customer-focused multi-product salespersons. As part of this cultural shift, credit officers also need to become more fully integrated into the marketing process. They must be willing to present themselves and be recognized as deal facilitators, while still preserving high credit quality. All too often today, credit officers view themselves and are seen by the RMs as deal blockers whose goal is to save the bank from the new salesperson mentality. This antagonistic relationship can be superseded by a mutual understanding of each area's needs and requirements, leading to cooperation and respect.

Credit Must Remain King

Even though this book stresses the importance of cross-selling of fee-based products and detailed account planning as elements essential to generating above-average returns, the foundation of a bank's performance remains its ability to make timely, high-quality credit decisions across all market segments. From the perspective of many mid-sized and large corporate customers, credit availability, even when unused, remains a key criteria when selecting a lead for a bank.

Although large corporates may borrow short-term only from the commercial paper market, they usually require backup facilities, foreign exchange lines, and trade finance, among other credit-related needs. For the middle market customer, choice of a bank remains largely credit-driven. In the small business market, while many customers use cash flow, equity, or trade payables to finance themselves, they still want access to credit. Also, business principals in this market often link their private banking to corporate needs.

Credit approval, loan and portfolio monitoring, and formal loan review processes must be rigorous and, in a word, excellent. At the same time, cumbersome processes need to be streamlined and nonessential activities eliminated to focus the RM on the external market rather than on internal credit approval and review hurdles.

Credit is and will remain a major product for corporate and middle market banking.

Virtually every corporate banker has heard the line about the hole dug by a poor credit decision: "It takes a $100 million of new loans to make up for one bad $1 million loan." Depending upon the spreads between bank costs and lending rates, the $100 million figure may be an exaggeration. The general warning, however, remains valid. It takes a lot of good loans to make up for one workout. Bad credit decisions inevitably have a very high cost.

This chapter examines the credit life cycle as four related stages.

1) Loan application process

2) Credit underwriting

3) Monitoring and loan review

4) Workout

We will review each area, evaluating how that activity is currently performed in many U.S. middle market banking operations and how it can be upgraded to meet best-practice standards for productivity and/or credit quality.

This chapter is followed by a case study of Norwest Bank, a bank that, many will argue, has one of the best credit processes in the world. Headquartered in Minneapolis, Norwest Bank has successfully balanced the requirement for high credit quality with its desire to show a consistent presence in the corporate middle market. The bank serves as one of the best examples of a financial institution, which, within a relatively short period of time, actively developed an excellent credit culture while placing a strong emphasis on credit and non-credit sales. While remaining a full-scale banking institution, Norwest Bank also manages to operate with the flexibility, directness, and focus of the best of the non-banks.

Imperatives for Change

Certain themes arise during an evaluation of the credit life cycle in the context of the changing financial marketplace of the 1990s. These themes include:

- *Cooperation and communication between credit and line officers.*
  While credit officers need to maintain independent judgment, more credit managers today are emphasizing a collegial, team-based approach to decision-making. This cooperation with line managers sharply contrasts with the previously common antagonism where credit officers distrusted the bankers and, in turn, the bankers viewed the credit area as an obstacle to surmount, avoid, or end run, often calling on senior management to intercede.

- *Opportunities for streamlining the decision-making process.*
  As portfolio credit quality deteriorated in the late 1980s and as government regulators required more documentation and tighter records for internal procedures, many banks added

steps to the loan approval and review processes. To meet these internal and external reporting demands, bankers, of course, spent more time behind their desks. Now, in light of more stable loan portfolios and flat asset growth, many banks are reexamining the need for and the affordability of a "belt and suspenders" approach to credit.

- *Realistic links between credit risk and credit return.*

  Banks are notorious for allowing the market to dictate pricing rather than requiring a return that achieves a target hurdle rate, both for the loan and for the overall relationship. Management's emphasis on detailed line-of-business profit analysis as well as internal competition for capital and human resources mean that loan pricing will now be examined closely.

- *New credit strategies for the "slow growth" 1990s.*

  Business requirements for success in the 1990s are, without a doubt, distinctly different from those required in the 1980s. Banks are beginning to evaluate each aspect of the credit process to determine opportunities for both front office and back office reengineering and to assess the impact on staffing and organizational requirements.

- *Application of cost-effective technology.*

  Technology is now available and even more should be available soon that offers increased leverage to RMs and credit officers seeking to monitor portfolio quality and customer stability. Systems improvements are giving heads of credit departments an ability to evaluate current portfolios online and highlight troubled areas. Before rushing to purchase new, technology-based solutions, however, credit departments must make a fundamental assessment of needs, especially before the introduction of tools such as artificial intelligence or credit file imaging. Many basic improvements can be made with little cost and in a relatively short time, that is, some are quick hits with significant impact.

Bottom line, a willingness now exists at many banks to examine the business dynamics of credit, an area that until recently has been considered sacrosanct. Most promisingly, senior managers of credit areas themselves are taking a leadership role in initiating such self-examinations. The following chapter sections—the loan application process, credit underwriting, monitoring and loan review, and workout units—should underscore the imperative for change within the credit process.

Stage 1: Loan Application Process

The loan application process, of course, consolidates the management, financial, and business information necessary to assess a company's creditworthiness. The opportunities to speed up the overall decision process are substantial, as are the benefits of changing the interactive dynamics between line and credit officers.

Banks can significantly increase leverage for their RMs by reengineering the application process. Most banks already use credit analysts or a centralized group of junior officers who spread the financials and, often, draft a preliminary credit write-up that the RM then edits. This delegation of tasks provides training for junior staff and allows RMs to concentrate on their areas of expertise, such as structure and pricing.

A Dynamic Process

Historically, putting together a loan package has been a static, linear process. At the best-practices banks, however, it is a highly dynamic one.

When the process is static, the RM or an assistant collects the piecemeal data and, only then, completes a formal write-up or makes a presentation to decision-makers. In these instances, very little active discussion or give and take with credit personnel occurs prior to the written presentation. Time commitments invested in the process are substantial because the great concern is to ensure that all possible objections have been anticipated and answered.

The negatives of this approach are many, among them slow decision-making, inefficient use of the RM's time and, in effect, implicit discouragement of an open, team-based decision process.

Contrast this static approach to one that encourages open communication between the line area and credit and informal "brainstorming" early in the credit evaluation process. This iterative process involving both credit and marketing can begin very early in the customer relationship, often after the first or second call reveals a potential business opportunity for the bank. It is largely an oral communications process rather than memo-driven and, therefore, both more informal and bearing lower risk for the RM and the credit officer.

One credit officer working in such an interactive environment described the spirit of cooperation between the line and credit, "My job is not to say no," he said. "My job is to help the bankers get their deals done. I consider myself a facilitator." This credit officer's ability to act as facilitator is further helped by the fact that he views his colleagues as being as concerned about credit as he is.

Many banks consider that maintaining distance between line officers and credit is an important means of protecting their bank's credit integrity. In fact in a recent interview the chief credit officer of a northeast regional said, "We tend to frown on credit officers meeting with customers."

Although not often stated as directly, the unspoken view can be that too much fraternization will compromise the integrity of the credit process. But excellent-performing banks are often the ones that promote the closest cooperation and development of trust between the two groups. At the best banks, a strong credit culture permeates the institution and its key activities, starting with the loan application process.

The Importance of Credit Culture

Many books and articles discuss the importance of bank cultures and how they develop. Credit culture emanates largely from the key officers of a bank. Lenders and credit personnel know intuitively exactly how involved in the credit decision or review process senior management is willing to get. At one large regional bank, for example, the chairman reviews each loan over $10 million, even though the bank has a lending limit for senior credit officers many times above that amount. His objective in taking personal interest is to show top management's commitment to excellent credit quality.

In another instance, the head of a regional bank has the reputation for reading credit memos and asking writers pointed questions to show that he is aware of the market trends and cares about individual performance. Of course, if senior level involvement goes too far, it can also be a constraint to the banker. That situation, however, occurs infrequently. At most banks, RMs greatly appreciate senior management's recognition of their achievements and their attempts to get new business.

Banks communicate their credit culture in seemingly insignificant ways. Just as in real estate where the three keys to success are "location, location, location," the physical location of credit personnel may indicate their stature within a bank's culture.

The importance of hierarchy was brought home to me most dramatically on day one of a client engagement several years ago. Since it was my first day consulting at that bank, I was walking around to meet various department managers. Virtually all lending officers were located on the same floor as the chairman and the other senior line of business managers. This was the "power floor." Most of the RMs had roomy windowed offices. When I asked to meet the key credit managers, I was directed to the elevator and sent to a windowless basement. Not surprisingly, the physical location of the credit group symbolized their lack of clout in that bank and underscored the internal power of the lending area. It was also not surprising that this bank was trying to recover from the fallout of very fast, although not high quality, loan growth. As our study subsequently warned, good market share and low stock price combined to make this bank a merger target. It has since been acquired.

Of course, in more recent years the pendulum has swung to the other extreme. Roles of credit officers and marketers have almost reversed, with lenders taking a subservient position to the credit specialists. Today, with relatively weak loan volume and a renewed emphasis on growth, the pendulum may be swinging back yet again, this time in the direction of more relaxed credit standards.

A strong bank credit culture leads to the loan preparation and the loan approval processes occurring, in effect, simultaneously. Pendulum-like swings where an emphasis on aggressive lending exists one year and an emphasis on triple-A credit quality occurs the next year are avoided. This balanced approach focuses the spotlight on high priority items that can be deal killers and also limits the time spent on deals that have a low likelihood of approval. The loan officer and credit officer prepare the credit memo together; formal memo-writing usually occurs toward the end of this process and is intended as much for after the fact record-keeping as for final decision-making.

Stage 2: Credit Underwriting

No two banks appear to use exactly the same credit approval process. From the top performers to the worst, credit approval processes vary. Some support the use of a credit committee, others value a concurrence or multi-signature system. Hybrids, of course, also exist. The fact that no one process is linked to top performance supports the conclusion that it is not the approval system but rather the training and skill of the credit analysts and bankers along with the strength of the credit culture that determines how well a bank's portfolio performs.

Alternative Approaches

Loan approval methodologies go in and out of favor. In recent years, the emphasis has shifted to a committee structure, at least partly in reaction to a stormy economy and high loan write-offs and delinquencies. A cynical observer might consider this transition to a committee structure as an example of the old adage of "closing the barn door after the horse has escaped."

Some managers view credit committees as allowing a bank to exert increased central control over the decision process and as providing more experienced eyes for evaluating individual credits. The typical committee consists of six to eight representatives who receive a collection of loan write-ups a night or two before the credit committee meeting. Very little time is available to review all the information in-depth and usually only one or two bankers do so. In any case, the smart RM pre-sells the deal to the key members of the credit committee to avoid unexpected glitches. Plus, when leadership is unclear, committees can lead to an avoidance of responsibility if problems eventually occur.

In contrast, a multiple signature system literally puts the signers "on the line" for the quality of the credit they are approving and pushes down responsibility in a decentralized manner. While an inexperienced banker may not possess the years to make a knowledgeable decision, the team leader or other senior banker should have earned the necessary gray hair.

In most cases, decentralized decision-making—exemplified by the multiple signature system—can be highly effective, allowing higher productivity and quicker customer response. Again, it is the people making the decision rather than the process used that will be the key to a successful loan.

Exhibit 7.1 summarizes some of the pros and cons of a credit committee system versus a signature or hybrid approach.

Just as "guns don't kill, people do," loan approval systems do not create good or bad credits; the quality of the analysis and the credit culture does. While the signature system with its qualities of empowerment and speed has many benefits, no one right answer exists for approving credits. Exhibit 7.1 presents an overview of the loan approval procedures existing at six regional and super-regional banks.

As might be expected, approaches differ. Even within the same holding company, individual bank loan approval processes often vary as shown in Exhibit 7.2. At this bank holding company, where much growth has resulted from mergers and acquisitions, the credit process in place at the time a deal closed has been allowed to remain in operation.

Within the banks that make up that holding company and within most banks overall, management bases its credit approach upon a

117

Exhibit 7.1   Signature versus Committee Loan Approval System

All approval structures have strengths and weaknesses. These can be countered by a strong, bankwide credit culture and close senior level involvement.

Signature Approval

Pros	Cons
• Clear responsibility/ accountability • Speed of decision-making • Customer knows decision-makers	• Subject to cronyism • Credit skills may vary within the signing group • Unit only perspective; may not consider the broader interests of the bank

Committee Approval

Pros	Cons
• Multiple "eyes" on each credit • Increased objectivity • Portfolio/bank perspective	• Few read memos in depth; one-two actual "influencers" on a committee • Accountability is unclear (who "owns" a transaction)

Exhibit 7.2   Existing Loan Approval Procedures

The loan application process differs greatly across banks. A number of approaches have proven effective.

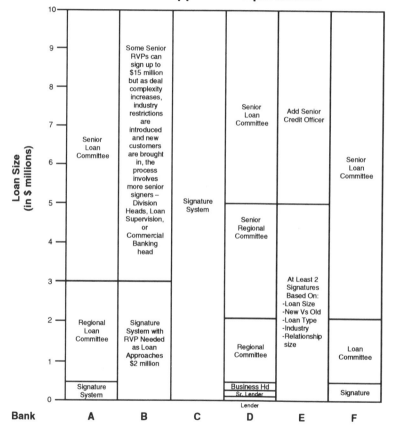

Preliminary

Loan Approval Requirements

Loan Size (in $ millions)

Bank A: Signature System (0–2), Regional Loan Committee (2–3), Senior Loan Committee (3–10)

Bank B: Signature System with RVP Needed as Loan Approaches $2 million (0–3), then: Some Senior RVPs can sign up to $15 million but as deal complexity increases, industry restrictions are introduced and new customers are brought in, the process involves more senior signers – Division Heads, Loan Supervision, or Commercial Banking head (3–10)

Bank C: Signature System (0–10)

Bank D: Lender, Sr. Lender, Business Hd (0), Regional Committee (~1–2), Senior Regional Committee (4–5), Senior Loan Committee (7–9)

Bank E: At Least 2 Signatures Based On: -Loan Size -New Vs Old -Loan Type -Industry -Relationship size (1–3), Senior Regional Committee (5), Add Senior Credit Officer (7–9)

Bank F: Signature (0), Loan Committee (1–2), Senior Loan Committee (6)

119

number of factors: the capabilities of its RMs, the strength of the credit culture, the bank's recent history and tradition. As shown in Exhibit 7.3, approval processes can differ within one bank holding company.

Pricing

If pricing, relationship profitability, and cross-sell requirements are not considered earlier, the proposed deal's return to the bank as

Exhibit 7.3 Staffing Approval Processes within a Bank Holding Company (BHC)

BHCs often permit individual units to determine their own approval systems.

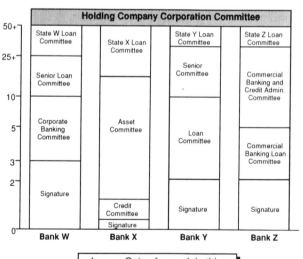

Intra-Holding Company Loan Approval Requirements

well as any other near-term sales opportunities should be evaluated during the loan approval stage. Ideally, banks want to see a clear correlation between a loan's risk rating and its spread over cost of funds. The shaded section within Exhibit 7.4 depicts the situation that should exist: risk-based pricing that allows for the achievement of the bank's hurdle rate—in this case an ROE of 17.5 percent.

Higher quality loans—those with risk ratings of 1—have relatively low spreads reflecting their quality. Higher risk loans are priced in a range to compensate for an increased level of delinquencies and write-offs. However, most portfolios are not built on an ideal pricing matrix.

The dots in Exhibit 7.4—which appear to follow an almost random design—reflect what we typically find when the individual loans within a bank's corporate middle market loan portfolio are plotted along the axis of risk and rate spread. Bluntly, little relation-

Exhibit 7.4   Linkage of Loan Risk and Return

While a close correlation between risk and return remains a goal, many loans within a portfolio fail to attain profit hurdles.

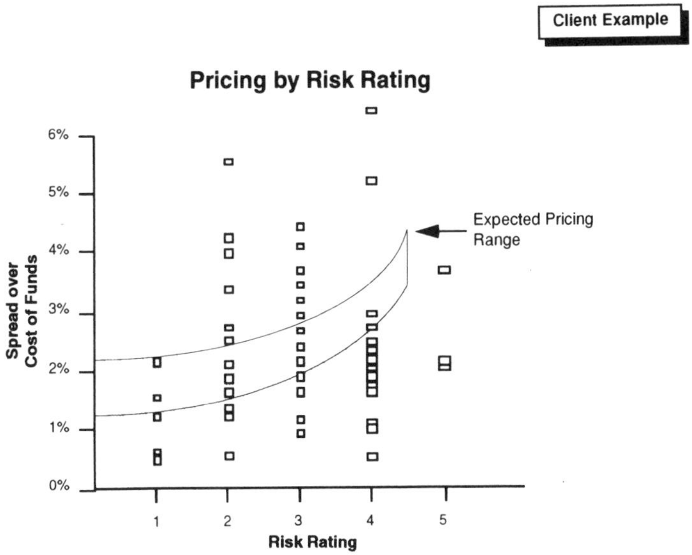

121

ship exists between risk and the return to the bank. The low return in the case of higher risk credits is particularly disturbing. For this disguised client example, most of the credits risk rated 3 or higher fail to meet the hurdle rate.

Loan Repricing Programs

Banks that perform the self-assessment of repricing their loan programs need to adopt an action plan to reprice their portfolios on a loan-by-loan basis. In one case, a west-coast bank decided to address pricing inconsistencies similar to those shown in Exhibit 7.4. Bank management developed a communications package for customers explaining why small rate adjustments were necessary. Senior management helped to deliver the message to customers, and their involvement demonstrated to internal staff members as well as to the customers that the bank was serious about fully implementing this program. Better quality loans faced rate increases of 1/16 to 1/8th of a percent; lesser quality loans had increases in excess of 1/2 a percent. Rates for the lowest quality loans, which were doubtful payers in any case, remained the same. Virtually no customers left the bank during this change, and the program increased the bank's bottom line by $7 million.

A senior bank manager commented that the greatest impediment to the program's success was not customer resistance but rather RM foot-dragging. Many RMs expressed concern that they would lose customers; in fact, that was not the case. As one senior manager commented, the RMs needed to be reminded that it was the bank and, only indirectly, the customers that were paying their salaries.

Beginning with day one of a new relationship, some banks will simply not approve a credit unless a sizable portion of non-credit business comes with the loan. At a minimum, a clear plan must exist for obtaining supplemental fee business. Norwest—which will be profiled later and whose president has described loans as "loss leaders"—pushes the RM to commit to cross-sell during the initial loan approval process. In instances where a loan gains approval without fee-attached business, Norwest will require the originating banker to obtain that business within one year. The RM's success is then reviewed, leaving open the possibility that the bank will reassess its relationship with the customer.

Stage 3: Monitoring and Loan Review

Monitoring and loan review are key components in the holistic approach to credit analysis that better bank and non-bank lenders are pursuing. When this after-the-fact review process turns up situations that also are affecting the wider industry or similar companies in the same industry, that information must be incorporated into a bank's upfront guidance policies.

Migration Analysis

One best practice that can influence the quality of decision making centers is learning from the past. Migration analysis can vastly improve both loss reserve and profit analysis accuracy. Too often the credit approval and loan review processes are viewed as separate, unrelated events. As mentioned in the chapter on marketing, loan review should play a pivotal role in setting industry and other exposure limits, ensuring sufficient risk diversification.

Loan review groups in a number of middle market banks also have begun to develop portfolio-based exposure management systems. These systems strive to apply an actuarial-like analysis and "cradle-to-grave" profitability measurements to loan performance by industry. Such evaluations review historic performance—usually over a five-year horizon—project future default rates based upon past results and can generate a risk/reward assessment for an industry. This migration analysis provides a major input into the loan approval process and allows for early detection of industries or business categories that may be deteriorating.

Early Warning System

Beyond providing input into credit policy and taking responsibility for portfolio evaluation, the loan review process creates an early warning system for uncovering problem credit.

RMs, always the first line of defense in pinpointing a deteriorating situation, require explicit encouragement "to pull the alarm" on a customer. An anecdote told by a senior credit officer at a large regional bank typifies the corporate openness required to encourage bankers to blow the whistle on loans they may have sponsored. About 15 years ago, when he had been at this bank for less than a year and had generated only a handful of loans, the quality of his largest loan began to disturb him. The numbers showed a downward trend, and the borrower failed to give satisfactory answers to the young RM's concerns. Rather than hoping that the problem would resolve itself or that his worst fears might be wrong, he brought the loan to the attention of senior line and loan review officers. They concurred with his suspicions and began a process that led to the account exiting the bank before the company's performance worsened.

To avoid surprises, the loan review process should be continuous, rather than once a year before the external auditors or regulators arrive. For example, several banks review loans shortly after they have been made and reevaluate the risk rating that the banker has applied to the loan. This follow-up can immediately set off a flashing yellow warning light. Many lending unit's risk ratings also are independently spot-checked twice a year. Additionally, the formal annual review process judges each lending unit on multiple criteria, including the accuracy of the risk rating that had previously been applied versus current performance and the loan's adherence to bank policies.

The Spirit of the Law

Quite simply, the more a loan strays from the bank's stated policy, the more likely it is to produce problems and require close management.

One recent analysis compared loan losses to the degree of the loan's compliance with bank policy. Out of the bank's total loan losses, only 20 percent resulted from loans viewed as following the letter and spirit of the law, as laid down by credit policy. Loans with minor exceptions to stated policy—often involving specific exceptions granted by line managers—resulted in another 30 percent of the total losses. Loans deemed "rule breakers" generated upwards of 50 percent of the losses.

The message here is unambiguous. A bank's culture and screening procedures must discourage exceptions. When they occur, both the RM and the loan review area must recognize them and train a constant spotlight on the loan in anticipation of future problems.

Outside of the loan review process, many banks also form problem-solving loan committees that usually meet once a month. These groups recommend the levels of charge-offs and reserves to be taken. Further, such a committee may recommend that deteriorating situations be transferred to the workout area for specialist attention.

Today, loan review managers may find a reduced need for the in-depth portfolio reviews considered essential only a few years ago. Along with the economy, portfolios are improving and reserves often are being reversed. In fact, the majority of weak borrowers have in all likelihood already been restructured or have exited the bank.

In short, the credit crisis of the late 1980s and early 1990s appears to be over. Loan review now has an excellent opportunity to play an active role in supporting marketing and assisting the line both in prospecting and upfront guidance. In effect, internal loan review can become an important part of the sales strategy, even though its role is invisible to customers.

Stage 4: Workout Units

Basic workout specialists usually have a singular goal: getting as much of a problem loan paid back as quickly as possible. Their customer is neither the borrower nor the line unit, which will absorb the loss should one occur. They represent the overall interests of the bank.

Unfortunately, however, workout groups are considered the last resort by many line units. Turning a loan over to the workout group is often a stigma of failure, a career breaker. Therefore, in many banks, RMs and their managers make the workout group's job more difficult by keeping the loans within the originating unit beyond a reasonable period of time. The justifications for this decision include a belief that a customer's problem will correct itself or a concern that a unit outside of the line's control will generate an unnecessary loss. In contrast, statistics demonstrate that early detection, tight initial structuring, and aggressive asset sales tactics have allowed some banks to unload emerging problems successfully before they become workouts.

During the 1980s, many banks formed specialized workout units, even though up to that point management had allowed the function to remain with the RM. Not experts in problem loans, RMs found their time for marketing increasingly consumed by non-performing assets. The sudden growth in number and dollar amount of problem loans called for a different skill set to manage them effectively.

A few major banks continue to have their RMs manage workout situations. In those cases, management feels that the RMs who originated the loans should have the learning experience of trying to fix the problems they created. The problem with this tactic, however, is that by the time a loan deteriorates, the responsible lender may have moved on to a different area or even left the bank. Further, specialized skills are required to make certain that the bank is not at a disadvantage versus other banks when it comes to a credit committee or the borrower. In most cases, banks will find that separating the "sell" process from the "save" process has measurable returns.

In fact, most banks choose to transfer a loan to the workout area away from the line units. They switch loans to workout when their risk rating is at the lower end of the scale and after management determines that the account should probably not remain with the bank. After that point, the RM will have little ongoing involvement with the customer. Ownership then belongs to the workout group, which will bear responsibility for all decisions. The line is kept informed and consulted only as necessary. Write-offs, however, are usually charged to the originating group's profit and loss statement.

During the high volume period of the late 1980s, most banks segmented their approach to workouts. As a loan joined what might be considered the bank's intensive care unit, specialists made a MASH-like triage decision. Loans were categorized either as "fix, forbearance, or foreclose." Depending on that initial assessment, the bank applied different timetables, negotiating tactics, and resources. This triage methodology did allow for some accounts to be "doctored-up" and returned to the line. Further, minimum effort was expended by the bank on lost causes.

As with the loan review process, the intensity of workout-related activities declined steadily during 1993–94 as the economy recovered. Today, however, banks may be able to afford the luxury of maintaining these groups as training areas for inexperienced bankers. As part of the holistic approach to credit, for example, issues that workout groups uncover concerning specific industries or loan structures must be communicated to other areas within the bank, including both loan review and the line.

The Cost of Credit

A recent survey of chief credit officers, which my consulting firm conducted for Robert Morris Associates, demonstrates the extent of the cost savings opportunity available to those banks that can simplify their credit decision process while maintaining high quality.

We surveyed 32 regional and super-regional banks from across the United States concerning the efficiency and effectiveness of their corporate loan credit processes. The corporate loan portfolios for those included in the survey ranged from $435 million to close to $17 billion; the median level was $3.8 billion in loans outstanding.

In order to understand the components of cost, we divided the credit process into the five related steps that are summarized in Exhibit 7.5.

Exhibit 7.5 Focus of Chief Credit Officers Survey

We evaluated the effectiveness and efficiency of the credit origination, approval, and maintenance processes.

Definitions

- Credit Analysis
  – Gathering of client information, statement spreading, reviewing applications, and writing formal analysis

- Formal Approval
  – Reviewing and implementing recommendations, attending and coordinating credit meetings, and committee approval and review

- Monitoring and Portfolio Administration
  – Reviewing current financial performance, maintaining loan portfolio information, and monitoring assets for compliance with covenants

- Loan Review
  – Reviewing loan deals for fit with corporate objectives

- Workouts
  – Reassessing credit for out-of-compliance deals
  – Restructuring, monitoring, and disposing of troubled assets

The impetus for the survey was chief credit officers' concerns about the costs involved in credit approval and maintenance, particularly in light of the need to increase productivity bankwide. The survey indicated that large gaps in cost performance did, in fact, exist. At the same time, no discernible improvement in credit quality was achieved by spending more on the credit process itself. In the current environment it may be that excellent credit quality is insufficient for success; efficiency is becoming increasingly important as well.

No matter how we cut the data—by geography, by size or portfolio, or by average loan size—the message remains the same: some banks are simply more efficient in the credit process. Exhibit 7.6 presents the cost numbers for banks with corporate loan outstandings of $2 billion to $5 billion.

The best banks in the size group require approximately $2,000 to underwrite and support $1 million in loan outstandings. While the average cost for this group was $4,500, the most inefficient banks generate costs that approach $6,000 per $1 million in outstandings, a dramatically higher figure. Obviously, those banks that have high costs are putting themselves at a competitive disadvantage. This cost focus becomes even more paramount when considering larger loan portfolios—those greater than $5 billion in outstandings. In that instance the average cost for the banks surveyed drops to approximately $4,200. As Exhibit 7.7 shows, the gap between the best and worst performing bank, however, widens to more than $4,800 for $1 million in outstandings versus about $4,000 for those banks with outstandings of $2 billion to $5 billion.

This limited data suggests that well run bigger banks may be able to create a significant cost advantage for themselves. But size itself does not result in better cost performance.

Similar cost performance gaps exist even within the same bank holding company. Exhibit 7.8 breaks out the costs of the credit process at two sister banks within a multi-state bank holding company. While regional market differences may play a part in their variance from best practices for their size segment ($1,520 per $1 million of loans), evaluating the areas where the greatest differences

Exhibit 7.6   Cost of Credit for Banks with Outstandings of $2 to $5 Billion

Top performers hold a strong cost advantage over competitors.

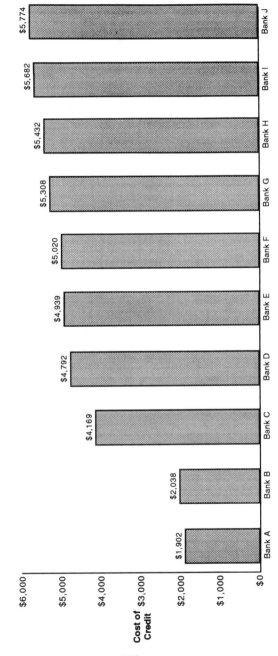

Exhibit 7.7   Cost of Credit for Banks with Outstandings of More than $5 Billion

The average large bank may have a cost advantage over smaller competition.

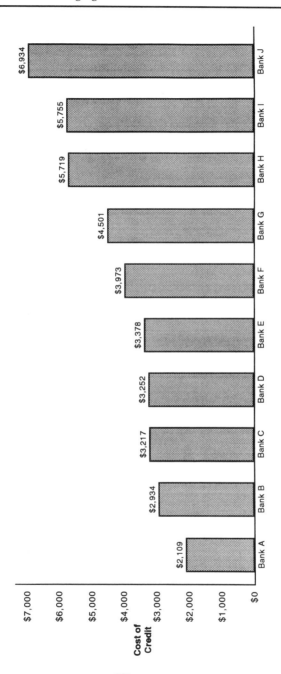

131

exist between these banks (in this case, the formal approval and monitoring areas) can lead to an understanding of internal best practices and, ultimately, their adoption across the bank. While whittling down the entire $1,900 gap separating the two banks depicted in Exhibit 7.8 may not be possible, any improvement goes right to the bottom line.

Lower costs can be achieved without harming the quality of the credit decisions by rethinking the roles and responsibilities of those involved in the credit process and by redesigning workflows related to this area.

Streamlining the Credit Process

The call for reducing the RM's involvement in the credit process is a product of simple arithmetic. The banker's time falls into one of three buckets: marketing, credit, or maintenance. A bank's growth in the corporate market depends on an increased marketing presence aimed both at current customers and new targets. To give the RM more time in front of customers, the bank clearly needs to determine whether any time can be freed up from the credit and the supporting customer service areas and reallocated to the sales effort.

Willie Sutton's line explaining why he robbed banks is applicable to this situation. If you remember, he reportedly said that he robbed banks because "that's where the money is." Therefore, we need to dissect and reevaluate the time that RMs spend on credit and customer service because "that's where the time is."

Streamlining the credit process calls for two separate but related initiatives: reviewing the RM's involvement in credit and examining the loan decision process. Today, that involvement ranges from relatively sophisticated tasks, such as credit structuring, to the more mundane, such as file maintenance and loan closings.

Many credit approval processes are not currently accomplishing what they were originally intended to do. Throughout the years, they have become a Rube Goldberg-like process where extra, complicated steps have been added on a demand basis. An exercise as straightforward as plotting out the process flows required to make

Exhibit 7.8 Cost Performance Within One Holding Company

Two unit banks from the same holding company had almost a $2,000 difference in their cost to produce and support $1 million in credit outstandings.

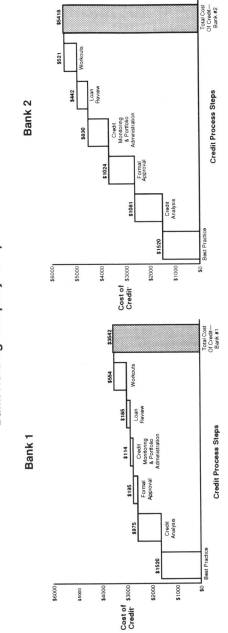

Bank Holding Company Comparison

a single credit decision can serve as the foundation for restructuring and streamlining the process.

Reduce the RM's Role

As discussed earlier, RMs typically spend their days on a blend of activities. What are broadly defined as credit activities consume approximately 30 to 40 percent of the average RM's time. That time can be reduced by at least 10 to 15 percent, and the RM can use the additional time to sell. Based on the experience of several major banks we have worked with, this restructuring can be accomplished without harming credit quality.

First, it is necessary to examine what specific tasks comprise the time spent on credit.

Exhibit 7.9, a composite example based upon actual client experiences, separates the 35 percent of time spent on credit activities into its component parts (column 1) and categorizes them into one of three groups: activities related to approving and booking a loan, the credit review process, and a catch-all miscellaneous or other category. Obviously, each bank completing this examination will discover that different amounts of total time are spent on credit as well as its component sub-tasks.

Column 2 presents the current time spent on each task. Interestingly, relatively few individual tasks involve a significant amount of time; only one—the initial credit assessment—requires more than 5 percent of the RM's average day. Eight activities comprise the miscellaneous category, each requiring less than 1 percent of the RM's time. These tasks, in particular, need to be closely examined, to determine if they can be offloaded to other personnel.

Column 3 presents the target level of RM "effort" to obtain credit approvals that can be achieved. Importantly, the loan decision process itself is only marginally affected. Much of the available time is connected to maintenance or reporting activities.

A number of activities currently performed by the RM could be shifted in their entirety to another group within the bank; in other instances the degree of RM involvement can be reduced. For exam-

Exhibit 7.9 Current RM Credit-Related Activities

As part of credit streamlining, the activities performed by RMs need to change.

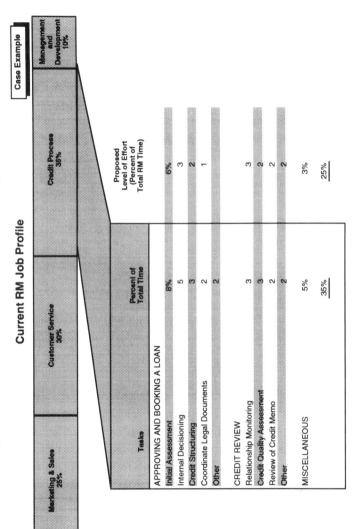

Current RM Job Profile

Tasks	Percent of Total Time	Proposed Level of Effort (Percent of Total RM Time)
APPROVING AND BOOKING A LOAN		
Initial Assessment	8%	6%
Internal Decisioning	5	3
Credit Structuring	3	2
Coordinate Legal Documents	2	1
Other	2	
CREDIT REVIEW		
Relationship Monitoring	3	3
Credit Quality Assessment	3	2
Review of Credit Memo	2	2
Other	2	
MISCELLANEOUS	5%	3%
	35%	25%

Marketing & Sales 25%   Customer Service 30%   Credit Process 35%   Management and Development 10%

Case Example

ple, the following hand-offs add up to a significant percentage of freed-up time:

- Both banks and non-banks have established loan closing groups to handle documentation, after a loan structure (which takes up 2 percent of the RM's time) has already been agreed to.

- An account administrator—whose role will be discussed more fully in Chapter 9—can handle sub-tasks, such as the initial loan disbursements, prepare loan system inputs, and be responsible for exception monitoring (which in total take up 3 percent of the RM's time).

- Centralization of core activities, such as workout and collateral monitoring, also can play a role in refocusing the RM.

Depending on the bank, these bits and pieces may add up to 10 percent or more of liberated RM time. This total demonstrates how nickel-and-dime changes can add up to dollars. Most bankers spend no more than 20 to 30 percent of their time marketing. If a bank can redirect 10 percent of their RM's current credit-focused effort toward marketing, the time spent marketing increases by 30 to 50 percent or more. Assuming the marketing approach is rigorous (following the path suggested in Chapters 4 and 6), the bottom-line impact can be significant.

Of course, promoting the merits of a specialized group is easy; but does it result in an increased infrastructure or centralization? Arguments founded on cost and quality issues can and have been raised against each of these initiatives. Banks that have particularly strong credit cultures are understandably reluctant to reduce their banker's involvement in areas related to credit. Detailed planning, a strong training program for those assuming responsibilities formerly lodged with the RMs, and a phased-in introduction of non-RMs to handle some tasks can address those concerns. None of these changes can be introduced overnight. However, banks can implement many of them within a few months.

Others may argue that a bigger infrastructure increases costs or that their bank's asset size cannot justify a centralized structure. The economic implications of redesigning the RMs' role and the infra-structure supporting them are discussed in Chapter 10.

Use Process-Flow Maps

One of the most telling exercises a bank can perform involves drawing process-flow maps of key decision areas—loan approval in particular. A work flow analysis can be developed with the full cooperation of key internal players or groups involved in perform-ing a function. In the case illustrated by Exhibits 7.10a, b, and c, line officers, credit personnel, and administrative assistants had input into these process-flow charts, which depict how the credit process currently operates.

An important addition to this analysis involves quantifying the cost of the various activities after management determines the time spent by each major participant on a particular task. Exhibit 7.10 is divided into three parts to focus more easily on specific opportuni-ties to streamline current processes.

In Exhibit 7.10a, the internal loan approval process begins with the account officer writing a call report and circulating it to the credit area. That group, in turn, may respond to the memorandum with a written request for additional information.

Exhibit 7.10b portrays the internal activities that occur when a credit memorandum has been written. Wide circulation of this memo occurs with substantial revisions preceding the actual sub-mission of a customer proposal.

Exhibit 7.10c focuses on the negotiation and proposal revision process. Again, many iterations of the proposal can occur prior to presenting a final structure to the customer.

Exhibit 7.10a illustrates a system that is largely driven by written communication. All loan requests follow a similar process, no mat-ter what the bank's previous credit experience with a customer. The activities covered in the early stages of the credit process also must encompass a clear understanding of the next steps required to get the deal approved.

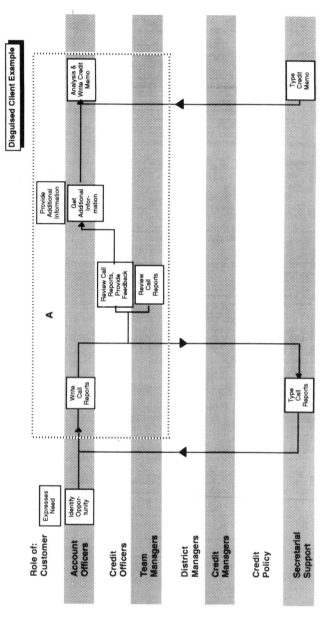

Exhibit 7.10a   Credit Approval Workflow

Workflow analysis identified several specific opportunities for streamlining the credit decision process.

Exhibit 7.10b Credit Approval Workflow

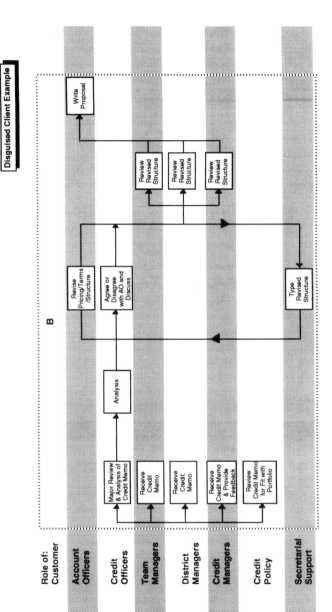

139

Exhibit 7.10c   Credit Approval Workflow

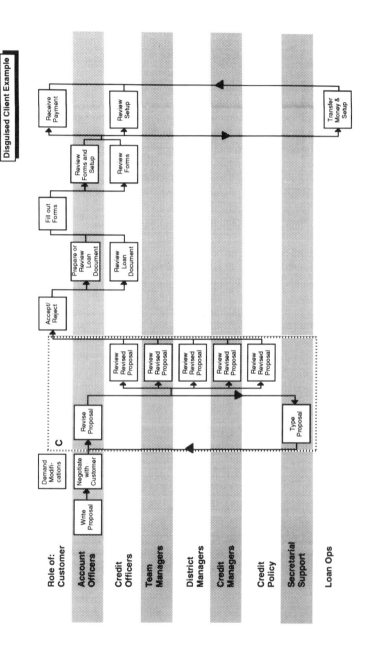

The back-and-forth movement from the line to credit illustrated in Exhibit 7.10b can be curtailed only if upfront planning is improved. Early meetings between the RM and a credit officer need to have the quality of an informal brainstorming session. Formal meetings with too much emphasis on the follow-up written word can create a tension that depletes the spirit of collegiality and cooperation and, of course, slows the approval process. Early discussions concerning the structure or acceptability of a loan have to avoid an internal us-versus-them mentality where the line officers feel this sales job is tougher than the one with the customer.

Streamlining the initial stages of the credit process also will simplify the steps required after the RM writes the credit memorandum (Exhibit 7.10b). Similarly, upfront decisions made prior to writing a proposal can avoid multiple revisions later (Exhibit 7.10c). For example, the period during which the proposal is being developed is the most appropriate time to agree on what pricing parameters the bank will ultimately accept and which terms are simply non-negotiable for the bank. This structure will give the RM a blueprint of the negotiating room available.

What often happens, instead, is that the banker delivers the proposal, the customer objects, and then an entirely new internal approval process begins. The inefficiency of that approach should be clear. Perhaps less clear, but as important, is how that process not only demotivates the banker but also demotes him to a "message-carrier" in the customer's eyes. Under the proposed new structure, empowering the RM to negotiate within the boundaries previously agreed upon can dramatically shorten the time to close a loan and, of course, allow the banker to get onto the next deal.

Substantial value can be gained from examining a bank's major functions using workflow analysis and detailed process flows to assess the time spent on individual steps and the costs of those steps on a per loan basis. This analysis often allows management to pinpoint specific areas for change; in fact, the dollars consumed by various steps may create a mandate. This process will only bear fruit, however, if management approaches it with a willingness to trust its employees' analysis and a corporate commitment to think about its business in a way that challenges time-worn assumptions.

Summary Thoughts

While credit quality remains the foundation of earnings quality, the credit approval and monitoring process should be subjected to scrutiny. Excellent credit must be complemented by increased efficiency, resulting from process streamlining and rethought job definitions and accountabilities. Portfolio growth can never be emphasized over credit quality, but quality can be maintained or improved while efficiency increases.

8

Linking Credit to Sales
Case Study: Norwest Bank

"Bank management must devote considerable time, effort,
thought, and leadership to . . . loan portfolio management."
—*Ed Morsman, executive vice president, Norwest Bank, Minneapolis*

Ten years ago, no one would have cited Norwest Bank in Minneapolis as an excellent credit bank. What Norwest has been able to accomplish in a relatively short period of time, however, offers an example to senior managers who wish to reengineer to initiate an efficient credit for the middle market process that both encourages RM marketing and still protects bank credit quality.

The changes Norwest Bank has introduced have neither been easy to implement nor have they been without internal controversy. In fact, the opposite is true. Yet, as with Chemical Bank's marketing program, successful change was achieved because of clear leadership and consistent, highly visible senior management commitment.

Rising from the Ashes

In the early 1980s Norwest Bank was a bank whose future was in doubt. Its headquarters had burnt to the ground in 1982. Net income in that year had decreased for the second year in a row. Its provision for loan losses had risen to $188 million from $26 million two years earlier. Earnings rose in 1983 but fell off in 1984, due in part to real estate losses. Skeptical industry observers debated whether real estate and other bad loans would sink the bank or force it onto the auction block.

By the mid 1980s, credit quality and earnings had improved, management imbued the bank with a strong culture, and a new course was established.

Part Process, Part Culture

Norwest Bank's approach to credit decision-making has grown in effectiveness throughout the past 10 years. In the context of the four parts of the credit process discussed in the previous chapter—loan application, credit underwriting, monitoring and loan review, and workout—we can find several themes that permeate Norwest Bank's approach to credit:

- Early informal involvement of credit officers in the marketing and loan application process, supported by a cultivation of collegiality between the two groups since "they think the same way."

- Decentralized decision-making and centralized review for credit underwriting.

- Focus of the RM time toward certain deals and away from others to increasing productivity and credit decision quality.

- Redirection of the RM away from internal credit control activities, such as evaluating specialized or complicated credits, and toward external marketing.

- Constant focus on cross-sell, beginning early in the customer relationship with the initial credit decision process.

Stage 1: Loan Application Process

Norwest Bank's credit culture with its emphasis on focusing the RM's time outward, or toward making customer contact and learning customer needs, pervades the underwriting process from the very start of a customer relationship.

Similar to many banks, at Norwest Bank a credit analyst who is a member of a centralized group spreads the statements. Depending on the type of loan under consideration, the RM may or may not be deeply involved in the write-up of the loan application. The RM will write up deals if they are simple, such as standard term loans or lines of credit; others will be immediately shifted to specialists. More complex transactions, such as asset-based deals, transactions related to mergers and acquisitions, and other more sophisticated credits are driven by the specialized financial services (SFS), asset-based lending, or equipment finance groups.

Shifting some transactions to these specialized groups accomplishes two goals: preservation of credit quality and focused marketing. This delegation of responsibility early in the loan process means that a specialized credit will be evaluated by officers who have extensive experience in that particular discipline, rather than by an RM who is a dedicated generalist. An RM can thus remain out in the market, rather than behind the desk or PC trying to understand and structure unusual credits.

Internal accounting systems at Norwest Bank also foster cooperation between the RM and product specialist groups. If an RM refers a deal to the SFS group, for example, that RM receives individual portfolio credit for the loan. For these deals the RM serves as the referral and delivery system and the SFS group becomes the underwriter.

While the RM gets credit, the deal will show up only on the SFS division's profit and loss statement. Although a shadow accounting system does not exist, cooperation occurs between units because, in one senior banker's words, top management "does not like infighting" and encourages cooperation and a one-bank approach.

Stage 2: Credit Underwriting

Essentially, Norwest Bank encourages decentralization of the credit decision process, empowering the RM or specialized officers to take responsibility by means of a signature approval system. As in other instances where banks employ a signature system, the number and top level of signatures required depends on the loan's size and risk rating. The sponsoring lender, whether an RM or a specialized officer, determines the loan's risk rating. After closing, the credit policy review department conducts what the bank terms a "flash rating" of all new loans.

Theoretically, a group of line officers could approve a credit without the approval or involvement of the credit area as long as it is within their authority; but that rarely happens. In fact, credit area involvement, although informal, begins early in any relationship and continues throughout deal structuring.

Extending credit facilities is part of an overall relationship. Before a credit can be approved, the RM must obtain a significant portion of non-credit business or, at a minimum, present a plan to obtain that business within a defined period of time, usually one year. The bank's emphasis on obtaining non-credit income comes from the top of the organization.

In a speech made to his officers in 1991, Richard Kovachevich, president of Norwest Bank Corporation, stated his business strategy in very clear terms: corporate loans should be considered a loss leader and effective cross-selling of other products must have the highest priority:

> "If we have a piece of business that is basically a stand-alone [lending only] relationship, we must have won that business by pricing it below our own standards [due to competitive pressures].
>
> We are doomed to making an unprofitable loan because the marketplace dictates it . . . If you look at where the real problems of banking are, it is the transactional lending banks who do one-off lending to corporations. These banks are being eaten alive . . . A suggestion to you . . . Go through your

portfolio. For every loan you have with little collateral busi-ness, either get some additional business or get rid of the loan. That's how convinced I am of this observation."

In addition to a focus on relationship profitability, Norwest Bank also makes certain that the credit fits into its portfolio parameters. The bank regularly examines its loan portfolio and determines its ongoing credit appetite for specific industries and loan types. The credit underwriting process, therefore, includes an evaluation of the loan against that criteria.

Norwest Bank's strong credit discipline is reinforced by its prac-tice of placing a relatively low ceiling on the amount of credit that the bank will make available to any one borrower. This philosophy grows out of a desire to avoid concentration risk and to limit putting all their eggs in one basket. As part of its credit process, Norwest Bank conducts a detailed credit review and negotiates hard on loan structure. Even with first-rate preparation and analysis, however, management's view is that portfolio diversity averts problems. At this point, Norwest Bank will lend more than $25 million to only a handful of companies, even though its lending limit far exceeds that amount.

Ed Morsman, executive vice president of Norwest Bank in Min-neapolis, in his highly readable book, *Commercial Loan Portfolio Management*, stresses this strategy:

"Concentrations occur in geographies, industries, products, and individual borrowers, and they can be career-stoppers. A small unit with high concentrations may seem innocuous . . . yet, it can produce unpleasant surprises.

High concentrations often signal laziness for they are the quickest and easiest means of producing volume . . . The best strategy for producing earnings consistency in a commercial loan portfolio is to diversify, diversify, and, when in doubt, diversify some more."

Of course, there are counter-intuitive elements to this view. Loan portfolio growth will likely be flat, at best, for the foreseeable future. Plus, the cost of putting on a large loan is about the same as a smaller loan. If customer retention is a key to profitability, what better way to retain customers than to lend them more money and uptier the relationship based upon credit?

Norwest Bank's coordinated credit and marketing thrust answers these points. The credit perspective is apparent from Morsman's comments. Basically, no matter how smart you are or how much analysis you do, something unexpected can happen. Loan limits reduce the impact of unpleasant surprises.

By not allowing RMs to rely on credit as the sole or even major foundation of a customer relationship, enforcing loan ceilings supports the bank's marketing strategy and a cross-sell discipline. The message to the RM and the customer is clear: credit remains an important product, but it is just one among many. A credit-only relationship is simply not acceptable within Norwest Bank's culture.

A conversation with a Norwest Bank RM underscored that point. He said, "RMs do not feel it is the loan that makes them bankers but rather bringing in any new business, including non-credit." When this philosophy permeates a bank, cross-selling becomes part of the fabric of an institution rather than a "nice to have."

Stage 3: Monitoring and Loan Review

One foundation of Norwest Bank's approach to loan monitoring is a portfolio-based exposure management system, based upon actuarial and industry analysis.

Exhibit 8.1 illustrates both the key inputs and potential outputs of this approach. Since 1987, Norwest Bank has been developing a database of information on all commercial loans made. The bank has applied what it believes is a consistent risk rating process for loans across its portfolio and has captured the profitability for each relationship from its start until the present time. Using this data, the bank can develop a profile on key industries based upon line and credit officer input. Other cuts of the database by geography or other types of segmentation can also be generated.

The center column of the chart outlines the analysis that can result from capturing sufficient data. On an industry-by-industry

Exhibit 8.1 Norwest's Actuarial Approach to Portfolio Management

Advances in actuarial and industry analysis have improved the portfolio management capabilities of banks like Norwest.

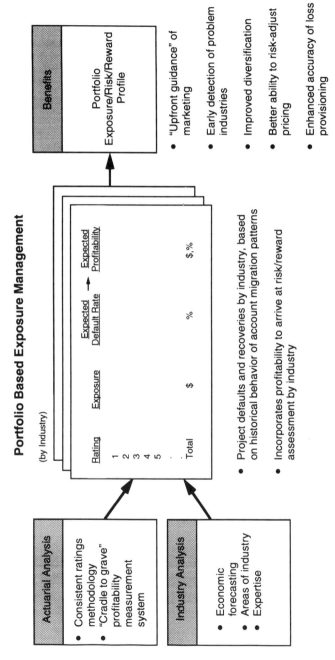

Portfolio Based Exposure Management

(by Industry)

Rating	Exposure	Expected Default Rate	Expected Profitability
1			
2			
3			
4			
5			
.			
Total	$	%	$, %

- Project defaults and recoveries by industry, based on historical behavior of account migration patterns
- Incorporates profitability to arrive at risk/reward assessment by industry

Actuarial Analysis
- Consistent ratings methodology
- "Cradle to grave" profitability measurement system

Industry Analysis
- Economic forecasting
- Areas of industry
- Expertise

Benefits

Portfolio Exposure/Risk/Reward Profile

- "Upfront guidance" of marketing
- Early detection of problem industries
- Improved diversification
- Better ability to risk-adjust pricing
- Enhanced accuracy of loss provisioning

149

basis, Norwest Bank can develop a loan migration report that projects yearly dollars of defaults and recoveries by industry, based upon historic account migration patterns. For each industry, therefore, the bank can estimate which accounts of a certain risk rating are likely to maintain their current credit status and which might deteriorate. Obviously, the bank's summary could lead to more detailed reviews down to individual relationship names.

In addition to forecasting risk migration by industry, Norwest Bank can also develop risk/reward profiles. Profitability data allows the bank to link the current and projected risk profiles to profits generated by particular industries, leading to a risk/reward assessment for each industry. Further segmentation of this data can lead to more detailed analysis and specific action plans to improve insufficient returns.

This approach allows the bank to catch deteriorating situations and establish early action plans either for improving a credit situation or moving the account out of the bank. Again, a tie also exists to the marketing process. This analysis leads the bank to emphasize some industries because of their strong risk/return characteristics and reevaluate others for the same reasons. Results from the portfolio analysis can and should feed the marketing process and serve as input into the upfront guidance system. For example, if Norwest Bank notices a decline in the credit quality and profitability of the franchise restaurant business, that information is communicated to the RMs across its network, allowing them to redirect their marketing efforts accordingly.

Conversely, the bank could find that it is experiencing high profit and high quality returns from lending to a segment within the manufacturing industry. RMs could then be directed to give marketing priority to companies in that business. The actual lending, of course, would be within concentration limits. The trend, however, is for profitable quality loans to be accompanied by profitable non-credit business.

Other potential benefits of portfolio-based exposure management include improved portfolio diversification, better accuracy of loan loss provisions, and a clear approach to pricing that links risk and reward.

Norwest Bank's management strategy, however, should not be considered a crystal ball. A good database is only one requirement. Such systems require a minimum of three to five years of comparable data before they can offer meaningful results. Of course, even then the results are history and cannot be 100 percent accurate for the future. But this approach does provide a strong analytic basis for decision-making. Again, to quote Ed Morsman:

> "Bank management must devote considerable time, effort, thought, and leadership to this [loan portfolio management] process. It is very hard, frustrating, and at times discouraging work in which the rewards are long-term and the pain immediate."

Morsman goes on to state that banks need an approach for "creating a planned and structured commercial loan portfolio with predictable results as opposed to the acceptance of a randomly created portfolio subject to economic cycles."

Norwest Bank's loan review process takes place both annually and on a continual basis. All lending groups are reviewed on a 12 to 15 month cycle, using a portfolio sampling procedure. Key criteria used to determine a satisfactory review include the accuracy of risk ratings for current loans and adherence to corporate policies concerning industry and concentration exposures.

The continuous review process occurs in two ways. Risk ratings for all new loans are reviewed shortly after they are booked. As a follow-up, current risk ratings are spot-checked twice a year.

Stage 4: Workout Units

Upfront guidance and portfolio monitoring are intended to lessen the number and severity of loans in the workout area. Recent results at Norwest Bank suggest that they have been effective in doing so.

Norwest Bank uses a seven-point risk rating scale for its loans. Once a loan reaches watch-list status, it becomes eligible for transfer to the capital lending group, which reports to the corporate bank's credit head. The transfer decision depends on the strategy the bank wishes to take with that account.

When an account moves to the workout area, the RM's responsibility ends, and account ownership shifts. Virtually all subsequent decisions are made by the workout group, which also handles operational issues. The mission of the capital lending group is to protect the bank by shoring up and cleaning up the account. Typically, 90 percent of the accounts sent to the workout area leave the bank. The area's customer, in effect, is the bank rather than the borrower.

Even workout activities at Norwest Bank are linked to the marketing process. Management has made the decision that capital lending should not be a permanent position for officers. Rather, workout officers rotate from the line for a two- to three-year assignment, taking the experience back to the line with them.

On Top of the Heap

In a conversation several years ago, Ed Morsman commented on why the Norwest Bank of the early 1980s was forced to change its approach to credit and marketing: "Why were we able to change? . . . We really had no choice."

Today, many other banks also lack choice if they are to remain competitive and independent in a rapidly consolidating marketplace. Norwest Bank's success is predicated in part on its willingness to undertake a self-evaluation and take the hard steps necessary to set the bank on a new course. Its recent performance—1993 earnings of $654 million, ROE of 20.9 percent, and ROA of 1.4 percent—indicates the potential pay off is substantial.

Summary Thoughts

The Norwest Bank view of credit and marketing as two parts of a whole provides several lessons for any bank manager contemplating reengineering the credit process. First, the four credit-related activities—loan application preparation, credit underwriting, monitoring and loan review, and workout—cannot be viewed as standalone activities. Rather, they are parts of a process.

Second, the most successful credit culture banks consider the credit process to be linked with the marketing effort.

Third, as generating growth becomes increasingly important and more difficult to achieve, a holistic approach such as Norwest Bank's will foster effective marketing while ensuring credit integrity.

Banks that fail to connect the marketing and credit areas, even though they maintain a rigorous credit process, will fall behind those financial institutions where teaming, cooperation, and a strong external focus predominate. Communication, respect, decision segmentation, and empowerment need to take precedence over hostility, distrust, and double-checking in credit underwriting. Bankers must come to view aggressive marketing and excellent credit not as opposites but as complementary elements of sustained success.

9

Growth through Infrastructure Change

> "Administrative assistants are the point of relationship continuity and the hub of customer service at our banks."
> —*a senior vice-president and head of middle market banking for a top-20 bank*

What senior bank manager would turn down the opportunity to increase an RM's marketing time by 20 to 30 percent or even more? In many banks, that percentage increase would double the time spent in front of prospects and customers. Similarly, who would turn down the additional opportunity to cut the bank's expense base by decreasing the per-relationship cost to service customers?

The combination of higher productivity, a lower cost structure, and a higher level of customer service may seem too good to be true. The fact is that banks can achieve these benefits by redesigning the front line of customer service, shifting responsibilities away from the middle market or large corporate RM, and assigning these duties to support personnel.

That group of support personnel—described as para-bankers throughout this chapter—has a decision-making role that requires extensive customer interaction and, in effect, day-to-day control over the operational aspects of a relationship. The shift of job

155

responsibilities to this group reinforces the middle market's and large corporate's emphasis on growth and demonstrates that management is willing to "walk the walk" as well as "talk the talk" in promoting productivity. Management that undertakes such a restructuring program shows that it is willing to provide the infrastructure required to allow the RM to market and sell. (A separate chapter, 15, deals with the small business market and the need for fundamental change in servicing the specific banking requirements of that customer base in a cost efficient manner.)

Impetus for Administrative Change

Few opportunities for a quick win exist in middle market banking today, and some readers may even dispute how rapidly the changes recommended in this chapter can have an impact. Nonetheless, creating a robust administrative support structure backing the RM and making certain that it is used to the fullest extent possible can have a very positive, near-term payback for a bank. Importantly, this change is one that the majority of RMs will whole-heartedly support because it increases their ability to develop a high-value relationship with customers and targets. Further, when implemented thoughtfully, this administrative restructuring strategy can actually improve, rather than decrease, the level of customer service that a bank offers.

Chapter 1 includes a chart (Exhibit 1.5), which indicates that most of the RM's time goes into one of two buckets, either credit or maintenance activities. Those two areas present the major opportunity for redirecting the RM toward revenue and profit growth—that is, if some tough decisions are made and if the RM's job is enhanced.

As reviewed in Chapter 7, banks have the opportunity to streamline their credit processes. However, any streamlining in that area must, of necessity, be carefully balanced against any adverse impact on credit quality. Because poorly implemented changes in the credit culture could "blow up the bank," change must be slowly introduced to that function. In contrast, banks can effectively limit the downside impact of changes in the account maintenance process.

Both for reasons related to portfolio excellence and to internal politics, customer service is by far an easier area to reengineer.

In Chapter 1, Exhibit 1.5 illustrates the current situation existing at many banks, regardless of their size. On average, RMs are spending more time on maintenance activities than on marketing, anywhere from 25 to 50 percent of their typical day. The focus of their time-consuming tasks is customer service, that is, making certain that current customers obtain high quality service across the bank. The importance of customer service is unquestioned, but as mentioned earlier, account retention and successful development of the existing customer franchise are the primary keys to future growth.

Customer service-related tasks consist of a myriad of activities, most of which are of a routine or maintenance nature. Among them are such time-eaters as: tracking receivables agings, following up on documentation exceptions, ordering UCC filings, and completing audit confirmation and credit checks. Few individual activities take up large chunks of RM's time. However, 2 percent here and 3 percent there adds up fast. The net impact of including maintenance tasks and customer service in the RM's job responsibilities is to chain down those officers who may wish to be in front of the customer and, ironically, to provide an excuse for those bankers who wish to avoid marketing.

Some banks have reduced the time that an RM spends on administrative activities, whittling the percentage down to the 5- to 10-percent range. They have accomplished this relocation of time by creating and empowering a new customer service position that provides leverage for line bankers. Management also has insisted that the banker use that new resource and increase marketing time.

Create a Customer Service Group

This new customer service position has a variety of titles at various banks, including account administrator, operations officer, and para-banker (PB). Whatever the name, one cannot overestimate the value of this group, and the way it provides a foundation that allows

RMs to grow business by getting out from behind their desks and into the customer's office.

Although some PBs may have been promoted from secretarial or clerical positions, this enhanced administrative function must be viewed differently from the administrative assistant (AA) positions of the past. To make this reengineering project successful, even the title of this function should be distinctive to differentiate it from previously perceived lower-status jobs. PBs need to be accorded the respect of professionals who are key members of the banking team. To support that new role—one that has the potential to lead to an officer title—banks must develop a meaningful training plan. This career path will both encourage commitment and reduce the high turnover that has often plagued administrative areas. To do this, management must agree on a clear definition of the roles and responsibilities of this group. Additionally, with a few exceptions, the role must be the same across the bank.

Many banks already offer their RMs an AA as support. Exhibit 9.1 graphs the ratio of AAs and secretaries to RMs for six banks. The support number varies from .65 down to less than .30 AAs per RM. As with other analysis of this type, a high degree of variability can be found within the same bank.

Exhibit 9.2 illustrates this inconsistency between seven units of one bank. Not only does the number of support personnel available for the RM vary, but how the RMs have used this support also varies. For example, in some instances in the past, bankers introduced the AA to the customer and nominated that individual as the customer service contact. The other extreme appears to be one in which the AA was relegated to the role of telephone answerer, copy maker, and coffee maker—all tasks better delegated to a lower-level clerk.

The misuse of AA time results from a distrust or disbelief that such individuals can even partially replace the RM. Therefore, let us consider what tasks a para-banker can perform. The short answer is: more than you think possible. In fact, the para-banker's role can touch upon all key banking areas, from lending and deposit generation to transactional activities. While the job description in Ex-

158

Exhibit 9.1   AA/Secretary Support Levels

Administrative support varies dramatically across banks.

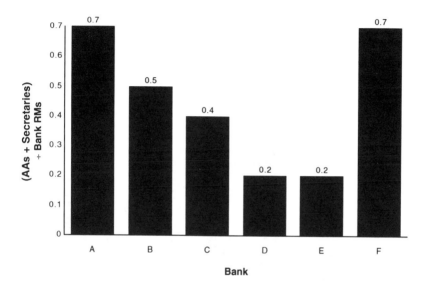

hibit 9.3 should not be considered all inclusive, the responsibilities do indicate the potential for allowing the RM to download time-consuming, non-marketing, or credit-related tasks. This list is not a consultant's daydream; it is a composite based on the actual structure of a para-banker's job at a top-20 regional bank.

Only the willingness of the RM, the training and skill of the PB, and the creativity of both will limit the activities that can be shifted away from the banker.

Implement the Customer Service Position

Writing the para-banker's job description should be a joint effort of the existing support group, RMs, and the operations area—all under the close sponsorship of senior management. Of course, specific tasks will vary from bank to bank, but a number of themes will certainly guide the job creation process.

Exhibit 9.2   Varying Levels of Administrative Support Within the Same Bank

Even within the same bank, support levels vary widely. Management needs to go beyond the ratio to determine root causes for the variability.

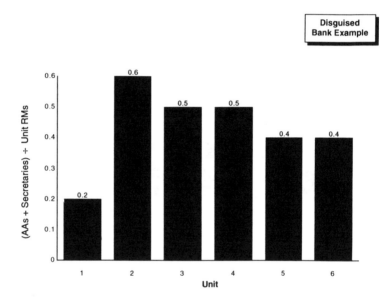

Assign More Not Less

The initial tendency may be to marginalize the para-banker position, that is, severely limit its responsibilities. This reluctance to transfer tasks may result from a concern that the PB will take time to ascend the learning curve. However, like mountain climbing, it is best to keep looking up and ahead, never down. Otherwise, a phased shift of responsibility may never occur.

That said, detailed preparation is critical. Offering strong upfront training, meaningful measurement systems, and close initial monitoring of performance will create a fuller job from day one.

Exhibit 9.3   Para-Banker Job Description

Para-bankers can fill much of the customer service role.

Lending
+ Coordinate loan bookings.
+ Prepare customer correspondence.
+ Make direct contact with agent banks and internal back office areas regarding syndicated credits.
+ Prepare management reports.

Marketing
+ Assist RMs in the account planning process.
+ Uncover and follow up on cross–sell opportunities.

Letters of Credit
+ Review documentation and transmit to letter of credit area.
+ Serve as initial customer contact for problem resolution.
+ Investments and Cash Management.
+ Research investment rates; communicate and confirm rates to customer.
+ Establish security safekeeping accounts.
+ Investigate cash management service related issues.

Administration
+ Coordinate loan documentation and loan closings.
+ Conduct documentation reviews.
+ Approve some check-cashing requests; issue bank checks.
+ Process and notify customers on payment of liens.
+ Initiate and execute wire transfers.
+ Assist RMs in the account planning process.

Ensure Success

The worst case when restructuring administrative support functions is one in where poor execution kills an excellent concept. Assigning top-level, excellent people—or, "people who cannot be spared"—to the design phase of the project is critical for the restructuring program to gain acceptance within the bank. PBs must not be viewed as "retreads" who have been given this job only because of tenure or politics. A strong internal hiring review process needs to be conducted along with an outside search for high-potential candidates.

Pilot Test

In most cases, a brief period of piloting or testing the PB structure in a limited way serves as an additional insurance policy. Testing this position in two or three geographic regions, for example, allows the bugs to be worked out and adjustments to be made. Roll-out to the entire bank can then proceed smoothly.

Those taking on the new PB responsibilities must believe that the position is not a dead-end. Rather, the position should be billed as one that allows for continued personal development and advancement. For example, one bank begins its administrative path with the role of receptionist, followed by several levels of administrator. Ultimately, high performers at a number of banks such as Bank of New York, Citibank, and Wachovia can earn an officer's title. Banks introducing this approach may need to find the right people rather than relying only on current employees.

Addressing Objections

Any reengineering project will generate expressions of valid concern within banks as well as cynicism and outright dissension. Senior managers can anticipate "pot-shots" at the idea of para-bankers and should be prepared to answer objections as well as defuse the tension that may threaten success of the program. The use of the para-banker is akin to the role of the nurse practitioner in hospitals, a well-qualified person who offers service which the doctor cannot or would not provide. Here are the most vocal objections those bankers trying to introduce change have encountered:

1. *"The customer will not like it."* When I began my career as a "wet-behind-the-ears" banker at Citibank, I was introduced to the managers at companies that comprised my portfolio. At one introduction, my new customer reacted by saying, "And, how long are you going to be my banker?" He went on to say that every two to three years his banker moved on and, in his own words, he "had to train a new one." But then he added, "Thank goodness for Richard."

The bank had an operations officer assigned to work with a group of bankers. Richard had been in his position for a number of years and, with an extensive internal network, he usually knew how to resolve problems quickly. Customers respected that skill and viewed him as a source of continuity. I quickly learned he was better able to service his customers and had more enthusiasm about resolving detailed problems than I or most of my colleagues. He was still serving his customers after I left the area less than three years later.

Without a doubt, customers want quick and efficient service. Banks that empower a para-banker with customer service responsibility find that when customers become familiar with that person, they do not hesitate to call them for routine matters and sometimes more complicated referrals and advice. While RMs often change assignments every two or three years, para-bankers can become a source of account management continuity.

2. *"The RM will lose touch with the customer."* In fact, the para-banker approach to customer service will allow for increased quality contact between RMs and their customers. Of course, the nature of the contact will change. The RM should be able to "uptier" in the customer's mind from an account manager who tracks money transfer requests to a consultant or solutions-provider. Elimination of routine chores from the RM's day frees up time for account planning, meetings with customers, and a focus on their more complex financing, cash management, and investment needs.

3. *"We have a reputation for personally serving the customer."* Also expressed as, "It's the way we have always done things," this objection is based on fear. Senior managers should note that the biggest pocket of initial resistance to the PB productivity opportunity will come not from the customer but from the RM. Understandably, RMs not only will resist those changes that they feel could threaten the quality of customer service but also those changes that threaten their turf. This latter

objection can and should be addressed quickly. Top management has to deliver a clear message that both supports the change and places the ball in the RM's court. RMs who continue as the main provider of routine customer service should be made aware not only of the negative economic implications but also of the career limitations.

Once the transition to a different account maintenance structure takes hold, the new structure will build on itself. One manager told me the story of an RM who was performing a task that had been reassigned to a para-banker. One of her colleagues, seeing her slipping into the PB's role, said "That's not your job. Give it to your administrator." She then stopped and asked the PB to complete the task. To change the work culture, the ball simply needs to get rolling.

4. *"We are already doing this."* Many banks already have administrative support, but most have fooled themselves into thinking that they have maximized the possibilities of this position. Only rarely is the bank-wide approach consistent or does the PB have full membership on the account management team.

    One example typifies the situation often found within banks. I was interviewing two groups of AAs supporting two different bank units within the same bank. They worked on the same floor of a bank's high-rise headquarters. One group appeared demotivated and talked about the RMs as "them;" the other group saw itself as supporting the client team and spoke warmly of the relationship between its members and the RMs.

5. *"We do not have the size to justify this approach."* Smaller banks and individual product areas should consider the opportunity to regionalize or centralize the customer service function. Although physical presence is optimal, phones, faxes, modems, and video conferencing allow for easy remote communication and can create what is being called a "virtual" bank. Very few customers actually need to come into the

branch office to resolve problems, and physical proximity is usually an irrelevant issue.

Individual product areas also can centralize. One sizable regional bank has created a cash management customer service front-line to serve as a contact point for product-specific inquiries. Even the insurance industry can offer lessons to banking in the use of remote sites for customer service. One New York insurer processes a portion of its claims forms from an office in County Kerry, Ireland.

6. *"The RMs will not use the time well."* Changing the approach to account maintenance does not automatically guarantee improved productivity. Unless effectively managed, increased administrative support can simply give RMs more time for reading *The Wall Street Journal*. Shifting the RM's time away from customer service has to be positioned as part of a wider program to redirect energies into the marketplace. This program should include the marketing and sales management training and support discussed in other chapters as well as the introduction of a strict performance measurement system that ties into meaningful incentives for strong performers.

7. *"Shouldn't we wait for a systems solution?"* Of course, banks must continue to take advantage of improved technology and systems capabilities. That said, management cannot afford to wait for the delivery of systems that are often as much as 18 months away from initial installation. The often-delayed imaging technology that IBM has been developing is indicative of the backup that can occur. This is also a backwards approach. Decide on the process, and then automate it. The changes recommended here can be introduced within three to six months and lower costs and increased selling time will quickly follow.

8. *"Isn't this expensive?"* By providing the RMs with increased administrative support, banks can leverage their marketers' time, increasing revenues and, despite any added administrative salaries, reduce their service cost.

Exhibit 9.4 illustrates the potential cost benefits from changing service delivery and redefining the RM's role. Prior to the introduction of a rigorous para-banker structure, management of 100 relationships at one bank required four RMs, one administrative assistant, and, on a full-time equivalent basis, one half of a secretary. After the introduction of a para-banker, as the right side of Exhibit 9.4 shows, only two RMs were required to handle the same account load. This change was due in part to the positive impact of economies of focus, that is, having well-trained support staff concentrated on administrative tasks. The per-relationship cost to service these accounts was, thereby, reduced by more than 20 percent. This economic snapshot does not include the impact of additional revenues resulting from the RM's added time in the marketplace.

Summary Thoughts

Best practices banks provide their bankers with a high level of quality administrative support, which is equal to one support person for every three to four RMs. The result is that RMs spend only 5 to 10 percent of their time on customer maintenance.

The creation of a para-banker function has a number of benefits which go far beyond operational support. Detailed job descriptions for the para-banker result in a refocus of the RM's efforts as well as ensure consistency in customer service across the bank. Furthermore, banks often benefit from the ability to consolidate operations into regional offices. The net result is increased customer responsiveness resulting from support personnel specialization, lower costs achieved by better leveraging scale economics, and a reinvigorated, marketing-oriented group of RMs.

Exhibit 9.4   The Positive Cost Impact of a Strong Support Infrastructure

By providing RMs with more support personnel, banks can leverage the RMs' time and reduce the banks' delivery expense.

RM Economics
(Different Organizational Structures)

Current Regional Structure
100 Relationships

Position	FTE	Cost
RM	4	$240k
Administrative Assistant	1	$36k
Secretary	0.5	$15k
Total	**5.5**	**$291k**
Per Relationship	**0.055**	**$2,910**

Best Practices Example
100 Relationships

Position	FTE	Cost
RM	2	$120k
Junior RM	1	$48k
Parabanker	1	$42k
Secretary	0.5	$15k
Total	**4.5**	**$225k**
Per Relationship	**0.045**	**$2,250**

23% cost savings

167

10

Reengineering the Relationship Manager

"In a world of high-loan spreads and attractive revenues from compensating balances, unmanaged by corporate treasurers, the luxury of relationship management was not questioned."
—*Paul Allen*, Reengineering the Bank

Increased growth and profitability in the middle market is directly linked to senior management's blueprint for redefining the role of the RM and, then, the successful execution of that plan.

Unfortunately, too many banks today find themselves without a plan and in the lower left-hand quadrant (current status) of the matrix depicted in Exhibit 10.1. Their middle market business is characterized by low productivity and high maintenance costs. The RM is all things to all people and, too often, sales and relationship development comes last on the list of priorities.

The X-axis of this two-by-two graphic represents low to high productivity; the Y-axis focuses on a bank's emphasis on maintenance versus sales. Based upon my consulting company's client work, and as demonstrated by the analysis prepared for this book, most banks serving small businesses or middle markets emphasize maintaining and servicing current customers. These tasks are con-

169

Exhibit 10.1   Sales Force Development

Creating a long-term sales culture results in part from a near-term focus on productivity.

Illustrative

Steps in Sales Force Development

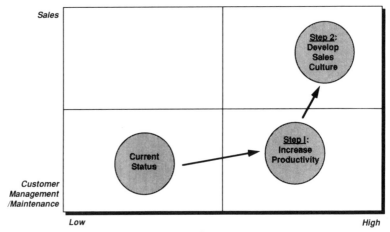

ducted at relatively low levels of productivity. The stated goal for most banks, of course, is to move to the upper right-hand quadrant (Step 2) and create a well-entrenched sales culture. That shift, however, cannot be accomplished overnight or without some pain. Instituting a sales culture is a step-by-step process that needs to be planned out as thoroughly as any marketing campaign.

Increasing productivity (Step 1) is the intermediate step required on the way to developing a sales culture. Represented in the lower right-hand quadrant of Exhibit 10.1, increased productivity has an immediate, near-term payback to the bank and sets up the framework required to transform the wholesale bank into a selling organization. Most banks that institute a change program, however, fail to climb this ladder for one of three reasons:

1) In at least 50 percent of banks that fail to make the grade, management lacks an information "database" on RM activi-

ties, key tasks, and workflows to restructure roles and responsibilities effectively.

2) At another 25 percent, quick-fix or simple solutions, such as new technology platforms, are chosen instead of rethinking the fundamental requirements of the key jobs.

3) At the remaining banks that fail, internal resistance to change weakens senior level commitment to the transformation process and leads to half-hearted implementation of essential changes.

A Program for Change

Throughout the past several years, my firm has developed a program for change management that not only quickly brings banks along the road to higher productivity but also builds both management and staff commitment throughout the process. To create the foundation required for change across the corporate middle market bank, this program first generates the information or database that serves as a benchmark throughout the process. An analysis of this database then leads naturally to a basic "rethink" of key jobs while also promoting technology-based opportunities to improve performance. This program benefits from substantial personal involvement of mid-level and senior management, beginning during the early stages of the project and continuing throughout its implementation, which is outlined in specific action plans.

While this program is most successful when customized to an individual bank, the key principles for change management apply to all financial institutions facing the challenge of marketing to corporations.

Step 1: Ensuring Success

Bank managers planning to reengineer the middle market should try to stack the deck in their favor well before kicking off the analytic phase of the project. Otherwise, substantial roadblocks to implementation may emerge. I recommend several tactics to gain commitment at all levels of the organization.

Sign Up Senior Management

Any change-related project is probably not worth the time commitment without the enthusiastic support of senior management from day one. Otherwise, creeping marginalism will set in. Potentially bold ideas will be reduced to small initiatives; "out-of-the-box" thinking will be discouraged; and, implementation either will never occur or will be diluted in an attempt to placate multiple internal constituencies.

The mandate and support for reengineering has to come from the top and be both public and unambiguous. Several articles published early in 1994 about Fleet Bank—which recently underwent a highly publicized restructuring—focused upon the high degree of involvement in that restructuring process by the bank's chairman. His personal commitment of time sent a clear message to bank staff that the program was not simply another consulting study but rather one that would lead to bankwide redesign. If such support is not forthcoming, beginning a change program with the hope of eventually attracting the endorsement of top management borders on the naïve, given the political factions found in many banks.

Create a Steering Group

Just as senior management must be involved in understanding and approving the changes that may evolve from a fresh look at the data, so too must a cross-section of marketing, credit, and support personnel be involved in designing and implementing the change process. In most cases bank management should empanel a steering group that has direct input into designing the change process. While consensus can be overdone, leading to a bureaucracy of meetings, an effective change management process requires that those individuals most directly affected by proposed changes play a meaningful role both in assessing the changes required and developing action plans.

This steering group, of course, not only needs access to but also the support of senior management. In return for that access, the steering group should be responsible for clear goals and deliverables tied to improving RM productivity and streamlining processes. Meeting those goals should become part of their individual management by objectives (MBOs).

Generally, this group is most effective when it is small in number, five or six people. A typical steering committee of more than 10 members creates an unwieldy situation that limits flexibility and creativity.

Two-way communications, down to the troops and back up again, is also essential. Frequent communication avoids concern over elitism or exclusivity and also encourages idea generation by those individuals closest to the customer.

One bank that was beginning a reengineering project structured a network-like reporting system to obtain input from various job levels and regions. Steering group members were each responsible for informing one or more colleagues about the progress of the group while soliciting their viewpoints on issues under discussion.

Step 2: Analyze Current Activities and Workflows

At "ground zero," reengineering the RM's role begins with an understanding of current responsibilities, that is, both how RMs spend their time and what processes they follow to meet key objectives. In most cases, the conclusion will be that RMs are spending too much time on non-marketing activities.

Individual banks, must, of course, evaluate performance on a unit-by-unit basis. Banks need to obtain a significant level of detail to chronicle precisely how time is being spent on various tasks. This information gathering is particularly important in cases where resistance to change may be high. A detailed activity survey can yield a treasure-trove of insights and provide a methodology for assessing time splits.

In Chapter 7, Exhibit 7.9 summarized how the RMs in one bank spent time on credit-related activities. Exhibit 10.2 provides another example of the power of such a database. This chart, based upon a disguised client example, provides meaningful background on both the amount and type of time bankers spend involved in administrative activities.

The RMs at this particular bank are spending approximately 30 percent of their time in activities related to the administrative process. While three main tasks eat up most of the RM's time—customer maintenance and reviews, customer contact, and exception analysis—multiple activities require one to two percentages of the RM's day. In terms of detail, while only 12 summary categories are illustrated here, an actual survey would consist of 20 or more separate activities related to the overall customer service process.

Surveying only bankers, while important, usually provides insufficient data. Conducting additional one-on-one interviews with those in relevant support and product areas can provide additional insight and creates a three-dimensional picture of the specific steps that the banker, administrators, product support specialists and others follow.

One responsibility of the steering committee will be to review the results of this detailed survey and agree on its action implications. By themselves, none of the activity percentages are necessarily good or bad. The bank's strategy must determine how the RMs should allocate their time. In the instance illustrated by this example, the steering group was particularly concerned about three time allotments: the time spent updating credit files, complaint resolution, and exception tracking.

In the particular case illustrated in Exhibit 10.2, administrators were being used with varying degrees of effectiveness. Oftentimes the RMs performed tasks that could have been completed by others. Instead of offloading low-value tasks, the bankers felt they were "putting the customer first" by taking responsibility for tracking down errors and researching problems. Similarly, routine requests were handled by the RMs, rather than permitting the qualified administrative staff members to handle day-to-day matters.

Exhibit 10.2 RM Time Usage

Management needs to evaluate the specific activities on which RMs focus.

Current Relationship Manager Job Profile

| | Marketing and Sales 25% | Customer Service 30% | Credit Process 35% | Management and Development 10% | Disguised Client Example |

Tasks	Current Percent of Total Time	Client-Specific Proposed Level of Effort (Percent of Total RM Time)	Comments
CUSTOMER MAINTENANCE AND REVIEWS			
Credit File Updates	6.0%	2.5%	No more recreating the file
Relationship Planning	2.0	2.0	Increased emphasis on cross-sell
Account/Relationship Review	3.0	2.0	Increased emphasis on cross-sell
Physical File Maintenance	2.0	0.0	Filing to be handled by clerical support
	13.0	6.5	
CUSTOMER CONTACT			
Customer Service – Phone	5.0	2.0	Routine C/S to Centralized Admin
Complaint Investigation/Problem Resolution	4.0	1.0	Only major problems handled by RM
Customer Service – Written	1.0	1.0	Routine C/S to Centralized Admin
Credit Inquiries	1.0	0.0	Routine C/S to Centralized Admin
Loan Advances – (Approvals & Exceptions)	1.0	1.0	Routine C/S to Centralized Admin
Account Set-up	1.0	0.0	Implementation shifted to specialists
	13.0	5.0	
EXCEPTIONS			
Exception Review and Reporting	3.0	1.0	Routine C/S to Centralized Admin
Handling Billing Issues (Credit and Noncredit)	1.0	1.0	Routine C/S to Centralized Admin
	4.0	1.5	
	30.0%	13%	

Step 3: Obtain Agreement on Change

The methodology proposed by this program for change management leads to a clear analysis of the current situation and generates some near-term, implementable solutions to address key issues. No study can result in a substantial leap in productivity or a change in marketing focus, however, unless agreement exists concerning the redefinition of activities, roles, and responsibilities of key personnel.

Here the steering committee will play a pivotal role in obtaining the level of agreement that will allow the process to move forward. Questions to be addressed include:

- What should an RM actually be doing? To which activities should time be allocated?

- Should the role of administrative staff be expanded? If so, what duties should be included?

- What is the emerging role of product specialists? How can this function complement the RM's role?

- How extensively involved should credit personnel be in the marketing process?

Banks need to agree formally on the appropriate roles and responsibilities for each major job function. Without doing so, individual managers and employees will inevitably continue to define their jobs—a sub-optimal situation for any bank. For most banks, raising fundamental issues such as the role of the relationship manager will uncover some significant disagreements.

In the case of one northeast bank, for instance, internal differences arose concerning the participation of the RM in ongoing customer service. Some senior managers felt convinced that customers expected close RM involvement in the day-to-day activities of a relationship; others believed that the customer would accept a change, if the high level of service continued. Some also believed that the economics of the business demanded a change to the RM's job.

Exhibit 10.3 summarizes some of the approaches to selling and customer management now in place at a cross-section of banks. This

Exhibit 10.3   Delivery Choice-Selected Strategic Options

A number of banks are breaking ground in determining the most appropriate way to serve various segments of the middle market.

Selling Focus	Emphasis on:	Selected Bank Examples	Issues
Business Development Officer (BDO)	• "Hunter/Skinner"	• Bank of America • Wells Fargo	• Coordination with RM
Multi-product Salesperson	• Account penetration	• Norwest	• Balancing product specialist strength vs. RM
Financial Engineering	• Sell solutions/not products	• NBD • Morgan Guaranty	• Probably appropriate for only upper end of market
Product Emphasis	• Sell product expertise	• Bankers Trust	• Unlikely fit with core middle market
Standardization/ Centralization	• Bring small business approach to the middle market	• Barnett	• Willingness of customer to accept standardized products and approach

177

list captures some of the alternatives available and raises serious "positioning" questions for top management. For example, the business development officer (BDO) discussed elsewhere in this book focuses only on marketing and requires separation of selling, underwriting, and maintenance activities within a bank.

As mentioned in the exhibit, the notion of a multi-product salesperson results in a support infrastructure, specialist group, and performance measurement system that clearly encourage non-credit sales. A more consultative approach to selling is exemplified by the financial reengineering concept pursued by NBD and Morgan; this approach requires a true relationship with the target company. Conversely, Bankers Trust, while it may be trying to shift its market image, is best known as a "product shop," albeit with many very strong products and services.

Finally, the standardization/centralization focus tries to bring "mass customization" to the middle market—fewer products, lower overhead, and much increased RM productivity because of the clear definition given to the banker's role.

The steering group plays a key role, not only in trying to smooth over differences of opinion within a bank but also in articulating the key questions and addressing them. This group cannot simply present the multiple aspects of an issue, however; it must weigh the facts and opinions. Input includes internal activity analyses and process workflows for current activities (such as in Exhibit 7.10); customer surveys and interviews and the evaluation of bank and non-bank competitor initiatives (as per Exhibit 10.3); and a frank independent assessment of the bank's strengths, weaknesses, and market opportunities. This varied data leads to a collective judgment made by the steering group concerning the approach that makes the most sense for the long-term profitability of the bank.

This is precisely the point where many financial institutions fail to "step up" to internal controversy and "do the right thing." Unfortunately, what begins as an energizing change process can then grind to a halt in the face of internal politics and the lack of top management sponsorship. In essence, a kind of corporate cowardice takes over. That is why senior management must support any project from its inception and why they must be kept informed as recommendations give shape to a new order.

Step 4: Create Specific Implementation Plans

As the foundation of the organization developing a more uniform approach to marketing, underwriting, and customer service, a bank undertaking a redesign of relationship management needs to agree on which job functions will be responsible for which tasks.

Exhibit 10.4 summarizes the key tasks and workflows associated with locating, underwriting, closing, and maintaining a new credit. In this disguised client example, management has refocused the RM on to certain key tasks and has enhanced the role of sales support staff, the junior RM, and the administrator. In actuality, these process flows would, of course, have additional details under each major heading and would be expanded to include more on credit and profitability monitoring, ongoing customer relations, and other areas.

This chart demonstrates how the different job types can each cover separate but critical responsibilities for the same customer. For example, the RM has primary responsibility for sales calls (e.g., telemarketing and centralized marketing), while the sales support areas have primary responsibility for lead generation, warming up the cold call and gathering financial information prior to the banker making the first call. Once a target becomes a prospect, the junior RM has responsibility for the first draft of a credit write-up. When the loan is closed, the administrator has primary responsibility for maintenance, giving the RM the time required to focus on a strategy for building the relationship.

The "economies of focus," which this division of responsibility promotes, allows more marketing by the RM, increases the number of accounts that can be handled by each team and, ultimately, improves profitability per employee. The corresponding positive impact on cost structure has already been noted in an earlier chapter (see Exhibit 9.4).

179

Exhibit 10.4 Process Flow for New Business Generation

The introduction of a team approach focuses the RM on high value-added activities.

Disguised Client Example

New Business-Related Acquisitions

	Responsibility			
	Sales Support	RM	Junior RM	Para Banker
Prospecting and marketing				
Lead generation/work up	●	○	◐	○
Preliminary prospect profitability assessment	●	◐	◐	◐
Sales calls	○	●	●	◐
Profitability (credit)				
Preliminary credit quality assessment		●	●	
Preliminary analysis/rough draft write-up		○	●	
Ratings assignment		●	◐	
Risk-based pricing		●	◐	
Profitability (non-credit) Assessment of:				
Contribution from fee-based services	◐	●	◐	○
Contribution from liability products	◐	●	◐	◐
Approval and closing				
Overall profitability assessment		●	◐	●
Final memo preparation		◐	◐	●
Approval		◐	●	
Closing/documentation		◐	○	
Maintenance set-up				
System account set-up				
Relationship management strategy		●		●

○ Involved as necessary
◐ Primary involvement
● Secondary involvement

180

Rebalance Account Loads

As the jobs and work flows are redesigned, productivity should increase. Today, little consistency exists between the accounts handled by one RM and another. Management needs to determine how to rebalance account loads so that RMs are handling portfolios of similar complexity and time intensity without harming the quality of credit or customer service. Gaining agreement on the "drivers" of RM workload (for example, size and type of relationship and servicing intensity), should be the starting point. Adding a complexity factor is an important part in ensuring consistent and comparable performance across the RM group.

Introduce Team-Based Marketing

Improved performance demands that the "lone ranger" status of many RMs give way to an emphasis on team-based marketing and customer service.

The traditional middle market organization is often similar to that depicted in Exhibit 10.5. The RM serves as the fulcrum of the organization. Staff areas such as credit and product specialists assist. Failure or success, however, clearly depends upon the talents of the RM.

This traditional approach needs to be reformulated to build a team approach to the customer, much as the junior RM, administrator, and RM mentioned above form a team that together handle or coordinate the handing of all customer requirements. Exhibit 10.6 places an emphasis on the role of a team manager, who might be considered a team leader "with teeth." The RMs report directly to this person. In addition, however, other key product and administrative personnel report to him on a dotted-line basis. The team manager concept can work for a number of reasons.

First, in this scenario the team manager has profit and loss (P&L) responsibility for the accounts in his unit. Compensation is tied closely to performance, and the team manager has meaningful input into compensation decisions affecting the dotted line reports.

Exhibit 10.5 Current Static Organization

Many banks fail to give loan officers the organizational support required to transform them into multi-product salespersons.

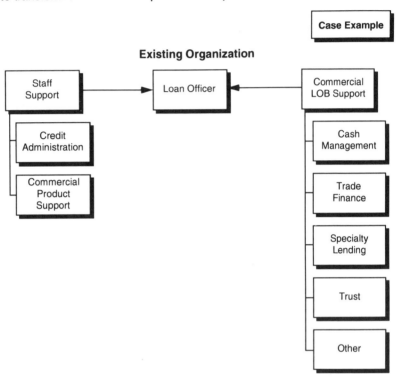

Second, team manager and specialty unit areas (including administration, credit, and product areas) work together to put their best "corporate face" in front of the bank's customers. Compensation policies that cross organizational units further encourage cooperation.

Third, selling opportunities lead to the development of a team selling approach.

For example, in the case of a potential cash management selling opportunity uncovered by an RM, the team manager has the responsibility for coordinating with the head of cash management to

Exhibit 10.6   Team Focused Organization

Relationship team managers have responsibility for fostering a selling environment.

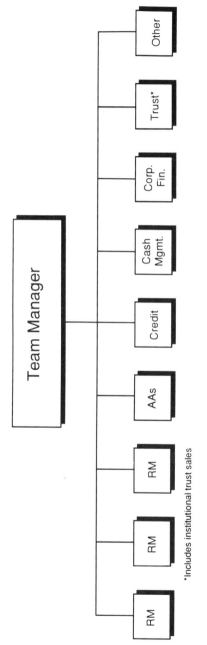

*Includes institutional trust sales

- Team manager has P&L responsibility.

- All positions are members of the "Sales Team."

- RMs report directly to the manager.

- All other positions have a strong matrix relationship to the manager.

183

select the best personnel for marketing that particular transaction. The leader for marketing the transaction may, in fact, be the cash manager and not the RM. The RM might make the necessary introduction and then back off in favor of the product specialist. This hands-off approach reaps the benefits of empowerment and allows the RM to continue marketing rather than make multiple calls in a situation where only product knowledge and expertise would make the sale.

Exhibit 10.7 provides an overview of the team manager's responsibility. The team manager (TM) trains, develops, and focuses direct reports and assesses those reporting directly to others. The TM makes certain that a rigorous relationship planning process is in place and that prospects are being pursued. The TM also will coordinate with the credit area to maintain both quality and clear, upfront communications. Importantly, the TM does not *simply* sit behind a desk or attend internal meetings. This job's responsibilities carry over to joint calling and continual RM assessment and knowledge building.

Step 5: Reap the Benefits

The bottom line impact of creating a strong support infrastructure and redefining the RM is to free up substantial RM time. This excess can be shifted to additional marketing or, perhaps, can result in a reduction in RM staff.

Freed-up time results not from one initiative but from many (Exhibit 10.8). In the example cited, on day one—based upon how they split their time—approximately 110 full-time equivalent (FTE) relationship managers are available for selling-related activities. The number of FTEs increases to 180 by a combination of successfully transitioning much of customer service and back-office activities to support personnel, streamlining the credit process, and introducing an effective upfront guidance system as well as more effectively managing the RMs already in place.

Exhibit 10.7   The Pivotal Role of the Team Manager

An "enhanced" team manager position assists in focusing the bank on better meeting customer needs.

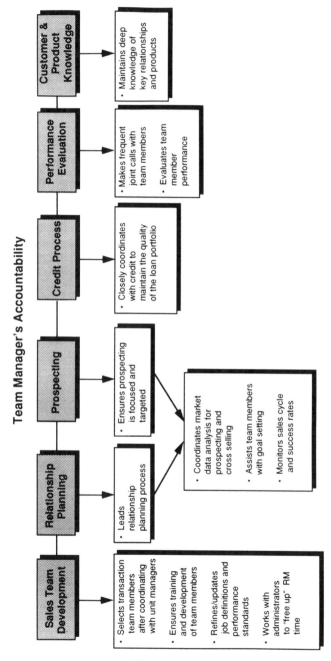

Team Manager's Accountability

Sales Team Development
- Selects transaction team members after coordinating with unit managers
- Ensures training and development of team members
- Refines/updates job definitions and performance standards
- Works with administrators to "free up" RM time

Relationship Planning
- Leads relationship planning process

Prospecting
- Ensures prospecting is focused and targeted

- Coordinates market data analysis for prospecting and cross selling
- Assists team members with goal setting
- Monitors sales cycle and success rates

Credit Process
- Closely coordinates with credit to maintain the quality of the loan portfolio

Performance Evaluation
- Makes frequent joint calls with team members
- Evaluates team member performance

Customer & Product Knowledge
- Maintains deep knowledge of key relationships and products

185

Exhibit 10.8 Steps in Creating Improved Productivity and a Renewed Marketing Focus

Increased marketing time is gained by reevaluating the level of RM involvement required in multiple areas, in particular day-to-day customer service and credit.

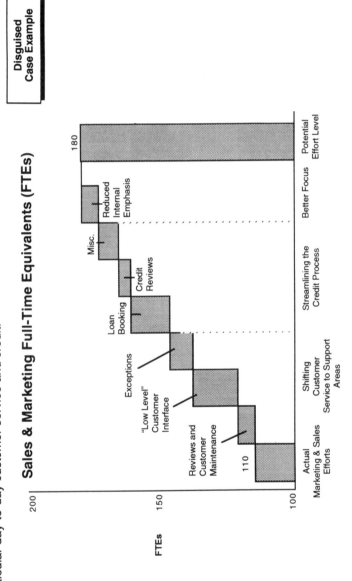

Sales & Marketing Full-Time Equivalents (FTEs)

Disguised
Case Example

186

Summary Thoughts

Creating a sales culture may take years, but it begins with a refocusing of relationship management activities and shifting the bank's perspective outward and away from internal meetings and politics. No matter how fervent the desire to change, we invariably find that the current organizational structure and job definitions of key personnel are at the source of the problems. A fundamental "rethink" is required if banks are to achieve the potential productivity available to them and if they are going to compete against those non-traditional competitors that are aggressively trying to attract business.

11

RM Training, Performance Measurement, and Compensation

"The universal regard for money is the one hopeful fact in our civilization."

—*George Bernard Shaw*

Role redefinition, a renewed and improved infrastructure, the streamlining of credit and administrative processes, and leadership from middle and senior level management are all essential in transforming a bank's approach to its middle market business. Obviously, this change process requires commitment and hard work to gain the substantial payback in employee productivity and sustainable profitability that it promises.

To successfully introduce the approaches recommended in this book and to make them stick long-term, management particularly needs to reexamine and upgrade its training programs, performance measurement systems, and compensation policies.

Training and Development

The banking industry spends hundreds of millions of dollars in training every year. Yet, commercial, middle market bankers are widely viewed as failing both to understand key product offerings and to anticipate emerging customer needs.

At most banks the training function itself is limited by tight budgets and senior manager reluctance to invest in new technology, curriculum development, and staffing. Also, in many cases, training does not keep pace with the needs of line bankers either in business content or the way it is taught, relying on traditional written presentations and formal lectures to teach bankers who are increasingly comfortable with interactive videos and CD-ROM databases.

Furthermore, RMs need to advance to a higher level of professionalism. In many instances, their corporate contacts will include not only the chief financial officer and the treasurer but also the chairman or president, those levels of a company that are involved in decisions related to areas such as employee benefits services and corporate finance.

Therefore, while improved product knowledge remains important, it is clearly not enough. For relationship planning programs to work, RMs also need both better listening skills and selling skills; they must be able to negotiate deals and evaluate deal relationship profitability; they must learn what it means to be empowered team members and to transition into becoming leaders of others.

Most banks currently offer inadequate training in these skills, which will become increasingly essential in the future. Too often, entry-level credit training is where a bank places the majority of its emphasis and training dollars. Ongoing product and skills training gets relegated to an *ad hoc* status, featuring courses that bankers can sign up for and then cancel out on without explanation or penalty.

Training has to become a continual process and value within a bank culture, beginning immediately after hiring and continuing throughout a banker's career. Rather than being a requirement that a banker gets promoted out of, training programs should continue to include senior and top management. While the nature and type of training and development programs may need to be tailored to the needs of those senior groups (for example one-on-one communications skills training), their inclusion in ongoing training sends a message to all officers and staff about management commitment.

While this chapter focuses on RM training, similar development programs need to be established for product and credit specialists and, most importantly, for those assuming the para-banker roles. That account administration group, which offers so much leverage to the banker, requires special attention. They need to be able to manage ongoing customer service needs and even pursue occasional cross-selling related to the products being serviced. No other area may offer a bank a larger return on its training dollar.

Entry-Level Training

Some of the best training programs that banks have put into operation begin with a rigorous introductory phase and continue throughout a banker's career. Introductory programs balance classroom sessions and team building exercises with rotations through multiple departments. The rotation process takes on the character of something like a mating ritual whereby the new employee tests the possibility of long-term involvement in a particular department while the manager of that area gets to check out the new recruit.

For example, one regional bank with an excellent approach to career development begins with a two-year entry program. Only the first few weeks, however, are classroom-based. During that eight week period, a number of key skills are taught or reinforced, including cashflow analysis, key products and services, and the bank's major policies and procedures.

Many banks include some form of testing during this initial period to make certain that the trainees are getting it and to weed out those few recruits where a poor fit exists. For both the bank and the employee, it is certainly better to cut losses early rather than continue to experience frustration.

When the RM completes the formal program at this regional bank, the business internships begin. This rotation is an opportunity for banks to highlight certain product areas. For example, some banks require that every RM spend several months in either the cash management, corporate finance, or trust areas. These work tours must be designed so that they are rigorous and allow the new banker to acquire and demonstrate product and process knowledge by the end of the rotation period. Each assignment should conclude with a formal and detailed evaluation process for which the area manager is responsible.

During this introductory period, many banks institute mentoring programs for new bankers. The mentor, an experienced banker, plays the role of advisor and confessor to the new hire. Mentors are assigned for a two- to three-year period. At some banks another mentor takes over after that period; in others, the one-time trainee becomes a mentor. Unfortunately, these programs can only be effective when management makes a commitment to them. Those banks that do support a meaningful program find that it increases employee retention and productivity.

As depicted in Exhibit 11.1, some banks have established multi-year training programs that focus on three key areas, analytic capabilities, sales and product knowledge, and management skills. In the case of one regional bank, senior management has made the commitment to 10 days of off-site training per year per RM to support their professional growth. Attendance is mandatory and enforced by senior management.

This exhibit shows that (as might be expected) the early years of this training program center around building key skills—in effect, creating the tool-kit that will serve as the foundation for bankers throughout their careers. In later years, the focus shifts to more sophisticated products and management skills. This emphasis is critical if the officer is to become an effective leader of the sales team. Telling someone to lead has much less impact than giving them interactive as well as instructional training in how to do so.

Even at this regional bank, which has as strong a program as any financial services institution, programs tailored to the needs of more experienced bankers do not exist. While the reasons for this omission are many—among them, time, necessary focus on junior bankers, lack of training staff experience, and the limited clout of the training group—this gap needs to be addressed to create a rounded program.

Exhibit 11.1   Multi-Year Training Programs

Best practice training continues to emphasize learning throughout the career cycle.

10 Days Per Year of Intensive Off-Site Seminars

Year	Analytical	Sales/Products	Management
1	• Lending case studies	• Cross selling: trust, leasing, retail, etc. • Cash management "college"	
2	• Analyzing personal financial statements • Documentation case study	• Selling skills	
3	• Credit structure, documentation & negotiation	• Public speaking • Sales negotiation	
4	• Evaluating quality of earnings	• Advanced investment banking products	• Selective interviewing
5–8	• Corporate finance • Advanced cash flow analysis		• Basics of supervision • Team building • Effective leadership • Employee empowerment

Two-Year Training Program (Examples)

Classroom (8 Weeks)
- Cashflow analysis
- ROA calculation
- Practice analysis

Rotation (2 Years)
- Middle Market
- Commercial real estate
- Asset-based
- Workout
- Cash management
- Loan review
- Trade finance
- Private banking
- National accounts

Beyond a seminar program, banks also offer self-training programs that use audiocassettes, videotapes, personal computers, and CD-ROM technology. The latter is particularly appropriate for corporate finance and capital markets training. The point is that a generation of bankers brought up on MTV and news dished out in 20-second sound bites require training methods that take advantage of their ability to grasp ideas visually and quickly through the medium of computer technology.

Banks should consider the value of testing RM knowledge as a performance measure. In particular, First Interstate Bank has taken a lead role in formally testing experienced bankers, and failing these tests has serious consequences. Unlike their brethren in the securities arena, bankers avoid any meaningful certification programs. As more banks move into servicing investment and corporate finance businesses that require exams, such as the Series 7 exam necessary for selling securities, similar hurdles are already being set in the bankers' path, whether with the assistance of an industry group, such as Robert Morris Associates, or by the fiat of bank management.

The result of both increased training needs and the call for new ways of training means that the training area itself will feel pressure to improve the professionalism of its staff and the quality of its products. Smart executives will invest in this area so that it anticipates the bank's business needs rather than reacting to them.

Performance Measurement

Recently, I questioned a banker concerning the annual goal-setting process that his bank undergoes. He said, "I sit down with my manager, and we set the next year's targets for my performance and for my group. He doesn't review them with me during the year. Then at the end of the year, we meet to set goals for the next year." Prior year performance is not discussed, and that banker and his manager do not review whether he has had a good, bad, or mediocre year. Obviously, the performance measurement and review process is a charade, a *pro forma* budgeting exercise providing no feedback and promising no reward. This process does a disservice to the bank and its employees, and I predict that unless changed will eventually lead to some unpleasant surprises in bottom-line performance.

A well-planned, bank-wide performance measurement system will support the bank's corporate culture and, like training, has to be viewed as a key factor in the change management process. Contrast the above situation where no feedback mechanism is provided to one in which managers periodically receive clear information about how their performance is valued across multiple criteria.

A Rigorous Approach

Most banks will envy the quality, rigor, and detail of the perform-ance measurement system approach my consulting firm found in existence at a major super-regional bank. This bank uses a four-part appraisal process consisting of goals addressing credit, marketing, financial performance, and staff development.

For unit managers, the credit goals includes specific, individually negotiated targets related to portfolio quality, documentation quality, and the timelines of credit renewals. For example, no credit lines for profitable relationships are to expire without renewal or cancellation.

Marketing success is tied to goals involving the number of sig-nificant new relationships, customer retention, the amount of monthly calling, business referrals to other product groups within the bank, and weekly sales meetings. In all, eight marketing goals exist. In one instance, a specific marketing goal for a unit with five RMs requires seven new accounts each with an ROE of 15 percent or more. The customer retention goal states that no customer can be lost for reasons other than credit quality or pricing.

Financial goals all revolve around exceeding the previous year's revenue and profit plan by a specific percentage or dollar amount. Staff development goals underscore the importance the bank places on managers completing detailed performance reviews and train-ing. This set of goals includes the identification and focused devel-opment of officers ready for advancement.

195

The four performance areas require 19 specific goals, a number which some banks may consider to be too many. Some goals are the same for every person at a particular level. Most are tailored based upon geographic or business differences or because of the level of experience of the manager or the team. As appropriate, goals related to credit quality are given the greatest weight. Importantly, once set, the goals are reviewed at least semiannually and provide objective input into the annual salary review and bonus approval process.

For this bank, the system is a well-used, dynamic process which serves to get all the bankers moving in the same direction. As with training, this appraisal system fully complements the transformation of the middle market effort.

A Means of Protection

Lack of a rigorous performance measurement system will have a particularly negative impact for banks during the next decade as the financial system consolidates.

Downsizing or rightsizing will undoubtedly continue to be part of the fabric of corporate banking. The implications of this include the need for changes in the type of employee hired and retained and changes to the bank's product delivery system. More customer service responsibilities can shift to administrators (Chapter 9) and smaller accounts will move to yet another specialized area (Chapter 15). Overall, relatively fewer RMs will be required to manage larger account loads. A different type of RM, manager, and administrator will be needed.

When the need to change and/or reduce the number of employees is mandated by the need to remain both competitive and profitable, bank management can find itself hamstrung by the personnel files of many employees. These reveal a history of reviews that judge employees known to be poor or mediocre at best, as adequate or better. This over-grading and the resulting paper file of good reviews complicates the process for dismissing employees who, in fact, have not been performing up to standard.

The unwillingness of managers to write honest reviews and discuss them frankly with employees has created an insidious situation. If managers are unwilling to reform their management practices, they themselves should face dismissal because their actions will put the bank at risk of lawsuits for wrongful termination.

Compensation

The importance of compensation and the value of linking pay directly to performance is a theme repeated throughout this book. Chapter 13, for example, makes the point that non-bank competitors have shown a willingness to increase the gap between the compensation of average and excellent performers.

Pay for performance and objective measures for determining salary adjustments and bonus payments are common practice throughout many companies within the world of financial services. These systems are rarities, however, in commercial banking.

When I began to examine corporate banking practices several years ago, I expected to find that the excellent banks had introduced sophisticated compensation systems that differentiated among the annual increases and bonus payments made to individual employees. In fact, I found that most banks had failed to emulate the advances made by other companies either inside or outside the financial services industry.

Why has little or no change occurred in banking compensation practices? One experienced banker commented cynically, "If you pay for performance, you have to eliminate the politics involved in compensation decisions." Others view the situation as an intellectual problem, stating that the chief difficulty revolves around the inability of banks to agree on what factors should be the basis of judging performance. Revenues? Profitability? Return on equity? Yet another group of bankers raises the issue that bankers will be pushed into making bad decisions to receive incentive payments, a sad commentary on ethics.

Banks need to put aside the politics, agree on standards of performance, and trust their employees to act in the best interest of

197

the bank. (Of course trust is somewhat less important if banks separate the selling and underwriting functions.) Non-bank financial institutions have dealt with similar issues and, arguably, they have done so with great success. While a rogue employee can probably subvert any system, extraordinary events should not be used as an excuse to avoid making changes to the compensation system that can encourage a positive change in performance.

Compensation programs can and should be structured to support the philosophy and interests of a bank. The Bankers Trusts of the world feel the need to pay for successful capital market performance in the near-term. Their employees demand and their management approach encourages that expectation.

Most other institutions will want to tie their employees into the long-term interest of the bank while meeting the near-term compensation requirements of the employee. In that case, incentives can be split between cash payments and other payments linked to a bank's long-term stock performance through awards such as options. What banks should not do is ignore the desires of their workers to be rewarded for top level performance. Bankers are no different than any other professionals.

Summary Thoughts

Training, performance measurement, and compensation policies all merit review in light of the new responsibilities in line for RMs, sales specialists, account administrators, and managers. Failure to evaluate each of these policies and introduce fundamental changes can jeopardize the success of any effort to reengineer a middle market banking group.

12

Leadership in Technology Planning

"You can look busy on your PC all day and not do any marketing."
—the head of relationship management at a major midwest regional bank

All too often bankers use technology—or more accurately, the lack of technology—as an excuse for failing to improve performance or take decisive actions. "We just don't have the technology to support that" is the answer often heard to questions on topics as diverse as account planning, profitability analysis, incentive compensation, money transfer, as well as new product capabilities.

However, the opposite situation also can be as true. When in place, technology-based innovation can serve as an entirely new excuse for RMs to stay behind their desks rather than head out the door to market. The above RM comment on the illusion of productivity generated by personal computers underscores the awareness that investments in technology do not always translate into increased customer contact or selling time. Job redefinition and management leadership are required coefficients.

One Bank's Experience

Recently, I had the opportunity to meet with representatives of a regional corporate bank whose operation is widely described as "paperless." Press reports indicated that unlike the backlogs at most banks, paper had been replaced by electronic images, and credit card files had been eliminated through the use of computer disks and fax modems.

During our discussion, it became clear that this bank had indeed made remarkable strides during a five-year period. However, management also made it clear that no magic computer existed, and multiple improvements were still being actively pursued by the bank. The executives spoke of a multi-year process requiring dedicated internal bank programming expertise as a necessary supplement to widely touted off-the-shelf software. Among the key capabilities that had to be added were on-line profitability analysis and electronic call memoranda.

While millions of dollars and years of effort had already been spent on creating a technology platform, many of the RM's traditional responsibilities at this bank had not begun to change. For example, the bank had created an on-line screen for collateral tracking, improving both the quality of the information and the time it takes to obtain it. Individual RMs, however, rather than a centralized collateral group or an account administrator, continued to have responsibility for collateral checking. This task continued to chain the bankers to their desks, at a computer, albeit for less time than in the past. Consequently, this bank was losing out on productivity despite the technology.

In contrast, at one client bank that we surveyed in detail, RMs spent about 3 percent of their time involved in the collateral review process. Off-loading those tasks to a centralized administration group freed up the equivalent of six RMs for prospect marketing and cross-selling. The simple calculation required multiplying 200 total bank RM days times 3 percent of freed-up time to equal six full-time equivalents (FTEs). In the short term, the technology used at this bank remained the same; the positive productivity impact on the RM, however, was immediate.

Technology Cannot Lead

The improvements in productivity that senior staff and line management can make with either virtually no technology or only rudimentary hardware and software are significant. In banking, technology follows and supports; it cannot lead the change process.

Rethinking the RM's role, developing a more complete and better trained infrastructure group, and empowering employees to take on increased responsibility all serve as the foundation for increased sales and productivity. Neither these actions nor many other powerful steps toward change require advanced mainframe technology or workshare networks to get started. They can, however, be greatly assisted by the information networks now becoming available.

The intent of this chapter is not to discuss the latest advances in hardware or software. These advances occur too rapidly to be included in any printed book. Furthermore, each advance needs to be reviewed not only with a skeptical eye but against the specific business requirements of an individual bank and its customers. I propose, instead, to offer guidelines on how management can seek out and evaluate technology-based decisions. Here are a few rules of the road to consider when restructuring the technology base of the corporate bank:

- Senior management must remain intensely involved in technology decisions, linking them to business objectives every step of the way. At the same time, management cannot be overly focused on immediate payback.

- Both projected costs and time to implement new information systems should not be underestimated. First estimates are also invariably too optimistic.

- Management may be able to get substantial benefit out of near-term job redefinition and process change, casting a new light on longer-term technology investment.

- Without the accompanying job redefinition phase, the value of the technology investment will be dramatically reduced.

- Technology-based change is always long-term. Management should think in terms of years, not months.

The Technology Trap

Frankly, a good degree of cynicism often appears the most appropriate initial response to proposed technology expenditures. Technological solutions can appear alluring and, admittedly, many are unproven. At one bank, a vice president who started life as an English major told me that he compared the computer sales representatives selling these solutions are somewhat like Circe, the beautiful enchantress from Homer's Odyssey, who magically captured men's minds and made them prisoners.

Transforming the corporate bank must begin with management's willingness to reevaluate the foundations of its business from target market to product delivery. If that reconsideration occurs, new technology can complement and support changes that are soundly based on reformatted processes, roles, and responsibilities. If technology leads rather than follows, it is a sign that management has abrogated its responsibilities, either to internal support areas or to external consultants selling a quick technology fix. Being seduced by technology results in throwing away a great deal of money.

A recent client meeting in which a group of bankers was discussing ways to increase efficiency points out how the technology trap can often ensnare bankers with a little bit of knowledge. One participant at this meeting was recounting a customer service problem where a customer (not so incidentally, a Fortune 100 name) ran a daylight overdraft. "Even though funds came in during the next hour," she said, "our system does not automatically update and allow disbursement." Only an RM or an RM's supervisor could okay the transfer.

She immediately offered her view of the solution required to avoid this situation in the future, "Why can't we fix the system so that it recognizes when funds have arrived and automatically releases them? It would only take a few hours of programming time, wouldn't it?"

One of the truisms of technology planning is that no improvement actually takes "only a few hours of programming time." Expecting a quick systems fix is usually bound to result in frustration—both for the RM making the request and for the systems area.

In the above case, the ultimate solution for intra-day funds transfer problems is, indeed, technology-based. The system should recognize when funds hit an account, and then automatically authorize the requested payment. Alternatively, the system should determine whether the customer's line of credit and the bank's position with the Federal Reserve will support an intra-day loan. A quick estimate for implementing these changes, however, revealed that a minimum of three to six months work would be required.

By default, the near-term solution, therefore, became people-based and process-based. Empowering the operations clerk and the administrator to authorize or, alternatively, co-authorize this type of transaction streamlined the decision-making process and allowed for a faster response to the customer's request. Of course, prior to allowing this delegation of authority, training had to be conducted, and security had to be ensured. The audit, legal, and credit departments needed to be made comfortable that the changes in procedure would not endanger the bank's daylight overdraft position.

Even with those important hurdles overcome, however, this change was introduced in a matter of weeks and at relatively little cost. Contrast that with the many months and dollars it would take to get a programming change approved and completed. More expensive technology solutions have to be viewed as years rather than months away from implementation. Managers cannot count on the "quick-fix, snake-oil salesman" to offer one-stop solutions to their productivity and sales management problems.

Beginning with an understanding of how a process operates today—who is and how many people and groups are involved—can often lead to a near-term reengineering of activities and provide a role redefinition against which a technology solution can then be even more effective.

For example, in future years more and more customer service activities will involve direct electronic links between the customer and the bank's computer systems. Ultimately, this change will allow for dramatic productivity improvements in the RM ranks, increasing the number of accounts that an individual can handle.

No More Backlog

Probably no other areas within a bank are more full of mystery and challenge for the non-technology-proficient senior manager than systems and technology planning. The nature of technology is that its capabilities constantly change, and its language is full of acronyms and buzzwords. How many times has every junior banker watched management, in effect, throw up its hands?

Yet, leadership in technology is critical to the success of a bank's business objectives. Senior management's inability to evaluate the options available should not make them either hostage to the systems gurus or the root cause of many banks' cost and performance problems with technology.

We know of one non-bank financial services senior executive, new to his job and not tied to the ways of the past, who challenged the status quo with great success. He sat through a day of committee meetings where technology solutions were proposed, one after another. Several times during the day, the head of systems and technology commented that the systems development queue was already long and that proposed additions would require hundreds of hours of programming time and more staff. In the system head's opinion, the window for new systems requests would not be open for at least six months and, more likely, considerably longer. A backlog had accumulated and was being addressed by priority as quickly as possible.

The executive listened to this quietly, although he may have been fuming inside. Finally, he said, "As of today, there is no more backlog." And, he meant it.

Following that meeting, all projects underwent an immediate review; priorities were reevaluated and shifted, and "business as usual" was no longer the accepted routine. Within a few weeks, an internal review panel involving both line and systems management reset priorities, matching them to business needs. In fact, after project sponsors learned about the review panel and the need to resubmit projects for scrutiny, many projects simply disappeared.

In this instance, the senior manager refused to be intimidated by a process that held both the technologists and the line officers hostage. The net result of this decision was stronger cooperation between the line and the systems area. Employees recognized that the old approval approach was inadequate and too linear to address the emerging needs of today's business environment. The systems area itself, which was inundated with requests, in turn, welcomed the opportunity to become more customer-focused.

Exhibit 12.1 presents one example of a simple format to use in this type of project review. Straightforward communication and brevity are keys to encourage a concise, but formal, description of each project. This format encourages that philosophy. Three sections on the sample form (see Exhibit 12.1) deserve special mention. The cost section is deliberately broken out into detail to present a clear picture of how well current projects are performing against budgeted costs. This will allow management to focus on and get behind substantial overruns. Project sponsors will know they can expect pointed questions at any review session.

Similarly, the schedule section is designed to catch any slippage in expected completion dates versus initial estimates. Pointing fingers at the systems department is not the reason for this exercise; understanding why timing slippage occurs and addressing the issues behind those problems is intended to reduce future gaps. In fact, delays often occur not due to systems group problems but because of ill-structured or changing requests by line managers.

Exhibit 12.1 Sample Project Summary

Project summaries assist in developing improved cost/benefit analysis and keeping projects on track.

Proposal:	**Area Requesting Project:** _____
	Project Leader: _____

Description:

Benefits: 1.
2.
3.
4.

Costs: Original Estimate $ _____
Current Estimate $ _____
Dollars approved for the current year $ _____
Actual YTD dollars spent $ _____
Percent complete   _____ %
Remaining $ _____

Schedule: Start Date
Initial estimated complete date
Current estimated complete date

Current Status:

Priority (1-3):

Finally, the form provides a check-off space to indicate whether the project priority is high, medium, or low. To make that assessment, however, management must agree on what its key strategic goals are and how essential a particular project is to those goals.

Creating a Decision Path

Harris Bank, Bank of Montreal's major entry point into the United States, offers an excellent example of a bank that has effectively articulated its approach to technology.

Harris set a strong framework for the use of technology by defining the key elements of its business strategy. These elements included:

- Improving the bank's knowledge of customers.

- Increasing the amount of time spent thinking about and meeting with customers.

- Becoming a key financial advisor to a company's decision-makers by providing value-adding knowledge, skills, products, and services.

- Delivering a customized mix of products and services through cross-functional teams.

Based on these objectives, the bank focused on areas for improvement. This approach developed the internal initiatives required to implement the strategy successfully. The bank came to the conclusion that it could group information technology opportunities into five functions that would:

- Provide easy, quick access both to internal and external sources of client, industry, proposal/bid, transaction, product, and market information.

- Develop and maintain standard material for demonstrating track record and execution capabilities.

- Promote interaction among team personnel by making the exchange of information on target transaction and product opportunities quick and easy.
- Develop, strengthen, and streamline the sales management processes.
- Streamline and upgrade production support capabilities.

Managers then developed what they termed their information flow, illustrated in Exhibit 12.2. This process captures data, converts

Exhibit 12.2 Harris Bank's Information Flow

Banks need to establish an approach that effectively captures data and distributes management information to decision-makers.

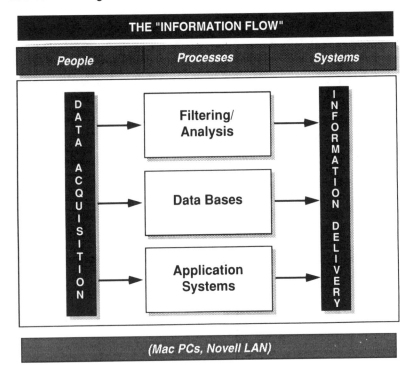

it into meaningful management information, and delivers it to users in a friendly format. The technology platform, which serves as the foundation for Harris' information flow, consists of PCs with an ability to access information over local area networks (LANs).

While Exhibit 12.2 illustrates the key components of Harris' process, Exhibit 12.3 peels away the outer layer to show the task areas that require management decision-making and the need to create priorities for the use of limited resources. Each of the eight organizational groups listed has projects underway as well as many other large projects in the proposal stage. Similar business items are

Exhibit 12.3   Inside Harris' Information Flow

Resource management involves people, processes, and systems.

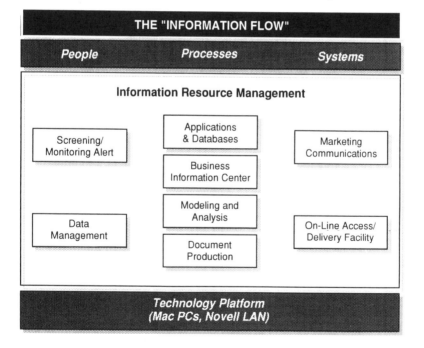

shared across the 30 or so key projects: increased bankwide standardization; better front-end access to internal and external databases; improved communications; and, additional marketing support tools.

Any bank using this planning process would have a clear picture of where it stands in each of these areas and have equally clear expectations for future capabilities along with a screen for evaluating the value of proposed projects. The analytic structure allows a bank to take its laundry list of projects and categorize them by key areas to be affected. Ultimately, this approach gives Harris Bank the ability to value one project against another.

Technology and Vision

The head of Deutsche Bank was asked about his company's vision. He commented, "The trouble with having a vision is that it often turns out to be an illusion." With that as a caveat, I argue that banks need to develop a technology vision that incorporates an assessment of the current business into an evaluation of current capabilities and leads to breakthrough planning and implementation. Exhibit 12.4 presents a three-part approach that has been used successfully with banks in the past to reassess the contribution of technology and maximize its value for senior management.

Stage 1: Evaluating Strategy and Objectives

Stage 1 begins with an evaluation of current business strategies, objectives, and the role that technology should play to support them. At this point in the analysis, the bank must reaffirm key customer segments, the products and services those customer groups require, and how the customers with those products are to be delivered.

To give an example, consider the technology requirements of a Bankers Trust or a Morgan Guaranty. Their primary focus on the sophisticated, international large corporate market will differ greatly from the needs of Chemical's Middle Market Group or a

Exhibit 12.4 Reassessing Technology Expenditures

A technology redesign approach defines key business processes and assesses current systems—processes, technologies, and organizations—to develop potential future system improvements for key businesses.

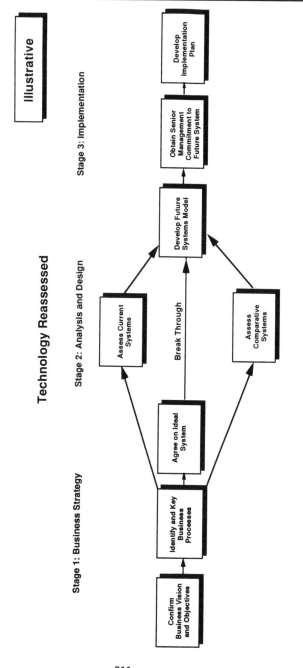

Illustrative

Technology Reassessed

Stage 1: Business Strategy

Stage 2: Analysis and Design

Stage 3: Implementation

Confirm Business Vision and Objectives

Identify and Key Business Processes

Agree on Ideal System

Assess Current Systems

Break Through

Assess Comparative Systems

Develop Future Systems Model

Obtain Senior Management Commitment to Future System

Develop Implementation Plan

bank's small business area. While each market segment requires a high level of customer service, the needs differ in several basic areas, such as product complexity, the degree of product customization, and the degree of customer connectivity to the bank's back office.

This first phase of evaluation should also involve the creation of process workflows for key activities. Not all activities need to be examined by means of a detailed workflow analysis. Focus should, however, be on those areas where a majority of internal opinion leaders agree that the process is critical to the bank and the need exists to effect change. Initially, it is important to concentrate on areas that are viewed as broken or at least in need of repair. Among the core areas that might receive attention are loan underwriting, product development, the cross-sell process, and back-office activities such as loan closing and loan documentation.

Stage 2: Designing and Measuring the Future

Stage 2 requires teamwork and farsighted projection of a successful customer/bank relationship. If successful, this phase is scenario planning at its most effective:

- Brainstorming how an ideal process would work.

- Assessing the current approach.

- Developing a measurement system to track success.

- Organizing to lever off technology more effectively by instituting meaningful cost/benefit analysis methodology.

At this stage, a competitive benchmark analysis can determine what other banks are doing and help break the mental chains that bind companies to old ways. A rigorous competitive analysis will demonstrate to management that many banks are already applying innovative approaches to the commercial bank business system.

The list of innovations could go on for pages and would range from small labor-saving approaches to major technological shifts. Among the innovations (in order of complexity) that such an analysis might find are:

- An electronic credit library with access both to marketing materials for targets and current credit files.

- The bar-coding of all credit file materials to avoid loss of documents and to feed a tickler system. One benefit, for example, would be alerting the RM if quarterly numbers are late or if loan documents are outstanding.

- Credit-scoring for small business accounts, such as looking at everyday retail practices for their application to corporate areas.

- Electronic underwriting; paperless transmittal of loan write-ups to line unit heads and credit administrators. Deals can be approved over the LAN system without any paper passing from department to department.

Exhibit 12.5 presents a menu of the areas to which technology might be applied. Each block denotes an organizational group that has been discussed earlier in this book: the RM team, marketing, administration, and credit support. Each area can take advantage of technology being applied to multiple activities, including the few listed underneath them. The link between these four customer servicing groups should be apparent, as should be the requirement for bank management to make cost/benefit and implementation timing tradeoffs that balance the requests of line, risk management, and other support areas.

The complexity of the situation facing bank management does not, however, stop there. Exhibit 12.6 illustrates the smorgasbord of choices to be made, even when the technology platform is in place.

As the graphic suggests, a LAN-based approach, for example, can offer extensive marketing, credit, and relationship information. Over a period of time the eight capabilities listed, as well as others, should be made available to the entire bank. Nevertheless, in the near- and mid-term, more limited access to fewer capabilities will be required.

During Stage 2, the bank will decide which technology solutions are appropriate for its business needs and for its pocketbook. Developing

Exhibit 12.5 Possible Technology Applications

Account officer productivity can be improved significantly through the use of technology to complement RM job redesign.

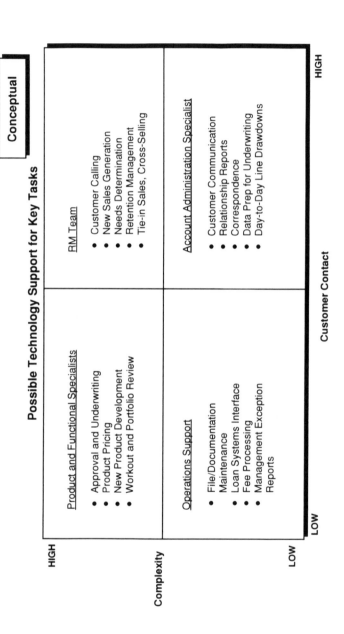

Possible Technology Support for Key Tasks

Conceptual

Product and Functional Specialists
- Approval and Underwriting
- Product Pricing
- New Product Development
- Workout and Portfolio Review

RM Team
- Customer Calling
- New Sales Generation
- Needs Determination
- Retention Management
- Tie-in Sales, Cross-Selling

Operations Support
- File/Documentation Maintenance
- Loan Systems Interface
- Fee Processing
- Management Exception Reports

Account Administration Specialist
- Customer Communication
- Relationship Reports
- Correspondence
- Data Prep for Underwriting
- Day-to-Day Line Drawdowns

Complexity (HIGH / LOW)

Customer Contact (LOW / HIGH)

214

Exhibit 12.6   Technology Choices Facing Senior Management

Lender workstations can be linked together to combine the power of individual PCs with the ability to share and retrieve information.

Sample Network Configuration

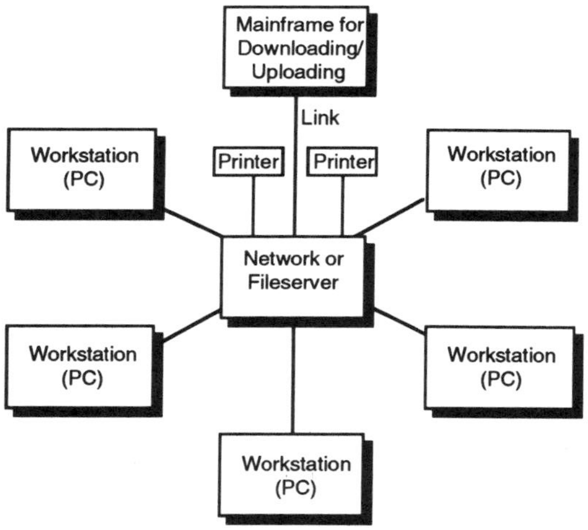

Potential Applications

- Business Development
  - Account planning
  - Prospecting
  - Sales tracking and pipeline reporting
- Customer Profitability
  - Loan and relationship profitability
  - Cost & market information
- Credit Analysis
  - Historical analysis/projections
  - Peer group comparisons
- Electronic Credit File
  - CIF data
  - Deposit and loan accounting data
  - Credit approval
- Loan Documentation
  - Loan documentation preparation
  - Exception and compliance monitoring
- Portfolio Reporting
  - Management reporting and loan review
  - Loan portfolio analysis
- Office automation
  - Word processing and electronic mail
  - Spreadsheets
- File Folder Imaging
  - Scanned document retrieval
  - Imaging of documents

a list of innovations is easy; choosing among them will not be. But by using the goals and objectives reaffirmed in Stage 1, the bank can now agree on its technology model for the future and the performance measurement standards by which it will judge success.

Those standards should include both productivity, performance, and quality measures and address areas such as head count, cost to serve an account, and time required to respond to customer inquiries. If one goal of technology expenditures is to free up the RM's time to make additional calls, the success of that expenditure has to be measured by the number and quality of additional calls that will be made. Any departures from expected performance need to be evaluated in detail. Again, holistic solutions are necessary, and each systems change needs to be recognized not only as a recommendation on the technology used but also in light of its potential impact on organizational structure and process.

Stage 3: Implementation

Clearly, a successful implementation process depends on project management. The use of detailed project-by-project workplans are, therefore, necessary in this third stage. These workplans provide a methodology for listing the steps required to complete a project, the person or persons responsible for a specific task, and a schedule for completion. The focus of this planning is ongoing communication and highlighting of emerging roadblocks.

Slippage can be caught early if the implementation process is effectively monitored and management can address problems as they occur rather than after they have grown in significance. As in the assessment and design stages, line and staff management must also share responsibility for project management with systems and staff members.

Summary Thoughts

Technology supports; it cannot lead the change process in transforming the middle market bank. Technology reform is also an area where senior line management must take a lead role rather than delegate authority to internal experts. They should see themselves as a person building a home who needs and wants to be involved in each decision along the way to completion.

Despite the arcane subject matter, senior management should not fear being involved. Structured approaches, such as those outlined above, will provide even computer-illiterate managers with the management focus and insight needed to use the breakthroughs technology will offer, instead of being sidetracked by inappropriate expenditures that do not support the key business goals.

13

The Non-Bank Success Story

"We pick our competitors."
—Sam Eichenfield, chairman, GFC Financial Corporation

Much of this book focuses on the market mandate pushing corporate banks to change themselves into customer-focused and profit-driven sales organizations. To understand and prepare for this transformation, bankers need to look beyond their industry toward their primary competitors: non-banks.

The strategies and approaches used successfully by non-banks provide excellent examples of skill and ingenuity. Most non-banks are unencumbered by the past. True, they may lack history and tradition, but they also lack the constraints of an entrenched bureaucracy. The best of them maintain excellent internal risk management procedures and focus intently on building lasting relationships with their customers. Whether non-banks concentrate on the consumer or commercial side of the business and whether they focus on the asset or liability side of the balance sheet, they intend to operate as virtual equals in the bank marketplace.

The financial community is certainly aware that non-banks will continue to grow in significance and strength as competitors to traditional commercial banks. An informal audience poll taken at an American Bankers Association (ABA) convention in 1992 revealed that bankers, from both large and small institutions, are increasingly coming up against non-banks in their markets. When asked, "Who is your main competitor?" more than 25 percent of the respondents answered "non-banks."

We expect that this percentage will rise steadily in the coming years. In fact, within five years, non-banks may provide the chief competition for the majority of medium- to large-sized commercial banks. As bank executives look for ways to position and defend their institutions in their emerging marketplace, most are beginning to realize that the non-banks' strategy is fundamentally different from the tactics used by most commercial banks.

Non-Bank Inroads

Non-banks have carved inroads into the corporate middle market in virtually all products and services from lending, trust, and investment management to back-office transactions. For example, Exhibit 13.1 summarizes the inroads commercial finance companies have made into businesses such as commercial and industrial (C&I) lending, which had been considered one of traditional banks' core product franchises.

Exhibit 13.1 shows that finance companies have gained share in C&I loans, asset-based lending and factoring, leasing, and real estate. In many cases, banks have "left the barn door open," walking away from or downplaying these products to focus on more traditional, unsecured "white shoes" lending. This vacuum has allowed non-banks to pick up significant market share at spreads that exceed those for straight, unsecured lending.

Non-bank success stretches far beyond commercial finance lending to tougher credit companies as several company examples illustrate:

Lending-Related Products

- The Money Store is now the largest Small Business Administration (SBA) lender. The erosion of the traditional bank

Exhibit 13.1 Commercial Finance Share Gains

Finance companies have been gaining market share in almost every commercial finance product area over the last several years.

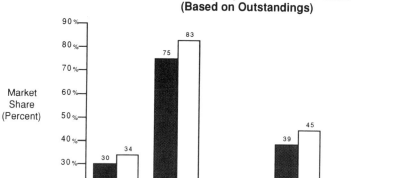

Select Product Examples

Finance Company Markets Share Shifts (Based on Outstandings)

franchise in the small business segment by new, non-bank players is likely to continue and will be discussed in Chapter 15. Unless banks renew their commitment to this market, they risk losing the franchise completely over the next 10 years.

- Merrill Lynch is the leading underwriter of commercial paper, with approximately 130 issues in 1993; Citibank, the most active commercial bank, had fewer than 20.

- In venture capital, Warburg Pinkus leads all other competitors with $4 billion under management. Chemical Venture Partners is currently the only commercial bank with funds managed exceeding $1 billion.

- Appropriately, commercial banks hold a strong position in the private placement of asset-based securities. Banks still hold six of the top 10 positions in that product area.

Non-Lending Products

- A recent *Euromoney* survey ranked Morgan Stanley Global Securities Services as 14th in global custody assets under management, ahead of Mellon, Northern Trust, and Bank of America. Morgan Stanley only entered this business in 1988, tripling assets under management from 1992 to 1993.

- Only five of the top 25 largest managers of 401(k) and 457 assets are banks.

- In the back office, companies like Electronic Data Systems (EDS), rather than major banks, have built a lead position in providing outsourcing services.

Although bank management may view itself as in a category separate from non-banks, such strong performances raise numerous questions that senior managers need to answer. Are banks, in fact, guilty of hubris in categorizing the aggressive marketing approach, pay-for-performance compensation policies, and selected product offerings of non-banks as inappropriate for banking institutions? Don't many customers see the non-banks' approach as creative and an indication of their understanding of the marketplace? Isn't the market demanding a more flexible, dynamic approach to product development and marketing?

Unless senior managers acknowledge the new market realities, banks will continue to lose corporate and middle market "share of wallet" just as they are losing share of the consumer wallet. Taken to its ultimate conclusion, banks may, in fact, become irrelevant for many of their corporate customers, whether small business or large corporate. One executive in a $30 billion regional tells of a customer stating that his institution was "a nice little bank."

The consumer who pays bills with his Fidelity money market checking account or with a Travelers Express money order, buys dinner with his Amex or GE card, and invests his pension funds through John Hancock or Travelers has, in effect, dropped out of the world of traditional banking. Except for the banks' current monopoly over the U.S. dollar payments system, many companies, too, could live without commercial banks. Even this last stronghold is threatened by technology-based innovations such as Electronic Data Interchange (EDI) and the entry of non-banks and corporations into the payment products arena.

Exhibit 13.2 contrasts banks and non-banks from the perspective of administrative bureaucracy and compensation. While many bankers would surely deny its accuracy, the exhibit represents how many non-banks and, more importantly, their customers perceive the competitive landscape.

Accepting these market realities and embarking on a path to operate like a non-bank requires an altered state of mind rather than a change of one's legal status. In fact, banks like Chemical, NationsBank, and Norwest often already have operating units that possess all the characteristics of the best non-banks. Still, such an approach is the exception rather than the rule in middle market banking.

Limited Bureaucracy

As Exhibit 13.2 suggests, non-banks operate in a world of relatively little bureaucracy, one in which alternative ideas and approaches are not only encouraged but also quickly evaluated without the need to jump over or across multiple internal hurdles.

This fast-track problem solving is characteristic of continuous improvement companies whose employees are empowered to make decisions. It is, however, in direct contrast to the structured consensus management style of most banks. The following case study of one bank's attempt to adopt GE's management style illustrates the discomfort many senior bank managers experience when confronted by newly empowered employees encouraged to offer opinions.

Exhibit 13.2   Comparison of Banks to Non-Banks

The best non-banks have performed more strongly and consistently than traditional banks in part because of management discipline and focus.

Banks Vs. Non-Banks

Banks	Non-Banks
Bureaucratic, consensus-driven	Greater flexibility to "get the job done;" lower operating costs
Primarily salary-based compensation	Closer linkage of pay-for-performance; large percentage of compensation tied to incentives/bonus
Breadth not depth/quality of products often emphasized	More specialized product/functional expertise; "less is more"
Price as a differentiating factor	Price based on low cost structure or "value added"
Competitors are many and increasing	"We pick our competitors."

224

Becoming a non-bank is not as simple as issuing a management decree. As the following story illustrates, one bank that tried to adopt GE's management style misunderstood the approach required.

GE, including its GE Capital subsidiary, is well known for what is popularly termed its "workout" program, which GE began in 1988. The town meeting format brings together employees of a business unit for very frank and direct discussions. Topics can include current or emerging problems, whether internal or external—such as management responsiveness, product quality, and worker relations. How to exploit market opportunities and organizational issues also can be the focus.

These sessions—which have gained a legendary reputation outside GE—are free-wheeling by nature, addressing those areas that both employees and management think need to be worked out.

Jack Welsh, the chairman of GE and someone who does not stand on ceremony, intends these meetings to be brutally honest and cover any area of importance with "no holds barred." Analysts understand this workout program is one part of a company-wide, ongoing process and view GE's willingness to confront itself and slay sacred cows as its key to continued efficiency and growth.

The achievements of GE's program looks all the more remarkable when compared to what reportedly occurred several years ago at a commercial bank that tried to introduce a workout session at a top officer off-site meeting.

An outside facilitator was hired to lead the group and was instructed prior to the meeting that he should be aggressive in raising issues of concern and encourage direct confrontations. During the course of the morning session, however, the head of this bank quickly became disenchanted with the facilitator's approach and uncomfortable with the direction in which the meeting was heading, even though the facilitator was doing what he had been asked to do.

"Workout," a popular buzzword, had became an ugly reality. The net result: after an early break, the workout was truncated, and the facilitator disappeared from the meeting, never to return.

Banks too often appear to be following a Japanese process termed *nemawashi*. Roughly translated, this phrase means "laying the groundwork" prior to making a decision. Multiple smaller meetings are held prior to a group meeting at which a proposal is slated for discussion. The net result is that the actual meeting avoids confrontation because it has been defused in advance. Unfortunately, the group meeting itself also may be largely valueless, a rubber-stamp procedure.

In contrast to avoidance, challenges to the status quo, combined with fast and flexible decision making and a strong emphasis on risk management, are the values given a premium at the successful non-bank players such as GE Capital, GFC Financial Corporation, Travelers Express, and Fidelity Investments.

Compensation as Motivation

Pay for performance is the compensation of choice at many non-banks. To differentiate salary levels and yearly increases, non-bank managers tier employees based upon the past year's demonstrated performance. Top performers may receive a sizable bump while mediocre players get little or no increase.

Contrast that compensation system with the situation prevalent at banks, which have not fully recognized the competitive situation they face, either for customers or excellent personnel. At banks, top performers usually receive salary increases that are marginal, that is 2 to 3 percent higher, than those given to the average banker. The best performers know that little differentiation in yearly increases is possible, and they resent it. Instead, they are dependent on bonus payments that are also often highly structured and limited by caps.

My consulting firm's client experience and several industry surveys we have conducted suggest that incentive pay, when offered at banks, is typically capped at about 15 percent of salary for mid-level bank officers, including RMs, product salespersons, and credit personnel. Banks are aware, however, that they compete directly with investment banks for trading and corporate finance personnel. Therefore, those specialists typically receive outsized incentives and bonus payments to attract and retain them. More and more, however, banks are competing with non-banks for RM and product salespersons as well.

Some non-bank managers weight total compensation strongly toward incentives/bonus. Salespersons can receive bonuses that are multiples of their salaries and face no arbitrary upside cap on potential earnings. In the words of one non-bank executive, "Compensation directly affects how we act." The result is a concentration on selling and dollars of profit (not volume) per account. Obviously, this philosophy is fostered by the possession of good profit data both for product and relationships, as well as having strong performance measurement systems in place.

Some bank executives undoubtedly see pay for performance as encouraging mercenary instincts and a short-term perspective. The best non-banks, however, both generate an increase in short-term earnings and record higher long-term productivity and profits. Kidder Peabody-like problems are in fact few and far between.

When approached to change their compensation strategy, bankers often balk and provide anecdotes of instances when incentives played major roles in "blowing up the bank." In one instance, a northeast bank encouraged loan growth by paying RMs incentives tied to new loan volume. Unfortunately, these bankers, however, also maintained their role in the credit approval process, rather than moving to a business development-only responsibility. Not surprisingly, volumes grew. The percentage of bad loans also grew dramatically with the expected negative impact on that bank's bottom line. Yet, the incentive system, rather than a flawed organizational structure, took the blame for that disaster.

Successful banks and non-banks protect themselves from such consequences by one or more fail-safes, including tying a significant percentage of compensation to long-term payout, penalizing business generators for past deals gone sour, and building a "fire wall" between marketing and credit.

The key issue that bank managers must recognize is how deeply this compensation disparity may be hurting their ability to attract excellent personnel. Without an easy-to-understand bonus and/or incentive system in place, many top performers are willing to walk out. In some geographies, competition for employees may still be limited. In most regions, however, banks will soon find that they need to face up to keen competition for professionals who expect to be paid when they succeed and are willing to accept the economic and professional consequences if they fail.

Product Selectivity and Focus

Banks also differ from non-banks in their self-imposed mandate to be "all things to all people." Non-banks, in contrast, do not usually attempt to match banks product-for-product. They are successful because they "pick their spots" and sell only those products through which they can demonstrate knowledge, achieve scale, or register another competitive advantage. Most important, non-banks make certain that a market opportunity exists before committing resources.

Many banks talk segmentation, but few have the discipline to do what their instincts and analysis tell them. Non-banks live and prosper with a focused approach. Given their higher profitability hurdles and, in some instances, more limited access to funds, they have no choice.

In cases where banks have exited product areas, the decision seems to have been based not on strategy or profit, but on senior management's view of what is an "appropriate" business for a bank to pursue. The customer's need for reasonably priced credit and bank services has little weight. Commercial finance and factoring activities on the wholesale side and low-end consumer business on the retail side appear to fall into this "inappropriate" category. When banks do pursue these businesses, they often want to find deals that can move into the core bank in a few years, rather than continuing to meet a long-term need of a profitable segment, as is the case for asset-based lenders.

Companies such as GFC, which will be discussed in the case example in chapter 14, have taken advantage of certain corporate opportunities and avoided others. GFC, Congress (owned by Core-

States but run independently), and GE Capital, for example, avoid competing for the borrower that can obtain funds at close to commercial-paper rates and, therefore, view lending as a commodity.

Such smart non-bank competitors focus on underserved or highly attractive markets using a specially designed product/service/delivery system for their chosen segments. Non-banks assess competitors and position effectively against them. How many bank executives can echo the words of Sam Eichenfield, chairman of GFC, when he said, "We pick our competitors"?

Companies pursuing this segmented approach to the corporate middle market include independent finance companies, some industrial companies, investment banks, and insurers. In addition to GFC's product offerings in commercial finance, leasing, factoring, and GE Capital's services for large, highly structured transactions, other competitors include Thomas Cook in commercial foreign exchange and Morgan Stanley in global custody. A number of strong players, including Merrill Lynch, Fidelity, and Prudential, are active in the employee benefits and investment arenas.

To this day, many banks still believe they must develop and provide the full catalogue of products required by the spectrum of corporate clients. Worse, many still fail to consider the value of outsourcing or joint venturing product offerings with bank or non-bank partners. Too often, pride wins out over profit. Contrast that stand-alone emphasis with the non-banks that tend to sell only those products generating an adequate risk-based return and to assess investments on the basis of a rigorous capital allocation model.

Cross-sell opportunities, while certainly not ignored by non-banks, have been historically less important because of the profitability of each product they sell. The request by marketers to reduce pricing to below hurdle rates "for the relationship" is rarely heard. In no small part, pricing toughness relates to the compensation systems described above which reward business generators for higher-than-expected returns for specific businesses.

Ultimately, for non-banks, relationship-based profit may be less important than generating profits on an individual transaction basis.

Fostering a Non-Bank Culture

It may be the exception rather than the rule, but non-bank cultures can flourish in banking organizations. Banks can become non-banks, in effect, not by giving up their state or federal charters but by remolding their self-image and refocusing their mindsets.

Multiple examples of non-banks within traditional banks exist. On the consumer side, Norwest's mortgage and consumer finance activities and Citibank's credit card business provide two excellent examples. On the corporate side of the business, Chemical's venture capital and Banc One's investment banking areas offer examples of semi-independent units operating within larger, bureaucratic organizations.

Characteristics of a non-bank-like operation within a bank may, for example, include a separate physical location. Banc One's investment bank is located several blocks away from its Columbus, Ohio headquarters. A specifically designed compensation and incentive pay structure is another characteristic that is usually seen in investment banks and venture capital activities. A culture distinct from the rest of the bank is a key sign of a non-bank attitude. As an employee in one of the above-example bank units said, "I am not a banker."

Why have the non-banks had such a large impact? Bank management is making a crucial error if they think there is a mystical formula. Little beyond fundamental good business practices, employee empowerment, discipline, and tough decision making is at the heart of non-bank success.

Unfortunately, however, bank managers often rely on excuses to explain what is happening rather than looking inside the bank at the root causes of its market disadvantage. They claim non-banks play a different competitive game, one where the rules are stacked in the non-banks' favor. Many banks also view themselves as hamstrung by tougher regulations, including the Community Reinvestment Act and other onerous government regulations.

Rules of Success

Non-banks, whether they operate in the consumer or corporate middle market achieve their success, in part, by adhering to three similar rules: focus, focus, focus.

Non-banks tend to have a clear sense of what they want and how to accomplish it, and they structure their internal organization and external delivery system accordingly. Furthermore, their organizations concentrate on the end customer and avoid becoming bogged down by addressing the concerns of internal constituencies. To have any possibility of success, banks need to consider three corrective actions: reduce bureaucracy, evaluate strategic focus, and rethink compensation.

Reduce Bureaucracy

Bank infrastructures have developed over decades, ostensibly to prevent fraud and keep management informed about current performance and emerging problems. The support areas—reporting to either the controller, chief financial officer, or senior line of business head—have grown in size and bureaucracy.

At its best, these support areas go far beyond number-crunching, and provide analytical back-up for decision-making, challenge unfounded assumptions, uncover fraud, and facilitate line management in achieving its business goals. Ideally, not being constrained by the responsibilities of day-to-day business, a support role empowers senior staff members to think "outside the box" and provides a spotlight on the leading edge for business managers.

However, what has occasionally occurred, particularly in larger banks, is that the control function becomes a self-perpetuating, members-only club. At its worst, this group (which in big banks can number in the hundreds) slows down decision-making and distances line managers from their direct reports. Further, while revenue generators are being dismissed, this group may avoid cost reduction initiatives. The implication is that rationalization will harm the risk management function and, therefore, ultimately the quality of bank earnings. Nonetheless, process streamlining and role redefinition can lead to significant cost savings in this area as well as changes to the corporate mindset.

Banks, of course, tend to operate by consensus and committee. As might be expected, this process can extend the time required to make a decision. The non-banks I have worked with are usually led by strong individual leaders who are willing to act quickly and to take the heat from investors. The best non-bank executives evaluate the analysis prepared for them, listen to their people, then make a decision and stick with it. They examine the various aspects of internal debates but then act in a decisive manner and demonstrate a willingness to put their neck on the line. Multiple committee meetings that allow equivocation and marginalism to set in do not usually take place in non-bank conference rooms.

A famous story, probably untrue, about Abraham Lincoln and his Cabinet effectively communicates the approach followed by any strong leader, regardless of industry. In a Cabinet meeting, a vote was taken. The net result: 10 nays and 1 yea. Lincoln reacted to the vote, saying the yeas had won. He had cast the one yes vote.

While some non-banks managers may disagree, my experience has been that non-banks operate less democratically than the typical bank, while still trying to be inclusive of multiple perspectives. There is a danger to this approach. Despotism, rather than leadership can be the cost, but despotism has been known to occur from time to time at commercial banks as well.

One advantage that non-banks have over their bank competition is that most have not been in operation long enough to develop the cultural mindset that mires them in the past. Non-banks are often start-ups or younger companies that have taken advantage of the opportunity to invent themselves. Rarely, thus far, have many non-banks been forced to reengineer or redirect an existing bureaucratic structure. Further, the culture itself encourages continual reinvention.

Admittedly, given a clean sheet of paper and the charge to design the ideal banking organization, few, if any, bank executives would design the complex structures in which they currently operate. To apply an analogy, building a new house is easier than remodeling and updating an old one.

Banks need to address that challenge by pushing themselves to think in terms of a clean-sheet approach. Why? Because their competitors—some known and some unknown today—are already doing so.

Evaluate Strategic Focus

Bank management needs to institute an approach that will regularly evaluate current businesses/markets and recommend changes in strategy and specific products. Some banks, however, appear to have their feet encased in concrete while their competitors are wearing the latest $200 athletic shoe and chasing the prize.

The banks are, indeed, in a race. Fortunately, they are playing with handicaps that management leadership and corporate willpower can overcome.

Rethink Compensation

A true program of pay for performance seldom exists for corporate middle market bankers, particularly in the critical mid-levels of management ranks. In many instances, bonuses or other incentive pay are small or non-existent. Ten to fifteen percent of salary may be too low a number to charge up the RM. In some cases, yearly bonuses are based on subjective criteria that appear to emphasize stereotypes of good citizenship over generating profits for the bank. As one innovative banker told us, "My manager said he couldn't stand it that I was always right."

Many non-banks see themselves as sales organizations and set up their compensation structure to encourage new ideas and constant selling. In the case of some commercial finance companies, a successful business development officer (BDO) can receive a bonus for substantially more than 50 percent of base salary by exceeding goals agreed upon at the beginning of the year. Since progress against goals is measured regularly, year-end surprises—whereby the BDO receives less than expected—are at a minimum. While some subjective good citizen goals are, of course, included, the majority of non-salary compensation is linked directly to performance.

While the responsibilities of the commercial finance or leasing BDO differ from those of a line lender, for example, in credit authority and responsibility for multi-product cross-sell, the model used by much of the commercial finance industry can be adapted to banking. We will examine how that model operates in the GFC case example found in the next chapter.

Simply stated, better compensation opportunities will continue to draw highly attractive top performers away from banking to industries where performance translates directly into more money in their pockets. Again, banks ignore the importance of compensation at their own peril.

Summary Thoughts

The best performing non-banks emphasize focus in their marketing effort and discipline in their approach to managing customer relationships. The qualities they emulate—organizational flexibility, individual accountability, and pay for performance, among others—merit serious consideration by banks as well.

14

Niching for Success
Case Study:
GFC Financial Corporation

"I sleep better with GFC in my portfolio than any other stock."
—*a portfolio manager for a major investment company*

GFC began 1992 as the subsidiary of a consumer products company, the Phoenix-based Dial Corporation. GFC's predecessor company was founded in 1954. Dial purchased that company in 1967.

By 1992, Dial management had come to believe that its shareholders were being penalized because the company was widely viewed as a conglomerate by security analysts and investors and, therefore, was trading at a reduced multiple. As a result, Dial management decided to spin-off its major financing businesses.

At the time of the spinoff, the resulting GFC holding company consisted of three operating entities: the core niche commercial finance operation, a mortgage insurance company that Dial was already liquidating, and a previously unaffiliated European finance operation whose results had suffered from the UK and European recession.

Once independent, GFC management assessed its current businesses and set out to refocus the company's operations to take advantage of internal strengths and external market opportunities. The company moved quickly. By May of 1992, it decided to phase out the European operation. By August, a decision was made to continue the "run off" of its mortgage insurance subsidiary rather than reinvest in the activity. As a result of an active desire to free-up and redeploy the capital tied-up in a nonstrategic activity, that company was aggressively marketed and subsequently sold to GE Mortgage Insurance Company, at a premium to boot.

That left GFC with one core operation: commercial finance. Perhaps surprisingly to some bankers, that business and the skills needed to be successful at it were chosen as the platform for future growth.

In 1992, GFC's commercial finance activities centered on five niche markets:

- *Resort Finance*

  In operation for 15 years, this group lends mainly to major developers of timeshare resorts and second home communities.

- *Commercial Real Estate Finance*

  The focus of this group is on three primary segments: owner-occupied commercial properties, retail outlets with proven cash flow, and hotel and hospitality properties.

- *Communications Finance*

  This group lends primarily to owners/operators of radio, television, and cable TV stations.

- *Transportation Finance*

  In operation since 1962, this group emphasizes used commercial railroad equipment and used aircraft.

- *Corporate Finance*

  Making secured term loans to medium-sized companies, this group focuses on low-tech industries such as services, manufacturing and processing, distribution, industrial, and consumer products.

GFC's overall business theme was to focus on underserved markets making loans of $2 million to $30 million.

As Exhibit 14.1 shows, GFC has demonstrated strong core earnings growth, both in the years prior to its spin-off from Dial, as well as in the two subsequent years in spite of the recession and its negative impact on corporate banking.

While banks have been suffering from a slowdown or contraction in corporate lending, GFC has continued to find profitable niche businesses (Exhibit 14.2a). Its borrowers are companies that both need funding and have limited alternative sources other than GFC. Excellent risk management and quick reaction to emerging problem situations have minimized write-offs (Exhibit 14.2b).

Importantly, GFC seldom finds itself in competition with commercial banks. When it does, the bank lender often lightens up the loan's structure to get the business, recasting what GFC and other

Exhibit 14.1 GFC Financial Corporation Earnings Review

GFC has generated consistent earnings for shareholders, both as a member of the Dial Corporation and post-spinoff.

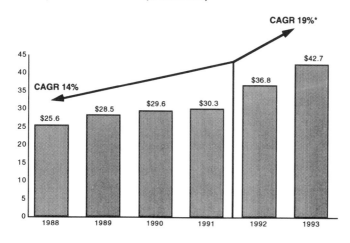

Income from Continuing Operations
(in $ millions)

Exhibit 14.2a and b GFC's New Business Volume and Portfolio Management Performance

New volume has shown consistent growth . . . while the portfolio quality has remained strong.

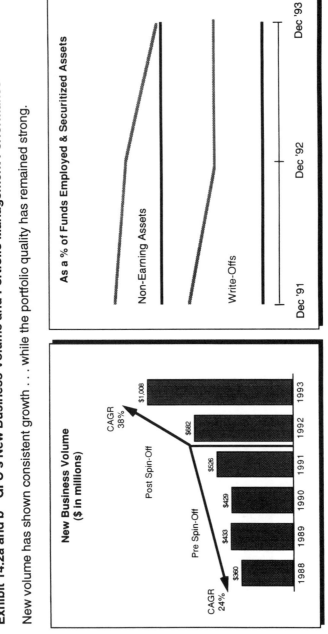

As a % of Funds Employed & Securitized Assets

Non-Earning Assets

Write-Offs

Dec '91   Dec '92   Dec '93

GFC, excluding Europe   GFC Pro Forma

*As a % of average funds employed & securitized assets.

New Business Volume
($ in millions)

CAGR 38%

Post Spin-Off

Pre Spin-Off

CAGR 24%

$360 $433 $429 $526 $682 $1,008

1988   1989   1990   1991   1992   1993

*Excludes pro forma results.

238

commercial finance companies might view as an acceptable secured credit into an unsecured or undercollateralized loan.

GFC's strategy is to be a low-cost producer; pick selected under-served niche opportunities; position its products to avoid substantial competition; focus its marketing effort in part by means of well-defined and well-communicated underwriting criteria; and, limit its exposure to any one borrower.

As stated in the 1992 annual report, management believes that success has resulted from its "highly developed sense of discipline." There are at least three ways in which this discipline is evidenced across the company: in the business strategy, in adherence to strict exposure limits, and through the incentive compensation structure. Each area provides corporate bankers with food for thought.

Corporate Discipline

GFC, like some other asset-based finance, leasing and commercial finance lenders, possesses a highly segmented approach to its business and a focused infrastructure. The defined job responsibilities, GFC's organizational structure, and its information systems all encourage increased productivity and a dedication to profitable growth.

Organizational Discipline

GFC uses what might be described as a cylindrical approach to business in which job responsibilities are clear. Salespersons are responsible for selling, credit people underwrite, and account executives maintain ongoing customer service. This structure is fundamentally different from the way most banks organize their core unsecured lending operations.

GFC's salespersons are, in effect, business development officers (BDOs). Their job is to sell and, while they know GFC's underwriting standards and deal structuring criteria, they have no credit authority. They pass along the deals they uncover to the portfolio management area for underwriting. This group consists not simply of credit specialists but also of individuals who are experts at the particular deals that GFC pursues.

Again in 1992, the annual report stated that GFC's Portfolio Management group which was "charged with the responsibilities of transaction approval, collection, and monitoring, has been instrumental in preserving the high quality of the company's loan portfolio during recent times of economic stress . . . and the group remains focused on maintaining the same degree of diligence."

After the transaction is complete, an account executive (AE) takes over. That person has ongoing customer service responsibility for a credit and will also conduct account reviews and gain approval for loan increases. In the case of term loans, an AE has responsibility for up to 100 accounts; because of the monitoring intensity of working capital deals, AEs monitor a smaller number of those transactions, in the range of 15 accounts.

Many bankers would reject this organizational model as being inappropriate for their unsecured corporate borrowers. Yet, it does work. A number of banks now use a BDO-like structure, and every few months one learns of another bank testing it. Several California banks use BDOs in their core middle market and large corporate segments. One major southeastern regional is in the midst of piloting a business development focus. Its goal is to shift marketing time not just to the 50-percent-plus level but rather to more than 80 percent of the calling officer's time.

Still, most banks reject this approach, arguing that their customers want to deal with a decision maker and that the only reason companies such as GFC can get away with a BDO-structure is because they are a one-time transaction lender rather than a relationship bank. That view is belied by the fact that cross-selling is growing in importance to GFC as it broadens its product niche capabilities.

In turn, the banks using BDOs reply that internal coordination alleviates many of the concerns that customers might, at first, fear. Further, many banks considering a BDO-structure feel that RMs and not the customers are most worried about the proposed change.

In fact, bank RMs—whose job has been refocused to put a greater emphasis on cross-selling and new business development activities—often have more difficulty adjusting to the BDO structure than do the customers.

Discipline in Lending

GFC's attitude to risk concentration parallels that of Norwest Bank. In the case of each of its businesses, outstandings to any one company, even on a secured basis, do not exceed $35 million. Additional limits exist based upon geographic concentration, industries, and products. No one mistake, therefore, can badly harm the company and a "bet the company" mentality is avoided. Exposure limits are, of course, one area where the interests of a BDO, who receives a bonus payment based in part on loan volume, could conflict with the company's best interests. Here, the policies of the portfolio management group guide and protect GFC.

A Third Discipline: Incentives

GFC ties a part of its incentive system to increases in the company's stock price, lining up shareholder interests with those of employees. Also, while BDOs do not have credit authority, they receive a charge against their bonus for any loans that deteriorate within two years of origination. That penalty serves to reinforce the company's emphasis on quality and helps to avoid some of the problems that occur with volume-based compensation systems.

Building for the Future

With commercial finance as its core, GFC has set out to grow its operations, both from internal and external sources.

Internally generated growth has been based upon adding more salespersons and improving its nationwide marketing reach by opening offices in selected cities where GFC either did not have an office or maintained only a limited presence.

GFC has also completed three major acquisitions: the asset-based finance subsidiary of U.S. Bancorp, Ambassador Factors which was the factoring arm of Fleet Financial, and in early 1994, Tricon Capital, Bell Atlantic's wholly owned finance company.

Exhibit 14.3 provides an overview of GFC's business mix following these acquisitions and presents the percent of total assets for each business. Diversification remains a priority for the company. This chart offers multiple examples of the combined company generating profits from areas that most banks avoid. Tricon Capital, for example, offers GFC an opportunity to expand its niche marketing approach. While Tricon is still in the process of being integrated into GFC, the acquisition appears to broaden the combined company's capabilities, extending them to medical equipment financing and remarketing, vendor and franchise financing, and several other potentially attractive niche businesses.

Exhibit 14.3 GFC's Pro Forma Portfolio Diversification

GFC's current business mix diversifies its earnings stream.

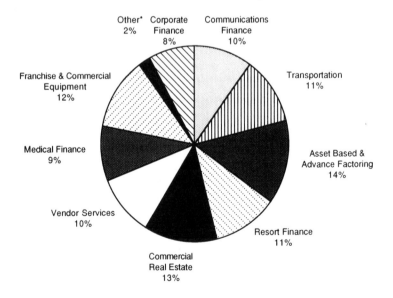

The acquisitions made up to this point have turned GFC into the largest independent financial services company focusing on the secured financing needs of middle market companies. As Exhibit 14.4 indicates, the company is now an expert in factoring, asset-based lending, leasing, and term lending. Industry expertise ranges from transportation and communication to medical equipment and fast-food franchising.

While maintaining its prior discipline remains a key to its future success, these acquisitions position GFC to continue along a path of profitability based upon niche businesses and "picking the competition."

Learning from GFC

Can banks learn anything from a non-bank company such as GFC? Or is GFC's focus so specialized and its market so unique that it presents an interesting success story but little more?

We think that only by evaluating and understanding how non-banks such as GFC, GE Capital, and Merrill Lynch, among many others, have been successful can banks position themselves to meet emerging customer needs. Banks should read at least three messages when looking at the GFC profile:

1. *Be willing to reinvent yourself.*

   As a new public company, GFC had the opportunity to examine itself and determine which businesses made long-term sense and which did not. It decided to go deeper into niche secured financing businesses, an area where senior management was most comfortable and where it had demonstrable expertise. At the same time, it eliminated those business areas where it possessed no competitive advantage. One of Sam Eichenfield's favorite maxims and one which the company seems to follow is: "If you don't have a competitive advantage, don't compete."

   This proactive approach is distinctly different than the trap many banks fall into, that is, providing too many products and serving too many market segments, regardless of profitability.

Exhibit 14.4   GFC's Niche Focus

GFC's recent acquisitions give the company extended product capabilities and multiple opportunities for targeted growth.

GFC Capabilities Post-Acquisition

Lines of Business	GFC	Ambassador	TriCon	GFC Pro Forma
Corporate Finance	X			X
Transportation Finance*	X			X
Communications Finance*	X			X
Commercial Real Estate	X			X
Resort Finance*	X			X
Consumer Rediscount Finance	X			X
Asset-Based Finance*	X	X		X
Factoring		X		X
Commercial Equipment Finance			X	X
Medical Equipment/Remarketing*			X	X
Government/Public Sector Finance			X	X
Vendor Sales/Services			X	X
Franchise Finance*			X	X
Inventory/Floor Plan Financing			X	X
Leverage Lease Portfolio Management			X	X

*Major market share.

2. *Think non-traditionally.*

As discussed above, bankers seem to view certain businesses as, in effect, beneath them. This attitude may result from the fact that many senior corporate bank managers began their careers as unsecured lenders and are most comfortable with that type of lending.

Companies like Cash America, Transamerica, and Travelers Express on the consumer middle market side and GFC on the corporate middle market side have stepped into attractive market gaps that banks have allowed to widen.

Going forward, the generalist lender will continue to be under pressure by the customer for lower rates and looser loan structures. Banks must respond, in part, by developing specialist capabilities, such as those which GFC and others possess.

3. *Emphasize discipline, communication, and productivity.*

Many bankers are surprised at the degree of discipline that companies such as GFC possess. These are not "wild cowboys" from Phoenix doing deals, but highly skilled business persons who understand the key drivers of their profitability, follow strict pricing models, and generate a deal flow large enough to allow them to book well-structured transactions.

Strong productivity results not simply from the "three cylinder" organizational structure described above but also from excellent communications across the company. Both because of their many years of experience and the strong working relationship between the portfolio management area and the line of business heads, BDOs do not pursue "off-the-wall" deals. Strong up-front guidance exists with the BDO serving as a responsible pre-screener of deals. BDOs center their activities on producing "do-able" deals because their bottom-line incentives as well as their future with the company depends upon profitability.

In the case of GFC, this results in the company regularly approving close to 90 percent of the transactions submitted for consideration—a measure of the efficiency created by sound communication and training.

Summary Thoughts

Of course, not all banks can or should attempt to transform themselves into non-banks. But the strengths that excellent non-banks possess and which have lead to continuing success can be emulated. Focus, clarity of purpose, an emphasis on productivity and profitability, and an insistence on excellent individual performance are characteristics that are worthy of adoption by banks and non-banks alike.

15

Building a Small Business Customer Base

> "Banks are losing the business banking franchise to more flexible, new competitors."
>
> *—a non-bank chief operating officer*

Small business banking is the forgotten middle market franchise. This core banking franchise is a market that, historically, banks have "owned." Perhaps because there has been no competition for this business that often walks in the branch door, little attention has been given to its profitability.

The push to restructure middle market banking, however, provides an excellent opportunity to take a fresh look at this forgotten market segment. While an efficiently structured small business franchise can significantly benefit from sophisticated management, not all small business belongs with corporate banking.

- *First*, small business—defined as companies below $5 million in revenues—is a large market (more than 90 percent of all businesses) with a self-funding loan portfolio that can generate substantial profit for successful banks.

- *Second,* this market segment is viewed, appropriately, as the engine of growth for the U.S. economy and that growth can translate into loan and deposit business for banks.

- *Third,* within many banks, small business gets lost in the shuffle. Bank management not only fails to give it priority but also fails to give it the resources and attention small business deserves.

- *Fourth,* customer needs and the economics of small business banking demand a different approach than what is appropriate for the middle or large corporate markets. For example, historically, much of the profitability of small business has depended upon branch-based deposits. Products, customer service, and sales distribution systems have to be rethought and customized to meet the needs of this segment.

- *Fifth,* recently, just as middle market banking has come under competitive attack by non-banks, so too has the small business franchise. The Money Store, investment banks interested in securitizing small business loans, commercial finance companies, and even consumer finance companies seeking to move upscale are taking increased share away from banks. A defensive response to these competitor attacks is needed, particularly with the advent of securitization. Failure to do so will lead to bank market share erosion, as previously experienced in other markets such as C&I lending, as well as concurrent erosion in consumer areas such as credit cards and mortgages.

Perspective on the Future

In my view, in less than 10 years, the way small business banking is conducted will look fundamentally different from the approach most banks use today. "High touch" will increasingly give way to "high tech," as this business takes on more of the operational characteristics of consumer banking.

Therefore, to get a perspective on where small business is heading, bankers need to look to the credit card and mortgage businesses. Just as those business banking systems have changed fundamentally and now resemble manufacturing production lines, so too will the management of many segments of small business banking change dramatically. Four areas will perhaps experience the most dramatic changes: marketing, credit, account monitoring, and securitization.

1. *Marketing.* Instead of a calling effort lead by branch managers or business development officers, banks and non-banks serving the small business market will turn to:

   - Use of proprietary databases for targeted solicitations.

   - Creation of "segments of one."

   - Pre-approved credit offerings.

   - Tie-ins to affinity groups.

2. *Credit.* Individual credit analysis is already giving way to:

   - Application of credit-scoring models.

   - Credit levels linked to model screening criteria.

3. *Account Monitoring.* Software rather than individual relationship managers will handle most monitoring and account maintenance:

   - Servicing will be accomplished by 800 calls to a central service center.

   - Monitoring will be by exception only.

   - Loan review will be centralized and software driven.

   - Emphasis will be on quick action (similar to credit card availability where use is suspended immediately and is not available again until a payment is made).

4. *Securitization.* As this technology becomes widely available, the competitive dynamics among companies offering bank services will change. This competitive innovation:

   - Allows new non-bank competitors into the business.

- Encourages disaggregation of the banking relationship, into segments such as, profitable, borrow-only customers.

Perhaps the most important lesson to be learned regarding securitization is that the credit card and mortgage businesses have largely eliminated what is the highest personnel expense in small business banking: the salesperson. A major percentage of small business owners may demand and, in fact, continue to receive personal attention for the foreseeable future. Nonetheless, a significant group (20-plus percent) will choose to access their banks directly by an 800 number, by computer, or by another means, particularly if the methodology cuts service charges or increases speed of resolution.

Again, a parallel example can be found in credit card banking. Late last year at LaGuardia airport, I discovered a Citibank terminal in a stand-alone kiosk. By following some very straightforward instructions, this terminal allowed users to apply for one among a selection of cards. Depending on individual preference, you could pick a no-frills, low-cost, or a higher-rate frequent flyer card. If personal data was entered, the bank kiosk promised a credit decision and that a card would be mailed out in a few days.

You may ask: how is this process relevant to small business banking? Can it be emulated in that market? Will small businesses ever be able to access credit without the human intervention of a business bank officer or branch manager?

The opportunities for non-traditional marketing approaches are tied to the economics of small business lending, which will be discussed later in this chapter. Most of the current profits in small business result from deposits and fee-based products, not loans. A streamlined, high-tech approach will increase profits from the lending business; it will also allow competitors to enter the business to pursue lending-only as the securitization market for small business loans expands. In fact, this "pull" marketing approach is now being promoted by banks that are using segmentation with direct mail or telemarketing to cut back on high cost, personal calling.

Affinity-based marketing has also come to this segment. For example, Amalgamated Bank, with branches in New York City, for its size has a greater than expected proportion of its loans with taxi drivers, financing their purchase of cabs.

A look inside our crystal ball finds considerable evidence that small business banking will be very different in the future than it is today. Therein lies the threat, as well as the opportunity, for bankers.

Protecting the Bank Franchise

The small business market segment provides the banking industry with a large and growing target market promising an excellent return on equity. Both to protect its customer base and to take advantage of growth opportunities, senior bank management needs to develop a coherent strategy that includes, but is not limited to:

- *Dealing with internal organizational issues.* A clear organizational structure and strategic focus for small business banking will be essential to business development.

- *Evaluating the business economics.* Bank management must become aware of profitability drivers and their implications.

- *Determining key customer segments.* Beginning with an analysis of the current portfolio and leading to internal agreement on key customer groups, segmentation in this business will be a foundation for success.

- *Addressing the product, distribution, and customer service approaches.* Tailoring these product areas to the requirements of profitable customer groups will ensure ongoing profitable growth. Maintaining the status quo is not an option.

An Attractive Market

Companies with sales below $5 million comprise well over 90 percent of the total commercial population in most U.S. regions. While many companies do, indeed, fall into the $2 million to $5 million range, the vast majority are below $1 million in sales.

Although the number of companies is high, that 90 percent of total companies usually generates as little as 20 to 25 percent of loan volume and approximately 40 to 50 percent of all commercial-related deposits.

A characteristic of this market is its deposits to loan ratio, which typically ranges from 2.5 to 4.0—that is, from $2.50 up to $4 of gross deposits remain with a bank for every $1 of loans. The richness of that deposit pool becomes apparent when contrasted with other segments of the corporate market.

Paul Allen in his recent book *Reengineering the Bank* estimates that for the large corporate market demand deposits as a percentage of loans declined from a high of 30 percent in the 1970s to about 5 percent by 1994. To underscore the contrast, the large corporate segment has reduced its deposits from 30 cents for every dollar of loans to 5 cents for every loan dollar versus the deposit of $2.50 or more for each dollar of small business loans. At the same time, fees that were intended to compensate for the lost balances in the large corporate market also have declined sharply.

Organization as an Obstacle

Despite its size, small business marketing often "falls through the cracks" between the commercial and retail organization of many banks.

When housed with larger commercial accounts, the segment may be largely ignored because of the relatively small size of each individual transaction and the corporate group's historic focus on loan generation. Some banks define their middle market segment as encompassing all businesses above $1 million to $2 million in sales. Corporate RMs, trying to attain loan goals and other sales targets, rightfully view small business as a poor investment of their time. This situation may be further exacerbated by accounting procedures that give credit for balances to the retail bank rather than the middle market bank even when corporate accounts generate those balances.

RMs are justified in asking: Why spend time on a relationship that you receive little or no credit for even though it generates a good level of deposits?

On the other hand, the retail bank also is often unprepared to deal with the needs of a small business commercial customer whose demands can be more sophisticated and time-intensive than the average branch consumer. Branch managers may be too busy and ill-prepared to act as the RM for multiple small business accounts. Training may have been nonexistent or spotty, and the broad goals by which a branch manager's performance is measured may work against the best interests of the bank in developing the small business market.

Economics Tied to Deposits

Understanding the potential of small business banking begins with evaluating current economics. As the deposit-to-loan ratio indicates, even in the low-rate environment of the early 1990s, deposits drive the profitability of small business banking.

Exhibit 15.1 presents the profit profile of two accounts. In the case of Customer A, most profits result from investable balances. Borrowings are infrequent, and for small amounts, therefore, loan income generates less than 10 percent of Customer A's relationship profitability. Customer B provides an even more dramatic example of the relative value of loans versus deposits. In this case, the imbalance between the high cost of selling and structuring a loan and the low level of net interest income that a small loan generates turns the lending product into a loss leader. Even with the loan-related loss, however, the overall relationship is highly profitable due to the high level of free balances on deposit.

John W. Ballantine, Jr., in an article in *Commercial Lending Review* (Winter 1993–94), poses the question, "Can banks make profitable loans to small business?" He points out the disparity between an average bank's overall return from its small business portfolio and the return from customers who are primarily borrowers.

Exhibit 15.1   Deposits Often Drive Small Business Profits

Due to balance levels, small business can be profitable even if lending is only breakeven.

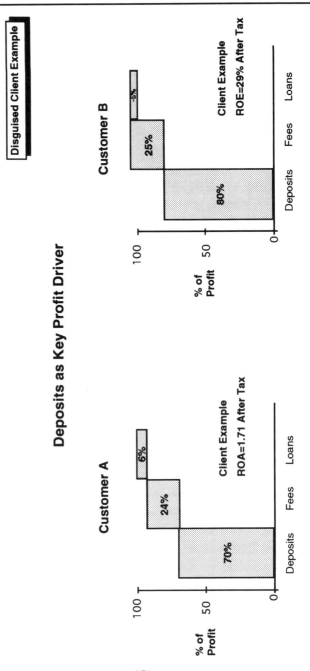

Many of those borrowers not only fail to provide the bank with free balances, but their loan amounts are so small that considering traditional marketing, approval, and monitoring structures, bank profits are minimal. In Ballantine's view, given the lending risks, the return may not be worth the effort for many banks. Certainly, the small business market should be avoided unless the bank is able to isolate those factors that result in profitability and, therefore, approach customers with a targeted strategy.

Focus on Key Segments

As in other bank businesses, an effective segmentation strategy is a key component of success in small business banking. The 80/20 rule—that four-fifths of profits come from a relatively small number of accounts—applies to this business as well as to almost all others. In the case of small business, however, the impact may be even greater. Major relationships can be 10 to 20 times more profitable than the average account.

The experience of one regional bank indicates the potential concentration of profitability. An analysis of the top 5 percent of their accounts shows that they generate more than 50 percent of the total balances for small business accounts at the bank.

Develop Needs-Based Segments

Segmentation can be based upon one or more factors, beginning with relatively straightforward characteristics such as company size, industry, or location. Typically, however, banks will find that a needs-based segmentation provides the best foundation for a meaningful strategy. For example, based upon the number of products and services used, banks can divide customers into basic, mid-range, and core user groups.

In many ways, basic customers are similar to no frills checking customers in retail banking and, in reality, are just as minimally attractive for the bank.

While those consumer accounts involve limited activity and low loan and deposit balances, their small business counterparts demonstrate similar activity profiles. Profits from this group of commercial accounts are unlikely unless the bank significantly reduces its cost to serve them. For example, a centralized phone-based service is preferable to servicing these accounts in person at a branch. The more expensive and personal approach should be reserved for high-value customers only.

When the majority of a bank's current small business customers are analyzed they fall into either the basic category of low potential or the mid-range needs categories. Mid-range customers maintain somewhat higher balance levels and provide increased opportunities for cross-selling. They are users of two to three services but offer the potential for added sales. In fact, some customers from this mid-range group may emerge to become core targets.

Core customers, those who are most profitable, usually represent less than 20 percent of the total small business customer base. They use the branch system more extensively (for example, for daily deposit making), leave relatively high balances, and merit a proportionately higher level of personalized service, bordering on a consultative relationship with the banker handling their account.

Cull Middle Market Portfolios

The portfolios of many middle market bankers contain relationships that can be slotted into one of the three small business groups defined above—basic, mid-range, and core users—to maximize productivity further.

For example, upon review, a substantial number of loans housed in the middle market are quite small, often under $500,000. This is particularly the case in many mid-sized regionals or smaller banks.

Another sizable group of middle market relationships are deposit-only. Both of these groups may be candidates for a centralized servicing group that caters to their needs. Their limited needs mean that these customers can be shifted from a high-cost RM to a central account servicing area performing a similar task for other small business accounts. Shifting these accounts out of the middle market area and into a small business delivery system not only improves the profits of the accounts but also frees up RM time for marketing high priority targets.

The central reasons why portfolios have not been culled in the past relates to the limitations of internal accounting systems and the self-interest of both the RM and middle level management.

Senior division managers in the corporate bank may be slow to shift account management and related revenues and balances (profits often being unknown) to the retail bank group, even though it may benefit the overall performance of the bank. In the near-term, this culling would reduce the numbers for the corporate group. When I asked one corporate banker if his group had accounts that could be serviced more efficiently elsewhere he answered, "Yes, but we have nothing to replace them with." Like this banker, some middle market RMs will not see this culling process as an opportunity to concentrate on their primary target market. Rather, they may want to avoid holes in their portfolios, as accounts transfer to the small business area.

This situation is a case in which individual interests can conflict with the bank's bottom line. Senior management will have to intervene in this process to ensure that the productivity increases offered by restructuring receive a serious evaluation and that the match between account needs and servicing standards is well-orchestrated.

Tailored Products and Customer Service

The crystal ball-gazing proposed at the beginning of this chapter suggested how dramatically product delivery systems could change. While "customization" and "personal service" may be the watchwords in the large corporate and middle markets, in small business "standardization" and "centralization" must become the mantras that focus the business.

In line with the customer base and segmentation strategy that a bank develops, management needs to tailor the mix of products it

257

sells to this small business market as well as the way in which it sells and services them. While exceptions will always occur, the long-term winners in the small business market will use that philosophy as the major signpost for their internal decision processes. The all-too-frequent requests for exceptions to standardization of products and centralization of underwriting and service must be granted only after the completion of quantitative analysis that supports proposed alterations to policy.

Product Standardization

A bank should only offer only a relative handful of products to the small business market compared to the mix offered to the middle market and large corporate areas. Loan product offerings might include Small Business Administration (SBA) loans, equipment leases, or lines of credit, automated to the extent possible. Other products offered could involve trade-related expertise and retirement planning. Uniform documentation and covenants exist for all these loans. Standardization not only speeds up and simplifies the underwriting process but can also, ultimately, provide the bank with a sizable loan portfolio that can be more easily securitized. Of course, a secondary market already exists for SBA loans.

Banks should discourage customization of any services for small business. When it is necessary, the added costs should be passed on to the customer as increased fees or through enhanced rates. On the deposit side, for example, the group of products should be limited to straightforward balance reporting and cash management services. Cash management queries, in turn, should be answered by PC-based technology or 800 numbers (an approach that Norwest employs), rather than branch visits or phone calls.

A recent project by Robert Morris Associates (RMA) has begun to address the need for standardized information from loan applicants. During 1993, an RMA task force developed a process for gathering financial information from private companies. These standards seek to improve the quality and detail of financial information available to bankers in making their credit decisions.

The *RMA Business Credit Information Package* provides a simple format for obtaining the same information from each prospective borrower. The package includes a format for a letter requesting information from the customer; a borrower's questionnaire, which requests a variety of information including key customers and suppliers; insurance information; company/principal transactions; a reporting and disclosure checklist for the borrower's accountants; a format for the presentation of financial statements; and an accountant's report form. This standard information package can be of value to banks that are new entrants to small business or have previously pursued the business with a high degree of decentralization. For more sophisticated banks, borrower responses can be input into centralized underwriting and portfolio analysis systems.

Underwriting Centralization

Centralization of underwriting will often result in taking credit underwriting away from a branch manager or a small business marketing officer. Using a centralized approach, credits are approved by regionally or centrally housed underwriters who will rely increasingly upon credit-scoring and artificial intelligence procedures. Only a handful of banks possess these capabilities now, but as technology becomes more available, automation processes will become the norm for small business. Servicing will also be centralized and conducted by phone for the majority of accounts.

Exhibit 15.2 illustrates the bottom-line impact of standardizing products and streamlining internal processes. This disguised example, based on client experience, indicates that for banks in which a manager handles 200 accounts, the small business ROE exceeds 20 percent. Conversely, banks that spend too much time on serving small profit customers generate unacceptable returns, below 10 percent ROE. The financial imperative for changing the traditional approach to this business segment is clear.

The small business selling process must also be redesigned both with economics and the customer in mind. For example, in the middle market and large corporate areas, the value of introducing a telemar-

Exhibit 15.2   The Importance of Increased Account Loads

Streamlined internal processes allow bankers/branch managers to handle high account loads.

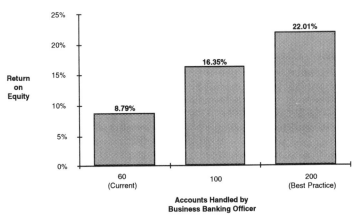

Discount Client Examples

Sensitivity of Small Business Profitability to Account Loads

Source: Mercer Management Analysis, CLS Database.

keting process to "warm up the cold call" for the RM, as Chemical Bank's success demonstrates, is recognized. In the small business segment, telemarketing and other non-traditional selling methods are simply essential if a bank is to generate high profits. Traditional sales tactics, such as cold calls, are unacceptable, and speculative in-person visits must be minimized. Based upon an institution's cost base, each bank should consider developing a customized profile of the "break-off point" below which personal calling becomes too expensive for the expected return from an account. In fact, in most instances, to ensure a high level of per-account profitability the target customer will need to be "pulled" into the branch system or a small business office to call on the account manager, after an initial database-driven and phone screening process occurs.

Best Practice Profiles

Profiles of two banks that have developed strong positions in small business banking provides a perspective on the major issues and tactics that players need to pursue to be successful.

Centralization and Segmentation

Bank A, an eastern regional, serves three large markets with close to 500 branches. Its defined small business market includes companies with sales less than $5 million or with average loan outstandings of less than $500,000. Because of customer preference for local management, some non-borrowers with sales greater than $5 million remain in the small business area. This bank generates an average ROE of 35 to 40 percent for small business, an outstanding result aided by the centralization of many functions and a strong, targeted marketing program.

Additionally, Bank A has enjoyed strong profits from its loan portfolio due to a high gross spread in excess of 5.25 percent, high-quality centralized underwriting, and a limited number of products. For example, the bank offers only three lending products: an automated revolving credit, a term loan, and an installment loan. The bank has also developed a highly effective approach to ongoing portfolio risk management.

The left hand side of Exhibit 15.3 presents the organizational structure for Bank A. The small business group and the branch system report to the same retail executive. Most branches have what is termed a "business banking officer" assigned to the branch, That officer and the branch manager are co-responsible for generating business, although the branch "owns" the business along with all revenues and expenses booked there.

The Market Support group, focusing solely on small business account maintenance, provides extensive data in creating a targeted sales effort. That group provides each small business sales team with a list of target prospects, identified by the history of profit within market and geographic niches.

Exhibit 15.3   Best Practice Organizations

Excellent performers can differ in their organizational structure, the responsibilities of small business banking specialists, and their approach to compensation.

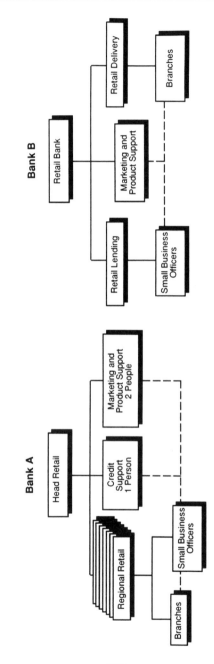

Success in adding new business often differs in particular from one region to another. Much like Chemical Bank's efforts in the middle market discussed in Chapter 4, the market support group creates promotions to assist the sales effort. Their effectiveness in pre-screening prospects has increased the yield and focused the calling program.

Notably, neither the sales team nor the branch manager have credit authority. Branches refer loan requests to a centralized loan approval and underwriting center that follows credit policy guidelines that the bank has developed for small business. That central group then approves loans, generates documents, and sends completed packages to the branch where the branch manager usually facilitates the closing process.

While the branch manager is responsible for account servicing, and on average more than 200 accounts are managed in each branch, the Central Branch Service group also assists. This service group facilitates new product introductions and interfaces both with the branches and the credit approval unit to ensure a rapid response to customer requests. A separate loan group has developed a highly automated, analytic, portfolio-based review system, and it performs hands-on loan reviews on an exception basis only.

At Bank A, both branch managers and business banking officers can be paid performance incentives for referrals of loans, and no conflict exists because these individuals do not possess credit authority. Branch officers also receive incentives for deposit and fee product sales, based on the profitability of those products to the bank. Since incentive compensation is tied to demonstrable performance, no limits are set.

Responsibility in Local Hands

Bank B, a regional bank with more than 200 branches, established its small business group in the early 1980s. The market is defined as companies below $5 million, but responsibility for credit intensive companies and specialized industries, such as contractors, is shifted to the middle market group. To underscore the bank's flexibility and willingness to match delivery systems to customer needs, the small business group also manages the local business of regional or national companies if no credit or sizable cash management relationship exists. Bottom line, this group has achieved significant market share growth since its inception and regularly generates an ROE in excess of 40 percent.

The right hand side of Exhibit 15.3 outlines Bank B's organization. In contrast to Bank A, differences exist in how the bank approves credits and, consequently, how it compensates branch managers and small business officers. Similar to Bank A, however, effective teaming appears to be at the center of this bank's approach. The sales officer and branch manager share responsibility for sales, service, and retaining customers.

Each of the regions has a small business unit headed by a sales manager. The small business officers assigned to a manager usually work with approximately six branch managers. These officers have multiple marketing and cross-selling responsibilities, which include:

- Developing new and existing relationships.

- Making credit decisions up to assigned limits. Individual credit limits are deliberately set at low levels, partly to de-emphasize loans while promoting deposit generation and fee-based product sales. The bank averages $3.40 of deposits for every dollar of loans.

- Presenting larger credits to senior management.

- Acting as team leader for their group of branch managers. Goals focus on: new business, deposit and fee income targets, new customers generated, and account retention.

All loans and deposits generated along with related expenses are considered to belong to the branches. This ensures the enthusiastic involvement of branch managers. The bank also employs shadow accounting to monitor the small business group's profitability.

In this bank, compensation for the small business officers is tied to goals that are heavily weighted toward deposit generation, new customer acquisition, and retention. Individual incentives are not tied to loan growth because of the credit authority that marketing officers at this bank retain. This absence of a loan volume incentive reduces the potential for conflict of interest. Additional incentive payments are made for internal referrals to areas such as Trust or Private Banking.

Several business practices are common to these two banks and others that have been highly successful in small business.

- Limiting the number of products (standardization) and a focus on non-credit areas.

- The use of marketing expertise, including telemarketing, to focus the selling effort.

- A willingness to reengineer credit and customer service processes to take advantage of economies of focus and of scale (centralization).

Dealing with Disintermediation

A number of "doom and gloom" articles and essays have examined the advent of securitization and its potential negative impact. A bank's ability to maintain market share and profitability in the small business segment will depend upon a long-term securitization game plan. Although most small business loans will remain unsecuritizable for the foreseeable future, securitization merits evaluation from both a defensive and an offensive viewpoint. Defensively, all banks are facing yet another attack by non-banks eroding what has been considered a natural franchise. By taking the offensive, some banks will be able to take advantage of the securitization business system to expand beyond current market segments and geographies.

To a limited extent, the securitization of small business loans has already arrived. During 1992, for example, close to 50 percent of the loans approved by the SBA were sold into the secondary market by lenders.

For example, in addition to government guaranteed SBA loans for which the Money Store is the market share leader, Fremont

Financial also has securitized portfolios of loans. This unit of Fremont General Corp., the Santa Monica-based insurance company, specializes in making working capital loans of up to $5 million. During 1993, it completed two securitizations. Typically, Fremont focuses on smaller, tougher credits and secures loans by a mix of receivables, inventory, and equipment. Before 1993 such working capital loans did not qualify for securitization, when the Securities and Exchange Commission's changed the Investment Company Act of 1940, which made those loans eligible.

Assisted by Merrill Lynch, Fremont set up a Small Business Loan Master Trust to emulate credit card securitizations. In total, $300 million in notes was issued in 1993. This allowed Fremont to reduce its reliance on bank debt and, therefore, its funding costs. Importantly, the institution also increased the number of loans it made because of its ability to package them into securities rather than keeping them on its balance sheet.

The Fremont Master Trust is only the first ripple of a more intense shock wave that will reshape small business banking. The impact of securitization on the competitive dynamics of the marketplace could be dramatic. By reducing capital requirements, securitization will allow non-bank lenders, including those with relatively low equity positions, to enter and expand in the market.

The only drawback for non-banks will be the importance of the branch to the small business market. To compensate, the non-banks may have to focus on targets who are willing to unbundle their choice of funding source from other banking needs.

In any case, the customer non-banks target for loan securitizations may not be the most attractive target for banks, because the majority of bank income comes from deposits. Since the economics of small business apply to non-banks as well as banks, success in lending will require extensive streamlining of the marketing, underwriting, and servicing processes—certainly beyond the best practices of banks profiled above.

As in other securitization endeavors, small business loan securitization consists of five key elements:

- *Origination:* generating the loan.

- *Underwriting:* approving the credit and structuring the loan.

- *Packaging:* determining which loans should be sold together.

- *Distribution:* selling the loan or retaining it in portfolio, i.e., self-distribution.

- *Servicing:* account maintenance and review on an ongoing basis.

Banks can chose to focus on one of these areas or specialize. For example, banks can originate and underwrite loans and then work with an investment banker to sell them to the aftermarket while keeping the servicing rights. Alternately, they can be originated, underwritten, and retained for their own portfolio. Still another approach is to develop a functional specialty, such as approaches to underwriting that can be sold to other lenders.

Banks also can adapt their business system focus according to geography, segmentation strategies, or the bank's appetite for holding assets on its books. For example, in its core geography, a bank might decide to keep and service the loans it generates. In a different geography or for a particular industry or needs segment (such as autos) management might decide to generate loans and package them for immediate sale with or without maintaining the servicing rights. Further, building an approach to securitization may allow banks to cross state lines and enter markets where they do not have a branch presence, echoing the focus of some non-banks on "borrowers only." Clearly, the choices are innumerable.

After a recent speech I made on trends in small business to an industry association, one banker expressed his frustration with securitization and his wish that this threat could be averted. To paraphrase, he said, "I don't understand why the industry doesn't get together and fight this." His hope was that the banking industry effort could forestall the securitization of small business loans.

While that tactic might result in, at best, a short-term delay, increased securitization is a virtual certainty. Whether promoted through a quasi-government agency, such as Velda Sue, or by the creativity of investment bankers, the writing is on the wall. Right now, the attractive spreads of this business and the strengthening capital positions of most banks may delay wholesale securitization of loans anytime soon. As soon as loan growth expands, however, and most banks' desires for assets begin to abate, securitization of small business loans will likely become commonplace. For now, non-banks will probably continue to be the pioneers in exploring securitization opportunities.

Building Profitability and Market Presence

Banks should consider a five-step strategic plan for building their small business profitability and market presence.

Step 1: Audit Profitability

As the two companies analyzed in Exhibit 15.1 demonstrate, the ability to evaluate profitability on an individual account is inestimable. Without this level of data, a bank must rely on guess work and hunches, putting its operations at a competitive disadvantage to those with better account tracking and analysis capabilities.

For any bank serious about improving small business profitability, an assessment of Customer B (in Exhibit 15.1) should lead management to develop an action plan to improve the profitability of lending to customers with similar characteristics. For example, product standardization, if introduced in the context of a centralized credit decision process, fundamentally alters the economics of lending and will increase Customer B's return on equity to the bank.

The deaveraged profitability analysis described in Chapter 3, as part of a discussion on the profitability of middle market clients, also applies to the small business market. Banks need to map the profit profiles of products, customer segments, and individual companies. Up until recently, however, very few banks have been able to do so. While they knew the profitability of their units, may have had a good idea of product profitability, and could also calculate the revenues an individual customer generated, few had a meaningful sense of a customer's profit or loss for the bank.

At a minimum, segment profitability is essential, particularly for those markets where levels of profit are unclear, such as "borrower only" customers.

Step 2: Build Off the Branch

An economic analysis of the small business market usually results in a recommendation for a combined branch-based front office and centralized back-office effort.

The branch is, without a doubt, the epicenter of small business banking. First, deposits are the key to profits, and branches service that deposit business on a day-to-day basis. Second, interviews with small business owners indicate that, for many, branch access remains a top decision factor in selecting a bank.

This branch-centered approach may appear in conflict with the statement expressed above that, in the future, a large portion of small business banking will no longer require a "high touch" approach. In fact, this conclusion carries with it the caveat that understanding segments is critical and that different customers will require a combination of approaches. Today, a branch system remains critical to most targets; tomorrow, it will remain essential to many.

Acknowledging the branch system as the focal point of the small business effort has multiple implications for the branch manager. Either a separate small business sales team needs to be established or the branch managers must take on a commercial sales role. Industry best practices demonstrate that the branch manager's role can be redesigned in more than one way and still be effective.

Banks must, nonetheless, avoid simply adding the small business responsibility to other tasks that the branch manager performs. If small business is recognized as a core focus, the manager's other responsibilities must be adjusted. Therefore, redefining the branch manager's role and performance expectations will be as important to success in small business as a redefined RM is to success in middle market and large corporate banking.

Step 3: Benchmark

Before a bank changes its small business strategy, its current efforts should be benchmarked—no matter where business management is located organizationally. Internal benchmarking will point out areas for further evaluation and should highlight best practices that can be introduced across the bank.

Exhibit 15.2, a disguised client example discussed earlier in this chapter, presents an example of benchmarking that demonstrates the value of this process. The branch manager at Bank A is managing 155 small business relationships; the manager at Bank B is handling three times as many. Based on benchmark data, senior management at Bank A would discover that account loads at typical banks range from 150 to 200 per branch. Given that the level of account loads per manager is a key profit determinant, senior management will determine why that degree of variability exists and whether the approach being used at Bank B provides any lessons for the overall small business effort.

As it turned out in this client example, the manager at Bank A was personally servicing many accounts, rather than taking advantage of his bank's centralized service center. In contrast, the branch manager at Bank B saw her role as that of facilitator and salesperson rather than as administrator or account servicer. Her personal attention was reserved for high profit or potential accounts. Therefore, she fully used the centralized support service group that specialized in the small business market. Her resulting account load was substantially higher because she followed a team management approach where roles are clearly defined and followed. This strategy gained her a high degree of leverage.

Step 4: Focus on Key Prospects

Interestingly, we have seen a lack of consistency between geographies in small business success. What works in one region does not necessarily work in another. Therefore, a marketing approach has to be designed with the peculiarities and sophistication of a specific geography in mind.

Regardless of the actual geographic boundaries, however, this step is founded on the creation and continual refinement of a customer database. It is, of course, possible to purchase databases. But the off-the-shelf data must be continuously added to and a profile of the successful customer constantly refined. The point of this exercise is to make suspects into high-priority prospects. The segmented profitability analysis of current customers, when completed, should lead to parameters being defined for new targets.

Step 5: Change the Organization

This final step in building a profitable small business banking franchise is really a prerequisite. Without a shift in organization processes as well as goals, the new strategy will be doomed to remain on paper, never realized.

Management must install streamlined decision-making and service processes. Doing things the old way because they worked in the past is simply unacceptable. Plus, just as Citibank restructured its retail bank in the 1970s and 1980s, a consumer markets' perspective must be brought to the small business market. Further, a pay-for-performance compensation structure must be introduced to encourage innovation. Finally, separating the credit decision from the marketing process will eliminate potential conflicts while cultivating the development of focus.

Summary Thoughts

Success in the small business market depends on a holistic approach to restructuring. Banks must become able to measure profitability down to the customer and product level; effectively segment their target market; design an organizational structure customized to the needs and economics of this market; and create a focused sales management process.

At the same time, banks must anticipate the growing impact of non-industry players and, in particular, the emerging role of securitization in this market.

271

Ongoing success in small business will, of course, be driven by understanding the customer's selection criteria and usage patterns, and then organizing and selling around these attributes. This market places a premium on strategies and tactics that break paradigms and which might appear in conflict, such as exploiting standardization and centralization opportunities while maintaining excellent customer responsiveness and high-quality service.

Bibliography

Allen, Paul H. *Reengineering the Bank*. Chicago: Probus Publishing, 1994.

Ballantine, John Jr. "Lessons of the Credit Crunch." *Commercial Lending Review* (Winter 1993–94): 37–47.

Bennett, Robert A. "Taking the Measure of Bank Profits." *U.S. Banker* (April 1994): 37–42.

Bower, Marvin. *The Will to Manage*. New York: McGraw Hill, 1966.

Grant, James. *Money of the Mind*. New York: Farrar Straus Giroux, 1992.

Graves, Marilynn W. "Loan Yield Analysis: A Tool to Improve Profitability." *Bank Accounting & Finance* (Winter 1993–94): 28–36.

Hamilton, Adrian. *The Financial Revolution*. New York: The Free Press, 1986.

Hammer, Michael and James Champy. *Reengineering the Corporation*. New York: Harper Business, 1993.

Kimball, Ralph C. "Calculating and Using Risk-Adjusted ROE for Lines of Business." *Bank Accounting & Finance* (Fall 1993): 17–27.

Lederman, Jess, Linda E. Feinne, and Mark F. Ozialga, eds. *The Commercial Loan Resale Market*. Chicago: Probus Publishing, 1991.

May, Joseph W. "Fundamentals of Commercial Lending." *The Bankers Magazine* (March/April 1994): 48–51.

McAleer, Linda. "New Approaches to Defining the Small Business Market." *Bank Marketing* (May 1994): 25–31.

273

Milligan, John W. "Can Big Banks Learn to Love Small Business." *U.S. Banker* (August 1993): 24–29.

Morsman, Edgar M., Jr. *Commercial Loan Portfolio Management.* Philadelphia: Robert Morris Associates, 1993.

Rawls, S. Waite and Charles W. Smithson. "Strategic Risk Management." *Journal of Applied Corporate Finance* (Winter 1990): 6–18.

Richardson, Linda. *Bankers in the Selling Role.* New York: John Wiley, 1984

Steiner, Thomas A. and Diogo Teixeira. *Technology in Banking.* New York: Dow Jones & Co., 1990.

Tichy, Noel M. and Stratford Sherman. *Control Your Destiny or Someone Else Will.* New York: Doubleday, 1993.

Walton, Anthony J. "Positioning a Foreign Bank in the U.S. Market: The Case of Westpack." In *Marketing Financial Services,* edited by David B. Zenoff. Cambridge: Ballinger Publishing Company, 1989.

Wendel, Charles. "Asset-Based Lending Presents Major Opportunities for Profit." *American Banker* (March 16, 1993): 4.

___. "Generating Higher Earnings from the Middle Market." *The Bankers Magazine* (July/August 1992): 14–19.

___. "How to Compete Successfully in the Middle Market." *Commercial Lending Review* (Winter 1992–93): 3–12.

___. "Meeting the Nonbank Challenge." *The Banker's Magazine* (March/April 1993): 12–19.

Index

credit approval workflow, 138-40
Product development, 22, 99-101
  product teams, 100
Productivity
  lack of improvement in, 5-11
    lack of marketing priority, 9-11
    low account prospecting, 9
    static account management, 6-8
  steps in creating improved, 186
Product specialist
  resistance to cross-selling, 96
  versus relationship manager, 96-97
Product standardization, 258-59
Profitability modeling, 33-42
  approaches to cost allocation, 37
  determining action steps, 40-42
  economics of lending, 39
  elements of, 36
  focusing profitability, 38-40
  segmenting/costing customer
    data, 35-38
Profit-assessment, example of, 31-33
Prospecting. *See* Marketing
Prudential, 229

R
Reengineering, 169-87
  account load rebalancing, 181
  ensuring success of, 171-73
  implementation plans to support, 179-84
  need for, 169-71
  senior management involvement, 172
  steering group, 172-73, 176
  team-based marketing, use of, 181-84
  team manager's role, 181-82
  workflow analysis, 173-74

Reengineering the Bank, 252
Relationship manager
  see also Reengineering
  account planning and, 101-3
  compensation for, 97, 197-98
  loan application process and, 113-15
  performance measurement, 194-97
  role of, 17-27, 134-37
    benchmarking/best practices and, 24-26
    business system, 21-24
    current credit-related activities, 135
    dysfunctional corporate bank structure and, 19-21
    and financial consultants compared, 18-19
    multi-product sales expectations, 18-19
    reducing, in credit process, 134-37
  technology and, 214
  time allocation, 10-12, 156-57, 175
  training and development, 189-94
    entry-level training, 191-92
    ongoing, 192-94
  versus product specialist, 96-97
  workouts and, 126
Return on equity (ROE), 30
  -based industry analysis, 43
  to evaluate line-of-business performance, 34-35
  segmenting by customer industry, 42-43
  value destroyers, 41
Richardson, Linda, 87
Risk adjustment, 34
RMA Business Credit Information Package, 259

About the Author

Charles B. Wendel is a Vice President in the Financial Services practice at Mercer Management Consulting, an international consulting firm with a major emphasis on the financial services industry. Wendel has focused extensively upon issues related to the corporate and middle markets throughout his consulting career. He has assisted numerous banks in redesigning their credit and sales management and product development processes. In addition, his background includes consulting experience with many of the non-banks that pose the greatest competitive threat to the banking industry.

Prior to joining Mercer, Mr. Wendel split his career between financial services consulting and banking. He has been a member of McKinsey and Co.'s Financial Institutions Group and had previously been a banker with Citibank, Schroders and Bankers Trust.

Mr. Wendel has spoken extensively on issues related to business banking and the middle market at industry meetings, including the American Bankers Association, Robert Morris Associates and Bank Administration Institute. He is also the co-author of *Business Buzzwords* (Amacom, 1995).

Wendel received a B.A. from New York University and an M.A., M.Phil and M.B.A. from Columbia University.